These children are reliving life in an early day rural school to gather data about questions they raised in an initiatory activity.

Social Studies
for the RealWorld

Social Studies
for the Real World

Maxine Dunfee

Indiana University

Charles E. Merrill Publishing Company
A Bell & Howell Company
Columbus   Toronto   London   Sydney

Published by Charles E. Merrill Publishing Company
A Bell & Howell Company
Columbus, Ohio 43216

This book was set in Helios, Univers, and Times Roman.
The production editor was Jan Hall.
The cover was prepared by Will Chenoweth.

Cover photo by *David Staver*.

Text photos courtesy of:

Donald Adair, University Elementary School,
Bloomington, Indiana, pages 38 (top), 85, 113,
117, 179, 198, and 300; *Randall Duncan,* Clear
Creek Elementary School, Bloomington, Indiana,
pages 35, 38 (bottom two), 131, 203, 216, 230,
and 232; *David Staver,* administrative assistant,
Monroe County Community Schools, Bloomington, Indiana, pages 7, 13, 59, 75, 147, 152 and
269 (top).

Library of Congress Catalog Card Number: 77–87428

International Standard Book Number: 0–675–08366–4

1 2 3 4 5 6 7 8 9 10—85 84 83 82 81 80 79 78

Printed in the United States of America

Preface

Social Studies for the Real World views social studies as the study of human relationships, the interactions of people striving to meet their needs and to solve the problems of their corporate life. Equally important, it takes the position that social studies is a method—a way of inquiring, finding out, and taking action.

Social Studies for the Real World recognizes that there are multiple strategies for social studies instruction and that teachers may develop their own teaching styles by combining elements of these strategies in various ways as the teaching-learning situation demands. It also takes cognizance of the fact that there are new textbook and media programs designed to improve instruction in social studies and to provide detailed assistance to teachers.

The book emphasizes that the social studies program which is most effective is one that helps pupils assume citizenship roles in daily living. It provides opportunities for children and youth to discover the generalizations that explain the world of people; develop values compatible with the principles of democracy; identify, investigate, and solve problems that are relevant to them; and put into action their ideas for making the real world better.

In the prologue, the reader is introduced to three groups of elementary school children, all of them wrestling with a modern community problem. Their experiences set the stage for consideration of the goals for social studies and an analysis of teaching strategies which are developed in the first two chapters. The following chapters investigate building readiness; planning for instruction; data selection, gathering, and processing; and generalizing and making proposals for problem solutions.

In its closing chapters, *Social Studies for the Real World* examines ways in which social studies goals may be achieved in the open classroom, explores techniques for value clarification, and suggests how learning in social studies may be evaluated. The prologue re-emphasizes the role of a relevant social studies program in citizenship education.

Readers will discover that *Social Studies for the Real World* presents a unified approach to instruction, suggesting how the components of inquiry and problem solving may enhance and bring to life social studies content, whether predesigned in published programs, planned within the school by curriculum specialists and teachers, or cooperatively developed by pupils and teacher. The instructional strategies and teaching techniques are illustrated by many examples drawn from the learning experiences of children, all of them based on the author's observations of elementary classrooms and experiences in working with children. In these vignettes, inexperienced teachers may glimpse how pupils make progress toward the goals of social studies; experienced teachers may compare and contrast the episodes with their own teaching.

Social Studies for the Real World is more than a potpourri of ideas for social studies activities; rather, it is an in-depth treatment of social studies instruction designed to achieve relevant goals and to help children see how their learning can function in the world around them.

Contents

Prologue

Social Studies
in the Real World

They had been talking for more than an hour about what they had seen on their fact-gathering tour of redevelopment centers in their city—thirty-six sixth-graders from Sheridan School in inner-city San Francisco—and then . . .

Teacher: Do any of you have any opinions or anything that you're still puzzled about in the redevelopment thing? Anything that you disagree with, ideas that you're not quite sure of?

Child: What I don't understand, all the houses in Diamond Heights, like there's a slope and then houses on it, another slope and houses on it. I want to know how come all of those houses are on hills.

T: Good question. Why did they build Diamond Heights on a hill? Anything else that puzzles you or any other problems that you think that the Redevelopment Agency hasn't solved, or do you think it's all solved?

C: Well, I think like in St. Francis Square they ought to think of something for the older children to be able to play with, and I think the Redevelopment Agency when we were down there that man was a little bit puzzled 'cause I don't think he really knew what was happening himself.

T: Happening where?

C: Around San Francisco like in places like the Japanese Cultural Center; when he started talking about it he started stammering and things when we started asking a lot of questions, 'cause I don't think he knew too many answers to 'em.

T: So you don't think he knew all the answers to the problem. Any other things you weren't quite sold on. Now Rowanda wasn't sold on everything they said down there. How about you?

C: Haight Ashbury.

T: Well, what about it?

C: It's got boarded up windows and doors, cracked sidewalks and everybody's sad over there.

T: Do you think that should be redeveloped, too? Any other things that puzzled you, that you're not sold on?

C: Like in St. Francis Square when you go through hallways, they all look alike. Why can't they have some decoration on it?

T: In other words, you don't like the all sameness of these projects that they built. Any others?

C: What they should do at Diamond Heights is to lower the cost.

T: Why is that so high there, do you think? St. Francis Square was so low. Why was Diamond Heights, Judy, way up?

C: Because the houses are more modern and stuff.

T: I wonder.

C: Maybe because you get a good view.

T: Maybe because of that view there—I wonder.

C: Well, Mr. Edison, the houses in St. Francis Square are modern, too, just like Diamond Heights.

T: So there must be some reason why the cost is so big, and you wonder why the cost is so big in Diamond Heights. Uh-huh. Gary, you had things that puzzled you that you weren't satisfied with even after all those experts we met.

C: What are they going to do about Hunters Point?

T: In other words, no one came up with a plan for Hunters Point yet; did they?

*   *   *   *   *

T: Any other things that you aren't satisfied with yet; or do you think those redevelopment people have all the answers? . . . Are you satisfied with what the Redevelopment Agency is doing? Shall we let them handle everything? I only see one person shaking his head; all the rest of you seem satisfied.

C: Well, like I said before, I don't seem satisfied. If they're going to fix up St. Francis Square and things like that, why don't they fix up the whole city that's all messed up; because like in Haight Ashbury, I looked around there: Even the schools needed redevelopment, I mean rehabilitation, because when I looked at William McKinley, it needed to be painted; it was all dirty and everything, didn't look like it was really taken care of.

C: I agree with Victor 'cause when I sittin' and we was in the bus goin' by, you could see the school houses, how the paint was all comin' off and the walls all cracked and everything, and the houses, when we was passin' by, it was turned all brown, and the windows were cracked, and the curtains all raggedy and everything.

C: I don't go along with the redevelopment, 'cause if they're goin' to fix up the rest, how come they don't want to fix up Hunters Point?

T: In other words, you think Hunters Point should be fixed up as well as some of the other parts. I see.

*   *   *   *   *

C: Mr. Edison, why are they taking so long to make up a plan for Hunters Point?

T: Did you hear that? This girl wants to know how long have they taken? When were those places out in Hunters Point built?

C: They were built after the Second World War about 1945.

T: That's how many years?

C: Twenty-seven.

T: Twenty-seven. You think they should have come up with a plan
        by that time?

C: I think they should have come up with a plan, too, because
        they've been buildin' all those other places.

C: And they should make a plan for Hunters Point because most
        of the houses were built in 1945, and they're old!

C: Well, I go with Julie and them. They ought to fix up Hunters
        Point, too, because if they don't fix up Hunters Point and fix
        up all the other places, San Francisco will still be lookin' bad.

C: They ought to have a place like St. Francis Square in Hunters
        Point because they got low cost; then they won't have to pay
        so much money.

C: I don't agree with the Redevelopment Agency neither.

T: Another person who doesn't agree with everything they say.
        Good.[1]

And so Mr. Edison and the sixth graders in Sheridan School made
their own plan for the redevelopment of Hunters Point! Were they studying social studies? Was the world they were concerned about the real
world?

Elsewhere another teacher is saying to pupils, "Can you answer the
questions that go with the picture on page 232 of your book?" (In the
picture, a large sign attached to the side of some old buildings announces
that they are being vacated for urban relocation.) "Susan, read it for us."

"When old buildings are torn down to make way for new, finding
homes for the people being moved out is often very difficult. Why is this
so?"

The teacher raises additional questions about the picture:

"What do you think might happen to the people who are moved out
of the buildings shown in this picture? Can you see a serious problem that
arises when apartments are torn down in order to build newer and larger
apartments? Can you think of some ways to solve the problems of moving
people out of old buildings so that new buildings can be built there?"[2]

Is this discussion a lesson in social studies? Are the pupils looking at
the real world?

In another classroom the pupils have been studying the *Evry City
Land Use Map,* which the teacher has posted for them, explaining that it

---

[1] Transcribed from an unedited tape. Used by permission of the teacher, William Edison,
Elk, California.

[2] Used by permission of Macmillan Publishing Co., Inc., from Teacher's Annotated Edition
for *Web of the World*, Teacher's Guide by Phillip Viereck, Bertha Davis, and Joseph
Decaroli, pp. 157–59. Copyright © 1973 Macmillan Publishing Co., Inc.

is a special kind of map for an imaginary city and that the different ways in which land is used are shown by different colors. The teacher inquires, "Who can figure out where the houses, stores, offices, schools, factories, and parks are located?"

The teacher explains that in the next few days they are going to play a game about Evry City. They will begin by listening to an imaginary letter from the mayor of Evry City, who asks the pupils to replan a part of the city which has been destroyed by fire.[3]

Are these children engaged in a social studies experience? Is the simulated world of Evry City like the real world?

The pupils in all these episodes were experiencing in varying degrees a social problem of the real world, exploring, analyzing, and eventually concluding. They were viewing human beings as active participants in a complex society, a society in which the search for the decent life is not always easy, a society in which people interact as they meet human needs.

America today, with its network of relationships with other nations, is the real world in which our children live. They are influenced by it, and their future will be determined by their success in meeting its demands and solving its problems. The real world impinges upon the thoughts of children and upon their life space. It reaches them through their daily contacts with those around them at home, at school, and in the neighborhood. It touches them through the problems their community is experiencing. It enters their awareness through the news and through the conversation of adults near at hand. Television, motion picture, and travel expand the children's world to include people in faraway places who are struggling with their own problems.

Children are keenly aware of the problems abroad in the real world, even when, like many adults, they cannot understand them; dilemmas of self-concept and interpersonal relationships, community development, environmental destruction, prejudice, world hunger and poverty, making democracy work, space exploration, and war and peace to name only a few.

That these problems come to school with children is evidenced by the questions they ask and the ideas they express. A good curriculum encourages pupils to identify problems appropriate to their maturity level and significant to them, to hypothesize about possible solutions, to gather data to support or reject their theories and to draw conclusions about possible actions. What better preparation for meeting the unknown world of the future than to gain experience in studying the problems of the real world of the present.

---

[3] From *Inquiring About Cities* Teacher's Guide by W. G. Fielder and G. Feeney, pp. 295–97. Copyright © 1972 by Holt, Rinehart and Winston, Publishers. Used by permission.

One
Identifying Content and Goals for Social Studies

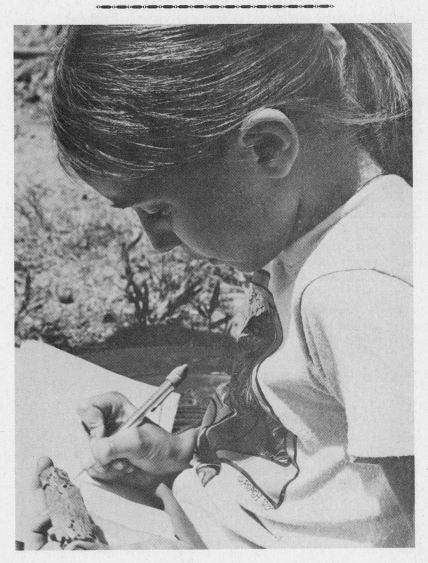

What *is* social studies? Social studies is the study of people and their reactions to and interactions with their physical and affective environments as they meet the problems of everyday living. The heart of social studies is the study of the real world and its problems—past, present, and future. Its overriding goal is the development of understandings, attitudes and values, behaviors, and cognitive skills needed for responsible citizenship in this world. Its methods are the methods of inquiry: to think critically, to use the scientific method, and to solve problems.

Social Studies and the Social Sciences

Social studies is one of the newest areas of the curriculum but at the same time one of the most misunderstood by adults. Some of the confusion may be caused by lack of understanding of the relationships between social studies and the social sciences. Older people, remembering their study of history and geography, question their seeming absence in many schools today. Others hear of experimental programs in anthropology or economics for elementary pupils and wonder why young children are being taught these adult subjects. We can be fairly certain that learning experiences like those in our prologue would generate questions about social studies among grown-up persons with whom the pupils are interacting. What is this social studies children are studying in school? What has happened to geography and history? How can elementary school pupils study something as difficult as sociology?

The social sciences are the origins and parent disciplines of social studies. In both, the core is the relationship of human beings to each other and to the environment. Both are concerned with the variety of activities in which human beings engage for the purpose of meeting their needs; in other words, human relationships are the common denominator in the social sciences and social studies. However, much social science content is beyond the grasp of elementary school children; its volume is too great for assimilation at any grade level. Determining the content of social studies is thus a matter of selection; the usefulness of the content in developing the goals of responsible citizenship is the selective factor. Social studies, then, is a synthesis, a composite of important generalizations about human relationships, problems, and institutions, drawn from the social sciences.

To be more specific, each of the social sciences offers its own discrete, distinctive body of knowledge made up of its own set of facts, concepts, and generalizations.

Consider, for example, the social studies generalization: *Through all times and places people have worked to meet common basic human needs and to satisfy common human desires and aspirations.*[1] How have the social sciences contributed to this significant generalization?

Economics: Ideas about people's producing and consuming activities.

Trade between people begins when there is a scarcity of resources in one group and an abundance of the desired resources in another.

Where there are not enough of the necessities of life, such as food, clothing, and shelter, to meet the demands for them, their cost to the individual increases.

Dividing the labor needed to produce essential goods and services increases efficiency in producing these goods and services, but it also increases interdependence among the producers.

Geography: Ideas about how people adapt to and use the environment.

There is a relationship between the climatic features of an area and the ways people in the area meet their basic needs.

Because people everywhere have certain basic needs that must be met, there are many similarities in the daily lives of people in all parts of the world.

Generally, the more natural vegetation there is in an area where people live, the easier it is for them to meet their needs for food, clothing, and shelter.

People's use of natural resources in meeting their needs is related to their desires and level of technology.

Anthropology: Ideas of culture and cultural change.

The way in which people meet their basic needs is influenced by their cultural level.

---

[1] Paraphrased from the *Report of the State Central Committee on Social Studies to the California State Curriculum Commission* (Sacramento: California State Department of Education, 1961), p. 41.

Each group probably prefers its ways of meeting basic needs, but it may be influenced to change if subjected to extended contact with another culture.

All human beings share some traits in common and have similar basic needs.

All cultures provide for the essential needs of their groups.

Political Science: Ideas about organizations and institutions.

Society establishes public institutions to assist its members to meet basic needs.

As competition for the use of the natural environment intensifies, political units legislate to protect resources.

When segments of the society are unable physically or financially to meet basic needs, government agencies are established to care for them.

In democracy, citizens may voluntarily choose the kind of work they will do to earn their living and to contribute to the welfare of others.

Sociology: Ideas about the structure of groups and group behavior.

There are many groups within a society which afford opportunities for people to meet their needs and aspirations.

Some groups in a society are based on the economic level of their members.

Ways of meeting basic needs are influenced by the expectations of the groups to which one belongs.

As societies become more complex, people become more interdependent as they strive to meet common needs.

History, usually considered apart from the social sciences, brings its own perspective to social studies generalizations.

History: Ideas about human relationships from the past.

Throughout time people have sought to meet their needs for food, clothing, and shelter.

In general, leaders of a particular period in history often are those whose ideas and inventions improved the welfare of the people among whom they lived.

Full assessment of a particular people's productivity in meeting their needs cannot be made without knowledge of their historical development.

History demonstrates that people have been motivated by ideas, values, and material wants and needs.

Does it seem impossible that all these social science generalizations have been synthesized to produce the single generalization with which we began this analysis? On the other hand, teachers would probably agree that to teach all this material as discrete ideas would be both impractical and impossible. Hence they are searching for broader themes which can be illustrated in the learning experiences of pupils. They welcome a synthesizing core of ideas that children can comprehend and that serve the purposes of social studies.

Do you suppose that the children described in the prologue were touching base with any of the social sciences through their activities? For example, recall the pupils in the sixth grade at Sheridan School who were making a redevelopment plan for Hunters Point, a slum they all knew. Can you attach one of the social sciences, or history, to each group of questions that may have been part of their study?

Group 1: In what kind of place is Hunters Point located?
How does the location of Hunters Point affect the lives of its people?
Does the location of Hunters Point make redevelopment difficult or easy?

Group 2: What social groups live in Hunters Point?
How do these groups relate to each other?
In what ways do these groups work together to solve problems?

Group 3: What persons or groups are most powerful in Hunters Point?
How can Hunters Point citizens organize to get the help they need?
How can officials be influenced to help Hunters Point?

Group 4: What kinds of work are done by citizens of Hunters Point?
Why is the economic level of the area low?
What can be done to improve living conditions?
How can business in Hunters Point be stimulated?

Group 5: What cultural groups live in Hunters Point?
          What things or ideas are most important to each of these
          groups?
          How do their beliefs affect living conditions in Hunters Point?
Group 6: How was Hunters Point settled?
          What changes have taken place in Hunters Point since World
          War II?
          How are the problems in Hunters Point related to things that
          happened in the past?

Were you successful in identifying the problems related to geography, sociology, political science, economics, anthropology, and history—and in that order? You no doubt also noticed that some of the questions relate to more than one of the disciplines. When the ideas from social sciences are translated into questions and problems children are investigating, the relationships between the parent disciplines and social studies do not seem too difficult for the young, nor threatening to teachers. Again the recurring theme is human relationships, people's never-ending interactions as they search for the better life.

Social studies as an area of the curriculum goes beyond, of course, the body of generalizations drawn from the social sciences and integrated in a content base for social studies. It is equally important to consider the methods of learning which children will employ as they explore social studies content in attacking significant problems. Consequently, mastery of methods of inquiry—the ability to think critically and to solve problems—assumes paramount importance in the social studies curriculum.

Still another dimension that must be considered in viewing social studies as an area of curriculum is the matter of values. Values and valuing are an integral part of inquiring. Few, if any, social problems can be analyzed without an awareness of the values involved and the consequences of holding one value or another. The development of social values remains a strong guarantee of social actions characteristic of responsible citizenship.

The Social Studies Curriculum Today

If the concern for social science concepts and generalizations, methods of inquiry, and development of social values seems to be a departure from traditional emphases in social studies, we may well wonder whether or not the scope and sequence of the social studies curriculum have departed from their earlier patterns.

Social studies draws on the content and inquiry methods of the social sciences and adapts them to experiences which are relevant to children. These pupils are engaging in a simulated "dig" to discover artifacts from a buried culture.

Traditionally, social studies has followed the ideas of expanding horizons, expanding environments, or expanding communities, a scheme based on assumptions about the development of children, their ability to deal with concepts of time and space, and their interests. This pattern has sometimes been illustrated in a series of concentric circles in which the smallest circle represents the environment with which young children are most familiar: home, family, school. Each larger circle represents an environment of greater scope; from each is drawn appropriate content as pupils become better able to cope with concepts of time and space. In some patterns the circles have been segmented to make clear that basic human activities are studied at each environmental level, as shown in Figure 1–1.

In other similar patterns the circles are diagrammed, as in Figure 1–2, to indicate that ideas from the social sciences and from history are being emphasized as pupils move outward through the environments.

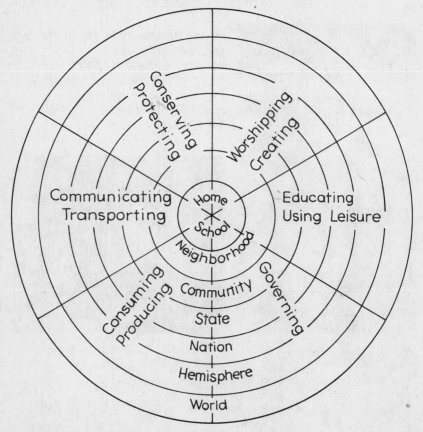

Figure 1–1. Basic human activities in the social studies curriculum.

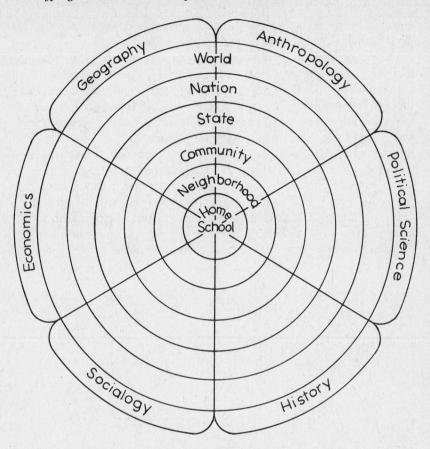

Figure 1–2. Social sciences in the social studies curriculum.

While research on children's ability to comprehend concepts of time and space makes it quite clear that these concepts do not become part of their understanding until they are well along in the elementary school, all teachers can cite instances when their pupils became very much interested in environments and happenings quite remote from the expected. Local conditions, travel, television, and unusual family experiences have influenced children's development of concepts of time and space and their interest in other times and places. For example, a first grade group who had in their class seven or eight children from Saudi Arabia became deeply involved in studying life in the country from which their new friends came; their experiences went far beyond the environmental circle indicated by the curriculum diagram. Similarly, during the Bicentennial celebrations in America, children at all grade levels dipped into content normally reserved for the fifth or sixth grade; in other words, they expanded their horizons in their own special ways.

It is also true that older children may explore in depth some concerns that focus their attention on environments very close to home: How can our community halt the discharge of dangerous chemicals into the water supply? Why are family life-styles changing today? How do federal welfare programs affect family and community living? All of these are problems which would take older pupils back into "horizons" or "environments" formerly reserved for younger pupils. As a matter of fact, some curriculum plans today introduce primary grade pupils to studies of people and places which contrast purposefully with the children's own lives. In these new programs, older pupils do not always deal exclusively with the wider horizons. Increasingly the concentric circles may assume uneven shapes, like those in Figure 1–3, as flexible curriculum plans encourage teachers and children to explore new interests and current concerns.

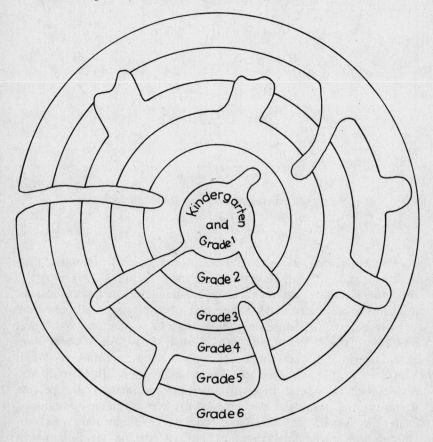

Figure 1–3. Flexibility in the social studies curriculum.

To what extent has the expanding horizons or expanding environments approach continued as an organizing theme? A look at some representative scope and sequence plans should provide data in response to this question.

A typical curriculum plan is shown below. It was constructed by a group of teachers for their local school system in a middle-sized Indiana city. The expanding horizons approach is clearly evident here, but contrasting people, environments, and cultures are also a part of social studies at each level. Here are their decisions for the years preceding their middle school.

Social Studies Framework

Grade One: The Family

1. Rural family
2. City family
3. Transient family
4. Pilgrim family
5. A changing family—Japanese
6. A family in Mexico, France, India, and/or Switzerland (choice)

Grade Two: The Neighborhood

1. The farm neighborhood
2. The urban neighborhood
3. The suburban neighborhood
4. The small town neighborhood
5. The historical neighborhood: American colonial
6. A changing neighborhood: Indians of the Southwest
7. A neighborhood in Canada, Israel, Nigeria, Greece, Germany, Columbia, Puerto Rico, and/or Italy (choice)

Grade Three: Community

1. A rural community (Monroe County)
2. An urban community (Bloomington)
3. A small town community (Ellettsville)

4. An historical community (Woodland Indians and settlement of Bloomington)

5. A changing community: Eskimo

6. A community in regions of Africa, Thailand, Mongolia, Arabia, Netherlands, Brazil (choice)

Grade Four: Our State

1. Indiana
   a. Rural aspects
   b. Urban areas
   c. History: exploration to present
   d. Geographical regions: cultural, political, and physical
   e. Government
2. Minority groups
3. Regions in New Zealand, Guatemala, Japan, USSR, Mexico, and/or Kenya (choice)

Grade Five: The United States and Neighbors

1. The United States
   a. History: Discovery to present
   b. Geographical regions: cultural, political, and physical
   c. Social, political, and economic systems
   d. Current social, political and/or economic issues
2. Canada and/or Mexico[2]

The curriculum outlines that undergird several modern textbook programs emphasize the disciplines that are the foundations of social studies. They also reflect some influences of the expanding horizons idea while pupils at each level are being taken beyond the local environment to contrasting cultures and regions. Note in the example which follows that Level 4 takes an interesting and divergent view of the idea of community, and that in Level 6 pupils dip into the past and present with some societies formerly not often studied at the elementary level.

---

[2] Monroe County Community School Corporation. *Conceptual Skills Guide for Elementary Social Studies in the Monroe County Community School Corporation* (Bloomington, Indiana: Author, n.d.).

Exploring the Social Sciences: Scope and Sequence

Level 1: Seeing Near and Far

1. Living in America (sociology, economics, geography, history)
2. Finding places (geography)
3. Farms, towns, and cities (geography, economics, sociology, history)
4. Learning (sociology, values, ecology)
5. Living in Japan (geography, sociology, economics)

Level 2: Observing People and Places

1. Neighbors and neighborhoods (sociology, economics, geography, values)
2. Outside your neighborhood (sociology, geography, economics)
3. Communities and their growth (history, geography, economics)
4. Buildings we see (economics, geography, art)
5. Transportation and communication (history, geography, economics)
6. People working together (sociology, values, political science, economics)
7. Greece—old and new (history, art, literature, geography, sociology)

Level 3: Comparing Ways and Means

1. Americans on the move (economics, history, geography)
2. Boundaries (geography, political science, history)
3. How Americans live (anthropology, sociology, history, economics, geography)
4. Indians of the Plains (anthropology, history, sociology, economics)
5. Americans at work (economics)
6. The region of the Great Lakes (geography, geology, history, economics, ecology, values)
7. Regions of Africa (geography, sociology, economics)

Level 4: Investigating Communities and Cultures

1. Exploring groups and communities (sociology, psychology, anthropology)
2. The culture community (anthropology, history)

3. The ancient community (culture, all aspects)
4. The urban community (history, archaeology, modern urbanology)
5. The economic community (economics, history, sociology)
6. The language community (language, history)
7. The interest community (sociology, ecology, values)
8. The world community (all previous concepts)

Level 5: Asking about the U.S.A. and Its Neighbors

1. Discovery, exploration, and colonization (history, sociology, anthropology)
2. Forming a new nation (history, political science)
3. The nation grows and divides (history, sociology, economics)
4. The nation rebuilds and expands (history, sociology, economics)
5. Industry affects American life (history, economics, sociology)
6. America in the twentieth century (history, political science, economics, sociology)
7. Canada (history, political science, sociology)
8. Mexico (history, anthropology, political science)

Level 6: Learning about Countries and Societies

1. Ancient Greece (history, sociology, economics, art, philosophy)
2. Confucian China (geography, history, sociology, philosophy)
3. Medieval France (history, sociology, political science, economics)
4. India (sociology, political science, geography, urbanology)
5. The Middle East (geography, history, sociology)
6. Nigeria (geography, sociology, history, political science)
7. Brazil (economic geography, history, anthropology, sociology)
8. The Soviet Union (geography, history, political science, economics, sociology)[3]

---

[3] *Exploring the Social Sciences,* brochure (Cincinnati: American Book Company, 1971).

The guides for the *Taba Social Studies Curriculum* develop a scope and sequence which combines the expanding horizons approach with strong emphasis on significant generalizations. Perusal of the content outline makes very clear this dual emphasis.

<hr>

Social Studies Curriculum

Grade One: The Family
- Unit   I: The socialization of children takes place primarily within family, peer, educational, and religious institutions.
- Unit   II: Families differ in life style and role expectations.
- Unit   III: The institutions of a society are economically sustained through a variety of means.

Grade Two: Communities around Us
- Unit   I: Community needs are met by groups of people engaged in many related activities.
- Unit   II: The nature of a particular community will influence the kinds of service it needs.
- Unit   III: The people of a community organize in different ways in order to attain their goals.

Grade Three: Four Communities around the World
- Unit   I: Differences in economics are associated with differences in the ways people use their environment and skills.
- Unit   II: Contact between cultures often brings changes in the social institutions within them.
- Unit   III: Interaction between a people and their physical environment influences the way in which they meet their needs.
- Unit   IV: Tradition influences the ways in which a group of people modify their behavior.
- Unit   V: The basic economy of a society has a major influence on the life style of its people.
- Unit   VI: Tradition and innovation interact to determine the modifications which will occur in a people's way of life.
- Unit VII: Same as Unit III.
- Unit VIII: People may develop new ways within their tradition to achieve their goals.

Grade Four: Our State—A Changing Society
- Unit   I: The cultures of different people influence the manner in which they use the same environment.
- Unit   II: Man's way of living is affected by the physical and social environment in which he lives.
- Unit   III: As societies grow, both their requirements and their problems change.

Grade Five: United States and Canada—Societies in Transition
    Unit   I: New discoveries result from the application of previously learned knowledge to the solution of current problems.
    Unit   II: The life style of a culture is shaped by the contributions of groups which make up that culture.
    Unit   III: Conflict may develop among groups when goals and expectations differ.
    Unit   IV: A mobile people tend to develop a way of life that differs from that in established communities.
    Unit   V: Technological development contributes to the nature and extent of cultural resources of an area.
    Unit   VI: The physical and cultural resources of an area encourage specialization in the use of land.

Grade Six: Middle and South America—Societies in Transition
    Unit   I: Cultures change in varying degrees when they come in contact with another culture.
    Unit   II: Though all cultures possess certain unique features, they are also similar in a number of ways.
    Unit   III: The human and natural resources and geographical features of an area influence the material prosperity of the people within that area.
    Unit   IV: Different cultures deal with certain basic problems in a variety of ways.
    Unit   V: Changes that occur in one part of a society often produce changes in other parts of the society.

Grade Seven: Western Civilization—Perspectives on Change
    Unit   I: Man's ways of living affect, and are affected by, the physical and social environment in which he lives.
    Unit   II: The actions of a people are influenced by the values they hold.
    Unit   III: Ideas and societies change as they come in contact with the ideas and achievements of other societies.
    Unit   IV: How quickly any change comes about depends not only on the nature of the change itself, but also on the pressures for and against the change.
    Unit   V: The beliefs, activities, and values of people are influenced by the times in which they live.

Grade Eight: United States—Change, Problems, and Promises
    Unit   I: Institutions tend to undergo continuous change.
    Unit   II: Political change results from dissatisfaction with the status quo; changes reflect attempts to deal with causes of dissatisfactions.
    Unit   III: Divergent ways of life tend to compete for available resources and political control.
    Unit   IV: As the nature of a society changes, new institutions arise to deal with those changes.

Unit   V: Men continually seek to improve their condition through obtaining those rights they consider essential to their welfare.

Unit VI: A nation affects and is affected by the other nations with which it interacts.[4]

Does it appear that there are many variations, too many perhaps, in the curriculum from place to place and from program to program? In fact, the possible variations and the flexibility inherent in most programs should be a boon to teachers and an opportunity to make social studies the most exciting area of the curriculum. It remains for teachers to be sure of the goals for which social studies is taught and to select the content and strategies to achieve those goals.

Goals for Social Studies

In our consideration of goals the critical question is how well are we preparing children for democratic citizenship. While it is true that all facets of the school program make contributions to this fundamental purpose of education, social studies has a particularly significant role to play. The qualities of the democratic citizen can be illustrated and emphasized by both the content and method of social studies. If the social studies curriculum has been planned with the intention of developing knowledgeable, concerned, and active citizenship, children will have opportunities to acquire intellectual understanding of what it is like to live in a democracy. They become aware of the values and attitudes that make the American way of life work. They participate at their maturity level in the actions that citizens take in improving their society. They become creative thinkers who can meet the problems of a changing, shrinking world. Mere learning of subject matter will not be enough. Goals for social studies must be directed toward helping pupils meet the demands of public life on a broad front.

Goals for social studies may be categorized in several ways, but presently they are being thought of in four groups: content goals, affective goals, behavioral goals, and cognitive goals. A clear understanding of these goals and their unique characteristics provides guidance in determin-

---

[4] *Taba Social Studies Curriculum,* Guides for Grades One Through Eight (Palo Alto, California: Addison-Wesley Publishing Company, 1969).

ing the direction for a program and instruction in social studies. Confusion and lack of clarity about goals make planning for social studies unnecessarily difficult.

Content

Content goals have traditionally been the priority goals of social studies instruction, with facts and information high on the list of desired outcomes. Today content goals in social studies go beyond facts and information. There is currently little support for content goals which stop with the acquisition of information, because fact-oriented goals afford little opportunity for pupils to become involved with problems, issues, or significant topics. On the other hand, it is recognized that facts and information form the data base for developing high-level content goals: generalizations, understandings, and their related concepts.

The highest order of content goals are generalizations drawn from the social sciences and now rather familiar to teachers who are using programs developed in recent years. These social science generalizations have been discussed previously in this chapter. Because lists of such generalizations may seem at times to be overwhelming in their scope, there have been some attempts to integrate the ideas from social sciences into a composite framework of generalizations for social studies. One such early effort served for many years as the basis for curriculum development in other parts of the country and is still an excellent example of the integrative nature of social studies. Although there were eighteen generalizations in this list, those identified here are among the ones frequently developed at the elementary school level.

1. CHANGE is a condition of human society; societies rise and fall; value systems improve or deteriorate; the tempo of change varies with cultures and periods of history.

2. Through all time and in all regions of the world, man has worked to meet common BASIC HUMAN NEEDS and to satisfy common human desires and aspirations.

3. INTERPENDENCE is a constant factor in human relationships. The realization of self develops through contact with others. Social groupings of all kinds develop as a means of group cooperation in meeting individual and societal needs.

4. The CULTURE under which an individual is reared and the social groups to which he belongs exert great influence on his ways of perceiving, thinking, feeling, and acting.

5. In the United States DEMOCRACY is dependent on the process of inquiry; this process provides for defining the problem, seeking data, using the scientific method in collecting evidence, restating the problem in terms of its interrelationships, arriving at a principle that is applicable, and applying the principle in the solution of a problem.

6. DEMOCRACY is based on such beliefs as the integrity of man, the dignity of the individual, equality of opportunity, man's rationality, man's morality, man's ability to govern himself and to solve his problems cooperatively.

7. ENVIRONMENT affects man's ways of living, and man, in turn, modifies his environment.[5]

It is obvious that statements like these are global in their application, and yet they stand as significant ideas which explain human interaction and relationships. They have broad application to many areas of living and yet do not in themselves specify particular studies. Generalizations do not refer to particular people, places, times, or activities. They do show relationships between concepts which also must be understood if the generalization is to have meaning.

Concepts are words or phrases which indicate a label for a group of objects or ideas. They may be simple classifications like *chair, tree,* or *baby;* but in social studies they are likely to be more abstract and inclusive like *change, basic needs, cultural contribution, interdependence, democracy, values, environment, culture.* Such labels or concepts may have specific meanings, but each also calls to mind a whole cluster of ideas and interpretations. When we try to express in words what the concepts stand for or how they are related to other concepts, we arrive at generalizations.

For example, consider the generalization, *Environment affects our ways of living, and we, in turn, modify our environment.* At least two very big concepts are imbedded in this statement (*environment* and *ways of living*) and how they are related is the point of the generalization. Similarly the relationship between *values* and *society* is stated in the generalization, *The basic substance of a society is rooted in its values.* In another generalization, *In the United States democracy is dependent on the process of inquiry,* the relationship of *inquiry* to *democracy* is highlighted.

Assuming that we wish to use these broad generalizations as the content base of social studies, there still remains the task of simplifying them to provide a realistic framework for the problems pupils will study. When

[5] *Report of the State Central Committee on Social Studies to the California State Curriculum Commission* (Sacramento: California State Department of Education, 1961), pp. 40–42.

generalizations are broken down into summary statements more closely related to children's study, they become lower-order generalizations called *understandings*. Understandings are more specific than generalizations previously listed, because they deal with particular times, places, people, or activities. Each understanding immediately reveals the nature of the content to be studied and corresponds directly to the problem being investigated. Note the relationships in each of the sets which follow:

1. *Generalization:* The way in which people meet their basic needs is dependent upon and influenced by the environment in which they live.
   Understanding: Because of lack of water and air on the moon's surface, living there will be different in many ways from life on earth.
   Problem: Why will living on the moon be different from living on the earth?
2. *Generalization:* The culture under which we are reared has great influence upon our beliefs and values.
   Understanding: Family life in Japan and family life in our community differ in some ways because of the traditions that people prize.
   Problem: Why are family life in Japan and in our community different?
3. *Generalization:* People of all races, religions, and cultures have contributed to our cultural heritage.
   Understanding: Minority groups in our country have made many contributions to music, literature, and art.
   Problem: How have our minority groups enriched the lives of people in our country?

Of course, generalizations are achieved through continual reinforcement, as understandings concerning many aspects of human relationships are developed by pupils. The strengthening of generalizations may take place in a kind of spiral as children become increasingly mature in studies of their world. Figure 1–4 illustrates how understandings provide cumulative learning toward a broad generalization.

It is possible also to make progress toward generalizations through a variety of content avenues. For example, note how understandings developed in the following series of studies contribute to developing the concept

The Generalization: Everywhere, past, present, and future, people strive to meet their needs for the basic necessities of life.

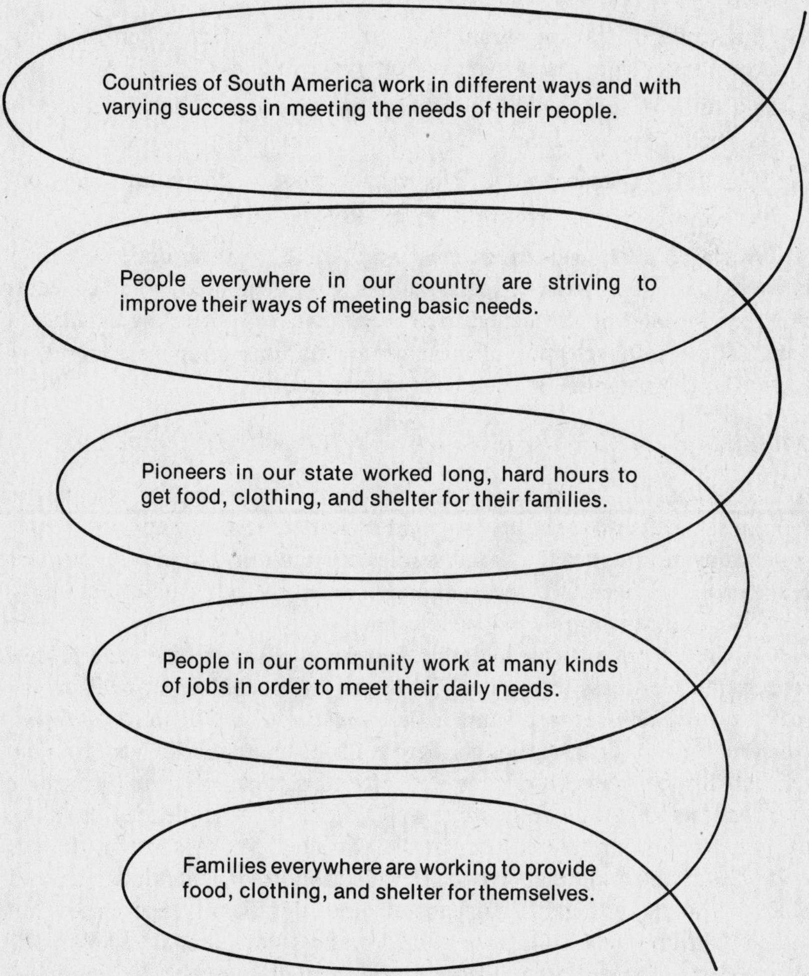

Countries of South America work in different ways and with varying success in meeting the needs of their people.

People everywhere in our country are striving to improve their ways of meeting basic needs.

Pioneers in our state worked long, hard hours to get food, clothing, and shelter for their families.

People in our community work at many kinds of jobs in order to meet their daily needs.

Families everywhere are working to provide food, clothing, and shelter for themselves.

Figure 1–4. Cumulative learning spiral.

of *change* and the generalization: *Ways of living change as people strive to meet old and new needs in better ways.*

1. In a study of families, this understanding: Family members engage in activities that are sometimes quite different from family life when our grandparents were children.

2. In a study of community, this understanding: As our community grows, the kinds of services needed are not the same as they used to be.

3. In a study of the farm: Farmers use many kinds of machinery that were unknown in pioneer days.

4. In a study of transportation: As our methods of transportation improve, it becomes easier to move from place to place.

5. In a study of schools: What children are taught in schools changes as the needs of people change.

6. In a study of environment: People have changed the natural environment in an effort to make their lives more pleasant.

Social studies generalizations and their related understandings become the content goals of social studies, complemented by the concepts inherent in each of the generalized ideas and supported by significant facts. The careful selection of these generalizations gives meaningful direction to the program at each level of instruction.

Affective

Affective goals in social studies are the attitudes and values essential to human survival and to the achievement of democracy; they appear in most statements of intent in the social studies curriculum, but very often their realization has been left to casual effort or, in the opposite direction, to approaches that resemble indoctrination.

Attitudes are difficult to define, but we may say that in general they represent a readiness to respond. They can be recognized as goals which seek *awareness, respect, desire, appreciation, willingness, interest, concern,* and so forth. Although there is little concrete evidence of a firm relationship between knowledge and attitudes, teachers usually assume that if pupils know and understand well an idea or principle they will more likely hold appropriate and compatible attitudes. In other words, there is a view that the building of broad, well-supported generalizations and related understandings through varied and significant experiences can and should influence children's attitudes and values. For the most part, attitudes are learned and generally are related to specific things and groups. They tend to persist but can and do change as people improve their insights and gain new views of persons, things, and issues.

Values are stronger than attitudes and usually become established through a process which has been described as choosing, prizing, and acting.[6] This process implies that values are not capriciously chosen and

---

[6] Louis E. Raths, Merrill Harmin, and Sidney B. Simon, *Values and Teaching: Working with Values in the Classroom* (Columbus, Ohio: Charles E. Merrill Publishing, 1966), pp. 28–30.

casually supported but become part of the fabric of an individual's personal and social actions. Developing values compatible with the American dream seems to be properly the concern of social studies education, although there is some reluctance on the part of teachers to undertake values education directly. And yet, it is impossible to avoid teaching values in social studies, for everything teachers do—establishing goals, selecting content, choosing teaching strategies—is a reflection of values. The classroom itself is a demonstration of the worth of the individual and the value put upon thinking, creativity, and freedom.

Selecting the values that should become the affective goals of social studies instruction is another matter, of course. And, while educators are stressing the importance of values, few have attempted to identify them specifically. Dunfee and Crump emphasize five values which they consider relevant to the social education of children and youth in modern society: self-concept, world friendship, environmental protection, democracy, and human rights.[7]

Among these values, especially prized are those that are derived from our heritage of great documents and the struggles to make them a reality. Such values as freedom, respect for law, worth of the individual, responsibility, and participation are crucial to the maintenance of a free society. They are given special priority because democracy cannot survive unless these values become part of the value systems of individual citizens and are exemplified in cooperative actions for the common good. How these values are to be developed is the question with which social studies educators are struggling.

Currently values education is emphasizing the process of valuing, which is designed to encourage pupils to examine values held by themselves and others, to study value conflicts and their resolution, and to arrive at a value system by which their lives may be guided. Valuing becomes an integral part of social studies as pupils consider these questions: Why do persons do what they do? How do the values people hold influence their behavior? How can value conflicts be solved? The social studies program that is concerned with affective goals affords pupils an environment in which they may question, express opinions, and explore motivations and consequences. In classrooms where values and valuing are avoided, these means of learning are closed to them.

Behavioral

Behavioral goals in social studies are the actions pupils will take now and as adults because of their convictions that the generalizations and under-

---

[7] Maxine Dunfee and Claudia Crump, *Teaching for Social Values in Social Studies* (Washington, D.C.: Association for Childhood Education International, 1974).

standings arrived at through their social studies experiences have meaning in everyday living. Behavioral goals assume that children will be able to translate their social studies learnings into their day-to-day existence, to apply them to problems that arise outside the school, and to make decisions compatible with them. What our pupils will do in the face of problems that arise in the life around them is a test of what they have learned in social studies. Will they perform confidently and resolutely? Will they make concerted effort to improve the well-being of others, strive to right the wrongs of the society, protect the environment so that others may enjoy it, work to make democracy a reality, and promote feelings of warmth and friendship among people?

On the other hand, these behavioral goals, however worthy, may seem somewhat idealistic unless we specify the particular actions which pupils may (ought to?) take as a follow-up of their involvement with and concern for a problem or issue. Are the behavioral goals associated with each of the following problems realistic for elementary school children? Try to add others to each set; eliminate those with which you do not agree.

1. The Problem: How do drugs help or harm us?

   Some Behavioral Goals
   The child removes drugs from container or cabinet only under the supervision of responsible adults.
   The child uses a drug only when prescribed by a doctor.
   The child refuses edible substances offered by strangers.

2. The Problem: Why do we have laws?

   Some Behavioral Goals
   The child cooperates in making and enforcing group rules.
   The child observes traffic and other safety regulations.
   The child obeys instructions given by police.

3. The Problem: Why is litter a problem at our school?

   Some Behavioral Goals
   The child disposes of litter in appropriate ways.
   The child admonishes others who are littering.
   The child participates in clean-up campaigns and encourages others to do so.

4. Why should citizens vote?

   Some Behavioral Goals
   The child participates in decision making at home, school, and community.

The adult studies issues and makes rational decisions.
The adult assumes responsibility for voting regularly.

━━━━━━━━━━━━━━━━━━━━━━━━━━━━━━

Cognitive

Cognitive goals emphasize the processes of logical thought. They differ from the content, affective, and behavioral goals of social studies, because they are more closely akin to skills than to particular problems, issues, or topics. In other words, cognitive goals are an integral part of the social studies curriculum and represent the methods used to identify problems, formulate hypotheses, gather and interpret information in order to test hypotheses, and draw some conclusions about possible solutions. While these goals are applicable to many areas of the elementary school curriculum, they are particularly significant in social studies. Based on extensive research on children's thinking, Fraenkel identifies these thinking operations: observing, describing, developing concepts, differentiating, defining, hypothesizing, comparing and contrasting, generalizing, predicting, explaining, and offering alternatives.[8] He recommends direct teaching of these skills as well as their continual use in pupil inquiry.

These operations are emphasized also in the following proposed framework of goals for social studies. It is a good example of a succinct statement of what pupils should be able to do as a result of their social studies experiences—in other words, the cognitive goals. Note also how relevant these goals are to the education of citizens in democracy.

1. Define issues, problems, and topics of study clearly, giving attention to values and other affective elements as well as to concepts and other cognitive elements.
2. Select and use appropriate modes of inquiry in terms of the problem or topic under study.
3. Select and use appropriate processes of inquiry in light of the mode of inquiry that is being used at a given time.
4. Interpret data meaningfully, assess the accuracy of information, and communicate these ideas effectively.

---

[8] Jack R. Fraenkel, *Helping Students Think and Value* (Englewood Cliffs, New Jersey: Prentice-Hall, 1973), p. 189.

5. Use concepts as tools to analyze problems, guide observation, make comparisons, classify data, interpret findings, and communicate ideas.

6. Contrast or compare events and activities as appropriate to explore identities, similarities, and differences.

7. Analyze rights, freedoms, and responsibilities in the context of relevant values and underlying conditions.

8. Propose and evaluate solutions to problems in terms of consequence-analysis based on a priority of values.

9. Make and test hypotheses and generalizations, taking account of relevant information and avoiding generalizations.

10. Express and demonstrate ways in which fundamental values are a part of our American heritage.[9]

These then are the goals of social studies: *content goals* identified as generalizations and understandings and their related concepts; *affective goals* representative of the attitudes and values of the society; *behavioral goals* that serve as action guidelines for citizens young and old; and *cognitive goals* which define the processes of logical thought. Modes of teaching by which these goals are achieved are the focus of the chapter which follows.

---

[9] *Proposed Social Sciences Education Framework for California Public Schools: Report of the Statewide Social Sciences Study Committee to the State Curriculum Commission and the California State Board of Education* (Sacramento, California: California State Board of Education, 1968), p. 3.

Other Points of View

Ellis, Arthur K. *Teaching and Learning Elementary Social Studies.* Boston: Allyn Bacon, 1977.
Chapter 1: Social Studies: Ideas, Definitions, Trends; Chapter 6: The Social Sciences.

Jarolimek, John. *Social Studies in Elementary Education.* 5th ed. New York: Macmillan, 1977.
Chapter 1: The Social Studies Curriculum—Its Nature and Purposes; Chapter 6: Contributions of the Social Sciences.

Manson, Gary; Marker, Gerald; Ochoa, Anna; and Tucker, Jan. "Social Studies Curriculum Guidelines." *Social Education* 35 (December 1971):854–66.
Definitive statements from the National Council for the Social Studies Task Force on Curriculum Guidelines.

Martorella, Peter H. *Elementary Social Studies as a Learning System.* New York: Harper & Row, 1976.
Chapter 2: What's a Social Studies?

Michaelis, John U. *Social Studies for Children in a Democracy.* 6th ed. Englewood Cliffs, New Jersey: Prentice-Hall, 1976.
Chapter 1: The Social Studies; Chapter 2: Organizing the Program of Instruction.

Preston, Ralph C., and Herman, Wayne L., Jr. *Teaching Social Studies in the Elementary School.* 4th ed. New York: Holt, Rinehart and Winston, 1974.
Chapter 1: The Nature and Purpose of Social Studies; Chapter 3: Social Studies Curriculums Old and New.

Seif. Elliott. *Teaching Significant Social Studies in the Elementary School.* Chicago: Rand McNally, 1977.
Chapter 1: Significant Social Studies in the Elementary School.

Welton, David A., and Mallan, John T. *Children and Their World: Teaching Elementary Social Studies.* Chicago: Rand McNally, 1976.
Chapter 2: Social Studies and the Human Experience: The Disciplinary Foundations.

Two
Exploring Instructional Strategies

Deciding how to teach social studies in the classroom can be quite complex if teachers take into consideration all the elements of the emerging social studies curriculum about which educators are thinking and talking. Relevant to selection are the nature of the social science disciplines and their role in social studies, social studies as an area of the curriculum, and the goals for which it is responsible. Furthermore, those charged with making decisions about social studies instruction must provide balance in their attention to content, affective, behavioral, and cognitive goals, making sure that the search for and acquisition of knowledge does not overshadow concerns for values, behaviors, and thinking processes.

Teaching Strategies in Social Studies

The teaching strategies teachers choose are influenced by their understanding of social studies, their attitudes towards the relative values of the goals of social studies, their knowledge of possible teaching strategies, and very importantly, their own personalities, strengths, and weaknesses in instruction.

Teachers who are most concerned with the content goals of social studies select the strategy which emphasizes that facet of social studies. Those who are convinced that social studies instruction should take as its priority goal the development of cognitive goals (inquiry and problem-solving skills) put their emphasis upon the thinking processes and give less attention to particular content. Figure 2–1 represents the range of positions teachers may take. Those who are concerned about content goals but still mindful of the cognitive fall into the left portion of the rectangle (teachers 1 and 2); those who use content to develop thinking processes but are not concerned primarily with content belong to the far right of the diagram (teachers 9 and 10). Other teachers are in between, depending upon their values. Even though social studies is both content *and* a method of inquiry, teachers are likely to tip the balance in terms of their own perception of the goals of social studies.

Teaching strategies are, then, a reflection of teachers' points of view about what is important in social studies. Assuming that teachers generally support content goals and the affective, behavioral, and cognitive goals identified in the previous chapter, we would expect most teaching

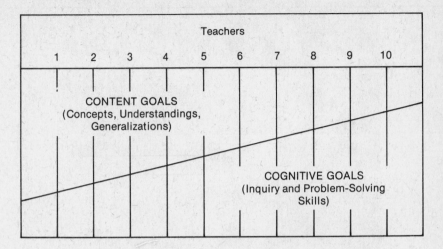

Figure 2–1. Teacher perception of content and cognitive goals.

models currently in use to reflect these goals in varying degrees of emphasis.

Teaching strategies relate not only to goal emphases, but they also indicate degrees of freedom ranging from directive methods of instruction to more open types of guidance. Everyone is familiar with the stereotype of the teacher who, textbook in hand, conducts children through the rigors of the lesson with planning, implementing, and evaluating entirely in adult hands. Few modern teachers fit this mold exactly, but they do differ in the extent to which their social studies instruction is closed or open. Usually the more open the strategy, the more opportunity pupils have to engage in creative thinking and to have input into the direction their study will take. In other words, it is probably possible to locate most social studies teachers on a continuum from closed to open, from teacher-centered to pupil-centered. Such a continuum is shown in Figure 2–2. At the far left of the line are the teachers of the most authoritarian persuasion; at the right are the most completely open teachers we can imagine. Probably neither of these types exists in the strict sense of the descriptions. On the line, however, as examples, we can locate several teaching strategies for social studies which are well-accepted by many teachers and which do not fall at the extremes of the continuum.

We should remind ourselves, moreover, that no teacher fits even one of these models exactly; and we can be sure that a particular teacher at various times alters the basic strategy so that it resembles one of the others or combines elements from several. Successful teachers know that not all

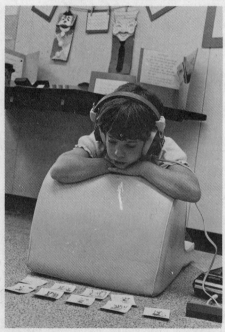

These pupils are using a variety of resources in their search for data about problems that are significant to them.

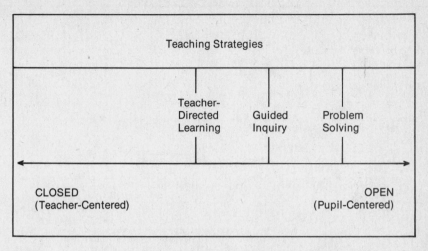

Figure 2–2. Continuum of teaching strategies.

things in social studies are best taught by a single strategy; they alter and change as the situation demands. For the purpose of clarifying these strategies, we can make some arbitrary distinctions as we consider each one.

Teacher-Directed Learning

Many teachers base their teaching strategy on a textbook or prescribed curriculum outline. They believe that there are many advantages: predetermined goals, well-defined content, and specific directions for procedures. Attractive format and supplementary teaching aids characteristic of modern textbook programs are also appealing to teachers and pupils.

Do you remember the teacher in the prologue who used a textbook to develop ideas about housing problems? As you study the lesson plan from the teacher's guide, consider these points.

1. What procedure is used to develop the content?
2. What sources of data are pupils using?
3. What goals are most strongly emphasized?
4. Who is responsible for developing the lesson?
5. How are pupils likely to be evaluated?

Macmillan Excerpt. How would you characterize this lesson? Is it like the social studies you remember from your elementary school days? In

Learning outcome: The pupil relates text and pictorial data on housing problems.

Material used:

√ *Web of the World*, pages 230–234
√ Study Prints 24-31 OR locally available pictures of urban renewal projects

Teaching strategy:

1. *Linking previous learning to the lesson of the day*

The pupil confirms ideas through reading.

● Pages 230–234 should be read to confirm the ideas developed in the previous lesson.

2. *Using pictures to expand concepts related to housing*

● These pictures in the text should be considered:

. . . recognizes the need for criteria in making evaluations or comparisons.

○ The pictures on page 231 show a radial (top) and grid (bottom) pattern of street planning. Pupils might compare these to local street patterns. They might also be compared in terms of efficiency (traffic, shopping) and aesthetic appeal.

● The caption question under the picture on page 232 should be answered by pupils. (The people who live in this housing can't afford or obtain better housing; they typically are low income groups who can't move easily.)

. . . interprets pictures by applying relevant information.

○ Additional questions should be raised about this picture:

—"What do you think might happen to the people who are moved out of the buildings shown in the picture? Can you see a serious problem that arises when apartments are torn down in order to build newer and larger apartments?" (The people in them may have no good place to live during the years that the new buildings are being erected.)

—"Can you think of some ways to solve the problems of moving people out of old buildings so that new buildings can be built there?" (Perhaps destroying only a few of the old buildings at a time, putting up larger apartments to accommodate the people in the next block to be destroyed, rehabilitating old houses instead of tearing them down.)

. . . gets data from graphs.

○ The table at the bottom of page 233 should be considered. Pupils should understand that:

—the figures refer to all housing, not just cities. (See caption.)

—the figures only establish minimum standards of electricity and plumbing, not the quality of the houses.

—the figures suggest the conclusion that there are many houses in the United States that are not desirable places in which to live.

● If Study Prints 24-31 are available, they should be displayed in random order, in such a way that pupils can examine them, read the captions, and suggest meaningful ways to arrange them. Pupils should notice that there are three "before-and-after" pairs that show large-scale urban renewal: 24-25, 28-29, and 30-31. Two study prints show the possibilities of renewal of individual buildings: 26 and 27.

The pupil sees cause-and-effect and other relationships.

● If Study Prints 24-31 are *not* available, use locally available pictures of urban renewal. These should be displayed and worked with in a similar way to reveal before-and-after situations.

● After a comparison of before-and-after pictures has revealed common patterns of change, discussion should focus on the quality of life that is available to people who live in both the "before" settings and the "after" settings.

. . . takes part in class discussion.

. . . makes inferences and draws conclusions. 1

---

[1] Used by permission of Macmillan Publishing Co., Inc., from Teacher's Annotated Edition for *Web of the World,* Teacher's Guide, by Phillip Viereck, Bertha Davis, and Joseph Decaroli, pp. 157–159. Copyright © 1973 Macmillan Publishing Co., Inc.

what ways does it seem innovative? How well does it match the description of teacher-directed learning which follows? In what respects is it different? Is it possible to locate the lesson strategy on the continuum in Figure 2–2?

━━

Teacher-Directed Learning

1. Instructional strategy is based on a textbook and/or curriculum outline.

2. Major emphasis is on information, concepts, and generalizations (content goals) with some attention to other goals.

3. Content of the textbook or curriculum outline follows a grade-by-grade scope and sequence pattern.

4. Supplementary learning resources are suggested and/or provided—pictures, maps, charts, graphs, etc.

5. Learning experiences are described in the textbook or curriculum outline and directed by teachers, with varying degrees of freedom.

6. Pupils are engaged in responding to the preplanned program—reading, discussing, reporting, etc.

━━

Guided Inquiry

Do you recall the classroom event in the prologue in which pupils were asked to replan a burned-out part of a make-believe city? The content of the lesson—city planning for housing—is similar to the content of the previous lesson. Study the excerpt from the teacher's guide, using these questions to compare the two lessons.

1. Is the procedure similar? If not, how does it differ?
2. How do data sources in the two lessons compare?
3. Has goal emphasis changed?
4. Is the teacher's role the same or different?
5. How do you think pupils may be evaluated?

Holt Excerpt. What do you conclude about the similarities and differences in the two lessons? Is the City Planning Game a teacher-directed experience or does it represent a somewhat different approach? To what extent does it illustrate the components of guided inquiry which follow? Where would you place it on the continuum in Figure 2–2?

INTRODUCING THE GAME

Point out the *Evry City Land Use Map* to the children. Allow them to inspect it closely if they wish. Explain that it is a special kind of map for an imaginary city called Evry City. It is a land use map. The different colors stand for the different ways in which land in Evry City is used. Who can figure out where the houses, stores, offices, schools, factories, and parks in Evry City are located?

When the children have had sufficient time to work with the map so that they feel comfortable using it, explain that in the next few days, they are going to play a game to plan Evry City. They will learn how to play it by listening to an imaginary letter. Read this letter to them:

> Dear Class:
>
> I am the Mayor of Evry City, and I would like to ask you a favor. Last month, we had a terrible fire in Evry City. Before we could put it out, many buildings in one part of the city were destroyed. The people who lived there lost their houses and had to move away.

Now we want to rebuild that part of the city, and we would like your help. Most of the people want:

1. to have open spaces for parks and playgrounds.
2. to be close to schools and stores.
3. to have safe, quiet, and clean streets without many cars.
4. to be able to move about in their neighborhood easily and to be able to get to other parts of the city quickly.

There are 75 families, with 232 children and 143 grown-ups, who are going to live in the rebuilt area. They own 100 cars which they have to park near their homes.

Can you help to make a plan for rebuilding this part of Evry City?

> Sincerely yours,
> J. P. Higgins,
> Mayor of Evry City

Write the requirements stated in the letter on the chalkboard where the children can study them. Answer any questions, and tell the pupils that the game will continue in the next lesson.

• INDIVIDUAL PLANNING

Remind the children of the letter you read at the end of the last lesson. Point out the list of requirements on the chalkboard. Then show the children the area marked in red on the *Evry City Land Use Map.* Point out that it is far from any parks, and it has homes on one side, warehouses on another, and businesses on another.

Then give each student a copy of Game 3 Data Master 1: *City Planning Site in Evry City.* Explain that each child now have learned about city mix in making their plans. If they seem confused, show them some examples of where they might put one or two types of structures on an extra copy of Data Master 1. Emphasize that there is no right or wrong way to

has his own map of the part of Evry City that will be rebuilt. Point out again that this is the area marked in red on the wall map. Each child is to draw his plan for rebuilding the burned-out area on his own map. The key on the large wall map will help him draw houses, apartments, schools, stores, offices, parks, and other structures. It will also help him to make his map drawings a good size.

Remind the children to use the chalkboard requirements and what they make a plan like this and that the plans will not be graded. Then ask each child to use the rest of the period to make his plan. The children may get up to inspect the wall map, to consult with each other, or to ask you questions if they need help. [2]

---

[2] From *Inquiring About Cities* Teacher's Guide by W.G. Fielder and G. Feeney, pp. 295–97. Copyright © 1972 by Holt, Rinehart and Winston, Publishers. Used by permission.

━━━━━━━━━━━━━━━━━━━━━━━━━━━━━━━━━━

Guided Inquiry

1. Instructional strategy is based on predesigned, nontextbook materials.
2. Major emphasis is on inquiry (cognitive goals) with some attention to other goals.
3. Content for inquiry departs from the usual scope and sequence pattern.
4. Various primary and secondary sources of data are provided—logs, databooks, films, tapes, etc.
5. Learning experiences are preplanned by authors and guided by teachers, with varying degrees of freedom.
6. Pupils are engaged in inquiry through reading, interpreting and summarizing data, discussion, role playing, projects, etc.

━━━━━━━━━━━━━━━━━━━━━━━━━━━━━━━━━━

Problem Solving

The continuum from closed to open, from teacher-centered to pupil-centered, in Figure 2–2 shows a third strategy: problem solving. Judging from its place on the line, how do you think it may differ from the others? Can we expect it to be more structured or less? More pupil involving or less? More concerned or less concerned with content goals? Recall the children in the prologue who were making a plan for the redevelopment of Hunters Point, a slum area in their city. Here is how their adventure started and what happened. As you read, think about these questions.

1. How does the procedure differ from previous lessons?
2. What data sources are pupils using?
3. What are their goals?
4. What is the teacher's role?
5. How will pupils' learning be evaluated?

The season of fall can be a hot one in San Francisco, and October 1966 was "hotter" in more ways than one. A policeman had shot a teenager in Hunters Point and the thermometer outside registered close to 100 degrees. . . .

The temperature in the classroom at Sheridan School rose to match the emotional climate outside. . . . I had 36 angry and highly motivated children ready to go on a safari into city problems.

The next few days brought a more dispassionate discussion. . . .

Deeper problems began to emerge. The villain of the piece [the cop] slowly faded into the background and the children wanted to know instead what the city was doing, for example, about housing, education, recreation for children, and transportation. The air had begun to cool, but the questions were just as intense: "What is the city doing about improving Hunters Point and other slums in San Francisco?" In a week's time, we had disposed of the cop—and had new questions that had to be answered, new problems to be solved. . . .

The gathering of information presented some problems. The average reading level of the class was possibly on a low fifth par. About eight children in the class were reading at third grade and maybe this same number were managing the sixth-grade text. But there were those happy bubbling faces poring over the newspaper every morning in class like a bunch of medieval scholars—grappling with new words, ideas, and concepts: Redevelopment; Rehabilitation; Western Addition; Federal Government; Integration and Segregation; Urban Renewal; Rapid Transit. . . . Who says children can't read?

. . . While the children were beginning to read and use new vocabulary they were also discovering the limitations of the written word. They even began to question the validity of some of the information, especially in the slick literature sent out by the Redevelopment Agency . . . .

The children invited many speakers and celebrities from all walks of life to come out and talk to their class. A local minister active in community affairs talked about the immediate local needs and problems. Higher-ups from the Redevelopment Planning Board spoke, and the class confronted them with annoying questions. . . .

Then it came time for us to see for ourselves. What was a slum really like? Were the new housing projects as good as they were said to be? . . . and off we went to explore the city. . . .

An excursion to the inner sanctum of the Redevelopment Headquarters. . . brought the insulting question, politely phrased, "Where are those plans for Hunters Point?" Alas, sadly, the children learned that there were tentative plans for the future. . . but nothing definite yet. (My class mathematician quickly figured that the Agency had been planning for some 26 years.) . . . The children were angered and disappointed by the Agency's slow progress with Hunters Point; but they were not discouraged. *If the city would not do it, they would organize their own plan for redeveloping Hunters Point!*[3]

In the Hunters Point experience there are some elements that did not appear in the other lessons on urban redevelopment which we have studied. Can you identify them? Where would you locate the experience on the

[3] Association for Supervision and Curriculum Development, *Hunters Point Redeveloped: A Sixth-Grade Venture* (Washington, D.C.: Author, 1970), pp. 5–7.

continuum in Figure 2–2? How well does it match the description of the problem-solving strategy which follows?

Problem Solving

1. Instructional strategy is based on problems identified as significant by teacher and pupils.
2. Major emphasis is on problem solving (cognitive goals) and on problem solutions (behavioral goals), with some attention to other goals.
3. Content relates to current situations or problems being investigated by teacher and pupils.
4. Many kinds of data sources are identified by teacher and pupils.
5. Learning experiences are planned cooperatively and are determined by problems and questions being studied.
6. Pupils are engaged in gathering data from community and print sources as they test hypotheses for possible solutions to problems.

If you are an experienced teacher, you probably have a teaching strategy that works well for you. You already may have identified where you are on the continuum from closed to open, from teacher-centered to pupil-centered. If you are an inexperienced teacher, you are in the process of developing your own teaching style. You will no doubt do considerable experimenting before you find your own place on the continuum. Further discussion of programs and processes may aid your choices.

Preplanned Programs in Social Studies

As pointed out previously, the preplanned program has contributions to make to instruction in social studies. It defines a body of content, thus relieving the teacher of responsibility for deciding what to teach. It identifies the goals which are to be achieved and suggests the techniques for achieving these goals. To the extent that the teacher agrees that the content is well-selected, the goals defensible, and the techniques compatible with present teaching styles and beliefs about how children learn, the preplanned program often works out well. The excerpts studied earlier in this chapter are representative of the ways in which teaching materials and teachers' guides combine to move pupils toward predetermined goals.

Textbooks

The demand for social studies textbooks is not likely to decrease, for they offer teachers the security they feel they need. Dissatisfactions with the textbooks of earlier years have led, moreover, to many improvements in both content and method. There are probably no textbooks in use today that adhere to the read-recite-test strategy common in the past, although it is possible for teachers to use the same time-worn and uninspiring formula on the best of modern textbooks. If a textbook is to be used as the foundation of social studies instruction, there are cautions for the teacher:

1. Become thoroughly familiar with the content of the textbook and the series to which it belongs. If the content load seems unduly heavy, make some decisions about content which should receive greatest emphasis.

2. Be sure you know how the content of the textbook fits into the scope and sequence of the entire program.

3. Study carefully the general philosophy of social studies instruction and the assumptions about children's learning upon which the series is based. Usually appropriate statements are included in the teacher's guide. If you do not agree, be prepared to make adjustments in the suggested teaching strategy.

4. Study the objectives to see how well they match yours; plan different emphases if you disagree.

5. Become thoroughly acquainted with the teaching strategy. Ask for one or more workshop sessions with the publisher's representative if the strategy is not clear.

6. If the teaching strategy is more closed than you prefer, consider how you can alter the techniques to give more opportunity for pupil involvement.

7. If you prefer more emphasis upon problem solving—the position farther to the right on the continuum—consider how you may use the textbook as a guide to problems pupils may identify and how they may use it as a data source in their investigations.

Criteria for Selection

Careful initial selection of the textbook series is of importance to teachers. Sometimes teachers have a voice in the choice for their school system; sometimes the decision is made by a committee of teachers or by the administration. If you have the opportunity to assist in finding the right textbook, these criteria may sharpen your search.

1. Does the textbook develop the concepts and understandings that you consider appropriate for your pupils?

2. Is the content likely to seem significant to your pupils, relevant to their daily lives, challenging intellectually?

3. Does the textbook teach the skills of inquiry?

4. Are attitudes and values which are compatible with a democratic society emphasized?

5. Is the style informal and interesting to children?

6. Are map skills and reading research skills systematically developed?

7. Do the visuals contribute to achievement of objectives identified by the authors?

8. Are there supplementary aids to instruction?

9. Is the reading level of the textbook appropriate for your pupils?

10. Is the format attractive and the textbook easy to handle and use?

In addition to these criteria, we must add those that will insure the choice of a textbook which emphasizes human dignity and depicts all human groups without bias. We should ask these questions about the textbook we are considering for adoption. Fortunately there are textbook series that meet these criteria successfully.

1. Does the textbook avoid use of content or phrasing which would be found objectionable by any group?

2. Does the textbook accept all groups as worthy of fair and accurate treatment?

3. Do the textbook illustrations portray individuals from various groups accurately in appearance and in cultural characteristics?

4. Does the textbook show integrated groups performing worthy services and cooperatively solving social problems?

5. Does the textbook emphasize the importance of freedom, justice, and equal treatment for all groups?

Textbook Programs

Some textbook programs in use today were developed initially under grants from the federal government or from foundations and subsequently found their way into publications by commercial companies. In all these programs there are many well-developed pupil materials: textbooks or booklets, complemented by a variety of other aids, including tapes, pictures, and slides. All of them propose to develop generalizations from the social sciences through inquiring and valuing processes. On the continuum of teaching strategies they fall somewhere in the range from teacher-directed learning to guided inquiry. Without attempting to evaluate, we will review briefly some of the better-known programs which originally were government or foundation funded.

Concepts and Inquiry: The Educational Research Council Social Studies Program (Allyn and Bacon, Inc.). A K–12 multidisciplinary sequence which places considerable emphasis upon subject matter in an extensive array of booklets. From them pupils acquire data from which to draw social science generalizations. Activities and resources supplement their reading. Pupils are asked to deal with expository content in an inquiry strategy. Teacher questioning is structured to encourage thinking about issues and topics outside the immediate environment.

Our Working World (Science Research Associates), formerly the *Experiment in Economic Education,* now encompasses all the social science disciplines and encourages pupils to draw upon their ideas in inquiry and decision making. Flexibility is possible in the implementation of the various textbook units, with choices to be made among many suggested activities and resources. Inquiry techniques are used in the analysis of social problems posed by the content of the program. Cognitive goals are of major concern, but affective goals are approached through choice-making. *Our Working World* is a carefully detailed program with a social emphasis.

The *Taba Program in Social Science* (Addison-Wesley), in its original format as a funded program, appeared in a series of elementary level curriculum guides, accompanied by a teacher's handbook designed to clarify the teaching strategy. Its primary focus is the development of cognitive skills through inquiry and the use of content as illustrative of concepts and generalizations. Its inductive approach is based on the studies Taba and associates made of children's thinking; knowledge of their theories and findings is basic to understanding the program. There now are textbooks for the program, and teacher attention has been directed to techniques for their use in achieving the original objectives of the program.

The *Georgia Anthropology Curriculum Project* (University of Georgia) is not a textbook program in the usual sense of the word, but it does provide a textbook-workbook format. It uses a highly expository method of imparting information about culture and the methods of archaeology. Its deductive character is rather unique among current materials and its place is to the left on our continuum from teacher-centered to pupil-centered strategies.

Multimedia Programs

Although almost all programs in social studies have built into them a variety of supplementary resources, there are some that rely somewhat less on text materials than the ones previously mentioned. The multimedia programs are designed to encourage pupils to use the methods and data sources of the social scientist to achieve program-identified goals. Data sources range from print materials, tapes, recordings, slides, films, and filmstrips to artifacts and other primary sources. The *Holt Databank System,* from which an excerpt was included previously in this chapter, is representative of these programs. Most of them use a *guided-inquiry* strategy.

Many of the multimedia programs, unlike the *Databank,* were origi-nally funded projects. *Man: A Course of Study* (Curriculum Development Associates) is one of the more controversial programs in use. This one-year course, originally planned for the fifth grade, has now been used at several levels and has been sufficiently challenging to interest high school students. Though the core discipline is anthropology, the program incorporates other disciplines as well, as pupils study humanity and our humanness in contrast to other creatures. The course uses a rather startling departure in content to develop concepts of life cycle, adaptation, and natural selection. The method is one of comparison and contrast, supplemented by simulation, role-playing, and independent investigation. Primary data sources play an important role in the program.

Similarly, *Project Social Studies* (University of Minnesota) is a K–12 program using the concept of culture as the content thread and drawing upon various social science disciplines. It places stress upon content organized in a sequential way and relies on resource units rather than on children's materials. Inquiry is the teaching strategy; pupils are encouraged to set up hypotheses and test them, usually through discussion. In later revisions, materials have appeared as multimedia units in the form of *Family of Man* kits (Selective Educational Equipment, Inc.), each containing books, visuals, tapes, and artifacts, as well as a guide for their use.

MATCH, Materials and Activities for Teachers and Children (Boston Children's Museum) is a series of kits containing a broad range of materials: realia, films, recordings, maps, games, reference books, and construction materials. Pupils manipulate the materials under the teacher's guidance to inquire about the city, about a foreign culture, and about an ancient society. Pupils are encouraged to inquire—to find out how to approach a problem, to hypothesize, to reason, and to formulate conclusions. A guide to the learning strategy assists the teacher in making the most of the resources to achieve the cognitive and affective goals of the program. Flexible use, however, is encouraged as teachers try to meet the varied learning styles of pupils.

This brief survey of some of the social studies programs now in use provides considerable evidence that guided inquiry as a teaching strategy is gaining in influence. Both textbook approaches and multimedia, non-textbook programs, share this interest in strategies that encourage pupil thinking and inquiring. The guided-inquiry strategy differs, however, from a problem-solving strategy, which is somewhat more open and which involves pupils more actively in problem identification and cooperative planning.

The Problem-Solving Process

The problem-solving strategy is dominated by the problem-solving process, a method by which we seek solutions to human dilemmas or answers to challenging questions. The process requires skills which are perfected best by practice. While it may be useful to tell someone how problems may be solved, such a description fails in one very important respect: it is not a substitute for experiencing the process. Furthermore, the description may fail to take into consideration the fact that there is no single method by which all problems are solved or the fact that some problems defy solution. Our verbal description which follows suffers from these shortcomings, but it may clarify the essential steps in the process and help us to understand how a problem-solving strategy may differ from a guided-inquiry one.

Essential Conditions

Problem solving depends upon at least four conditions. The first is obvious: There must be a problem. The problem may be a real-life one that appears in the home, school, community, or larger environment, or it may be an intellectual one which intrigues pupils. In any case, a problem exists when the learner's previous knowledge or patterns of behavior do not provide adequate data for a satisfying solution.

Second, the problem must be recognized by the pupils. They may sense some disparity between what is and what ought to be, but they may not be aware that it could touch them in some way or that there is anything they could do about it. It is the teacher's task to set the stage in such a way as to capture the interest of the pupils and encourage them to become involved with the problem. How to build this readiness to investigate is the focus of Chapter 3 in this book.

Third, the problem statement must suggest clearly the nature of the solution; in other words, what are we looking for? What will be the product of our search? Some problems are so global that pupils have little idea about how to attack them; others are so broad that a solution is hard to visualize. By contrast, a sharp definition of the problem makes clear the solution being sought. Compare the sets of problems which follow. Does the first of each pair seem more explicit than the second?

Set 1. How have shopping centers changed the way people in our town meet their everyday needs?
Why do things change all the time?
Set 2. How do big cities try to provide better housing for their people?
Why do big cities have so many problems?
Set 3. How can we make our school grounds more attractive?
Why don't people stop littering everywhere?

We must hasten to point out, however, that pupils may very well identify these very broad problems as something they think is important to study. If they do, then teachers must help them break down the problem into questions which they can handle. For example, assume that children are concerned about littering. The teacher suggests that there may be some subproblems or questions that pupils can begin to investigate. They suggest some of them:

1. In our community, where does litter collect?

2. Who does the littering in each of these places?

3. By studying the places, can we hypothesize about why people are littering these spots?

4. How can we find ways to observe places where littering seems the worst?

5. How can we find out from people why they throw things away carelessly?

6. What can we do to stop our own littering?

There is yet a fourth condition upon which problem solving depends. The solution for the problem must be within the realm of possibility. It is discouraging to pupils to discover that there is no hope of finding an answer to a question in which they are vitally interested. Problem solving makes much more sense if there is promise of some tangible or at least possible solutions, some product in which they may take pride. On the other hand, it may be important for pupils to find out that some problems have no solutions at present and to understand better than before why there are unsolved problems in the world today.

Steps in Problem Solving

The *first step* in problem solving, then, is defining the problem and stating it clearly. Study the following problems. Does each exemplify the third and fourth conditions previously mentioned? Does each one indicate the nature of the solution? For each, is a solution possible? In other words: What is the investigator looking for? Are data available to solve the problem? Can the data be gathered by pupils?

1. How will living on the moon be different from living on earth?
2. Why does almost every town have a school?
3. Why is it dangerous for a city sanitation department to go on strike?
4. How would life in our community be changed if there were no ways to travel about except on foot?
5. Why did many people in our community fail to vote?
6. How does prejudice keep women from choosing their careers freely?
7. Why did Indiana pioneers have to depend on their environment for what they needed?
8. Why was it difficult for Vietnamese immigrants to learn to live in America?
9. How can we help other countries understand American ideas and values?
10. Why is television an important influence in everyday life?

Once the problem is identified, the *second step* follows naturally; it involves formulating hypotheses for testing. As pupils begin to pinpoint their concerns and interests, they quite often are eager to offer suggestions for solutions or state their ideas about why things are as they are; these are their hypotheses, their educated (or not so educated) guesses based on the information they have or think they have before investigation gets underway. While teachers may feel that some of the predictions are in fact already supported by known data or are quite obvious, if children state them seriously, they are worth considering. Then pupils can be readily challenged to gather data which will support or reject their predictions. It may be inappropriate for the teacher to discount or disparage a well-stated hypothesis simply because the outcome has been established or is known to others. If we are interested in the act of hypothesizing, then we value the thoughtful ideas of pupils and accept them at this point without trying to correct them or channel them in other directions.

For example, assume that pupils have chosen to investigate this problem: *How will living on the moon be different from living on earth?* Pupils, eager to begin answering the question at once, begin to formulate hypotheses in their own ways.

1. It will be necessary to provide a continuous supply of oxygen for those who live on the moon.

2. Houses will have windows that will not open because of the need to seal in the air.

3. People will need special outside clothes because of the temperature and lack of air.

4. There will be no recreation outside because of the heavy clothing we will have to wear.

5. There won't be many stores because of the difficulty of getting supplies to the moon.

6. Water will have to be manufactured in some new ways or brought from earth.

7. It will be impossible to drive the cars we now have on the surface of the moon.

8. Daily life on the moon will be easy because the weather doesn't change.

9. Foods will have to be grown without water.

10. Houses on the moon will not be built of lumber.

The *third step* in problem solving is the collection and ordering of data. Clearly stated problems and hypotheses suggest the nature of the data to be collected. These in turn imply appropriate sources. As will be discussed later in this book, there are many data sources, formal (current materials in print, special references, authoritative accounts, visuals, etc.) and informal (persons, organizations, environment, etc.). When these existing data sources are subjected to data gathering (reading, surveying, interviewing, observing) for a specific purpose, they become functional; otherwise they remain inactive until the learner calls upon them and relates them to a particular problem or hypothesis.

For example, in the problem about living on the moon, pupils have available much of the nontechnical knowledge astronauts and scientists have accumulated. However, until particular data are sought to support a hypothesis (Windows on the moon houses will not open because of the need to seal in air) or to answer its related problem (How will moon houses use windows?), the data will be buried in an inert mass of information. Furthermore, the value of data is their relationship to a problem; data seldom have intrinsic value.

Furthermore, a single source of data is rarely adequate to test a hypothesis or to solve its related problem. Pupils ask themselves whether or not they have sufficient data to cover all aspects of the hypothesis. Following are some of the questions that may guide data collection related to a single hypothesis about windows in moon houses.

1. Are the houses likely to have windows?
2. Will the windows be needed for ventilation?
3. For what purposes will windows be used?
4. How will air be kept inside houses?
5. Will doors and windows be used in the same way?
6. Will windows be made of the same materials we now use?

When data from an array of sources have been gathered in response to fact-seeking questions, they must be sorted and classified to render them serviceable. Data will be most readily related to hypotheses if they are ordered in such a way as to facilitate summarization. Without such ordering—outlining, charting, mapping, diagramming—data may remain fragmented.

The *fourth step* in problem solving requires pupils to study the ordered data to discover what they mean. When children have sufficient well-organized data to support a leap from facts to meanings, they are inferring from the data. In other words, given the information they now possess, they can make some inferences and apply them to hypotheses set up previously. These inferences are lower-order understandings, which refer directly to the time, place, or people being studied. Pupils, having firm evidence about conditions of life on the distant terrain of the moon, are ready to formulate understandings when the teacher asks, "What statements can you now make about what you have discovered?" The pupils reply:

1. Limited supplies of air and water on the moon's surface will make living there somewhat inconvenient unless new inventions improve the situation.
2. Many of the activities people engage in on the earth will be restricted on the moon because of environmental conditions; in time these limitations may be overcome.
3. Inventing ways to meet the problems of living on the moon will be a significant, continuing activity.
4. Living on the moon will require an adventuresome spirit, since new ways of doing things will have to be learned.

The *fifth step* in problem solving is the formulation of higher-level generalizations, with pupils taking still another leap to broader statements when the teacher asks, "Suppose you were interested in similar problems on Venus, or Mars, or even in some unknown part of the earth. What do you think you could predict about living in these places?'' The question is a likely lead-in to this high-level generalization: *Since the ways in which people live are affected by the environment, whenever they move into a new and very different one they have to adjust to these conditions, and they may have to change their old ways of living.* Or: *When people move to new environments, their ways of living change to the extent that the new surroundings are different from the old.*

These generalizations become then very general hypotheses to be tested with other content at some future time. Were they true of pioneers in our country? Of Europeans who came to America in the seventeenth century? Of those who first went to Australia? Are they true of farmers who move to the city? Of a neighbor who moves to Florida? Of those who will someday go to Mars?

In the very core of problem solving lies something more solid, more deeply dimensional than accumulation of information. To be sure, acquiring information is necessary in problem solving, but it is not an end in itself. It is analyzed, interpreted, and culled until its essence becomes clear. But this essence bears the stamp of logical, organized thinking and makes possible the identification of generalizations from which to infer new information and on which to base new hypotheses.

A *final step* in problem solving follows when the problem solution requires action, though it is obvious that some problems may not lend themselves to immediate implementation. On the other hand, when the big ideas at which pupils arrive indicate that something can or should be done, that some action ought to be taken, then this final step represents one of the most significant outcomes of social studies instruction.

Efficient Problem Solvers

Will it be possible to recognize those citizens who can be entrusted with the problem solving society requires? If social studies education does its work well, many pupils will have an opportunity to develop skills needed to solve the problems that are apparent now, skills which will be equally useful in some future time when problems may be quite different. Who are the effective problem solvers? What behaviors do they exhibit?

First of all, efficient problem solvers examine problems carefully in order to define them clearly, narrowing them to manageable proportions if necessary, not wasting time on problems of obvious irrelevance or insignificance. They acquire sufficient background so as to be dissatisfied with a narrow or one-sided view of the problem or with a cursory examination; they recognize that it is more efficient to linger at this point until every facet is sharp and clear than to run headlong into a morass of undefined dilemmas.

Effective problem solvers become actively involved in the process; they secure their own data to test hypotheses they have identified; they do not rely on others to gather their evidence, though, of course, they share with others in order to confirm or reject hypotheses on the widest base of evidence possible. They do not accept readily the untested solutions proposed by others. They either reject them, require that the proponents supply adequate data to support the proposals, or themselves set about to test proposed solutions.

Effective problem solvers maintain flexibility in their approach to problems. They recognize that the problem-solving process does not always proceed logically and they allow for insights and accidents along the way. They abandon avenues that appear unprofitable even though at first these routes may have had great promise. They "brainstorm" frequently just to get the creative ideas flowing, knowing that a seemingly unlikely possibility may be the key to the problem. Creativity is a hallmark of persons who are successful problem solvers.

Importance of Teaching Strategy

Among the more crucial decisions in social studies are those relative to teaching strategies which will achieve agreed-upon goals. Experienced teachers are not likely to explore alternatives to their present teaching styles unless they are dissatisfied with the outcomes of current instruction. For beginning teachers the problem is different; you are embarking on a new teaching adventure with little personal evidence of the possible success or failure of a particular instructional model. In either case, decisions about modes of teaching social studies are relevant to the achievement of socially significant goals and to the development of a functional social studies curriculum. Upon your choices will rest the interest and involvement of your pupils in social studies and the satisfaction you experience in guiding pupils to be good stewards of their heritage, to be challenged by the future, and to become efficient problem solvers.

Other Points of View

Banks, James A. *Teaching Strategies for the Social Studies.* 2nd ed. Reading, Massachusetts: Addison-Wesley, 1977.
Chapter 2: The Method of Social Inquiry.
Beyer, Barry K. *Inquiry in the Social Studies Classroom: A Strategy for Teaching.* Columbus, Ohio: Charles E. Merrill, 1971.
Ellis, Arthur A. *Teaching and Learning Elementary Social Studies.* Boston: Allyn and Bacon, 1977.
Chapter 4: Learning Alternatives; Chapter 10: Inquiry and Problem Solving.
Fraenkel, Jack R. *Helping Studies Think and Value: Strategies for Teaching the Social Studies.* Englewood Cliffs, New Jersey: Prentice-Hall, 1973.
Chapter 5: Teaching Strategies for Developing Thinking.
Hagen, Owen A., and Stansberry, Steve T. "Why Inquiry?" *Social Education* 33 (May 1969):534-37.
Michaelis, John U. *Social Studies for Children in a Democracy.* 6th ed. Englewood Cliffs, New Jersey: Prentice-Hall, 1976.
Chapter 6: Developing Thinking and Inquiry Processes.
Ploghoft, Milton E., and Shuster, Albert H. *Social Science Education in the Elementary School.* 2nd ed. Columbus, Ohio: Charles E. Merrill, 1976.
Chapter 7: Inquiry for Children in a Democracy.
Preston, Ralph C., and Herman, Wayne L., Jr. *Teaching Social Studies in the Elementary School.* 4th ed. New York: Holt, Rinehart & Winston, 1974.
Chapter 8: Teaching Strategies I: Promoting Inquiry and Critical Thinking.
Seif, Elliott. *Teaching Significant Social Studies in the Elementary School.* Chicago: Rand McNally, 1977.
Chapter 2: What Are Significant Processes and Skills in Social Studies?
Turner, Thomas N. "Making the Textbook a More Effective Tool for Less Able Readers." *Social Education* 40 (January 1975):38-41.
Welton, David A., and Mallan, John T. *Children and Their World: Teaching Elementary Social Studies.* Chicago: Rand McNally, 1976.
Chapter 6: Teaching Modes: From Expositing to Inquiring.

Three
Building
Readiness for
Social Studies

Building readiness for selected content assumes a high priority in whatever strategy the teacher decides to implement in social studies instruction. Whether the scope and sequence of the curriculum are clearly prescribed or whether teachers and pupils exercise some measure of freedom in choosing their directions, teachers cannot assume that children will be interested in particular content. Many problems do generate interest because they touch pupils' lives closely, but other subject matter, equally significant, may not. Children's interests are closely related to their everyday lives; these interests may not be immediately transferred to more remote times and places. Too, children's interests tend to be of short duration and easily dissipated before teachers can capitalize upon them.

Thus, when teachers decide to introduce pupils to selected content or to take advantage of real problems, they assume responsibility for stimulating pupil interest and for creating a need for learning. Children's enthusiasm for social studies and their readiness to become involved with problems depend upon the interest teachers are able to generate through readiness activities.

Techniques to Build Readiness

Building readiness serves several important functions that go beyond stimulating general interest. Regardless of teaching strategy to be employed, readiness activities preview the content, provide common experiences that will unify pupil interests and purposes, capitalize on expressed interests as well as stimulate new ones, and encourage pupils to inquire and investigate.

Readiness for social studies instruction can be developed in a variety of ways. In all of them there are two common elements: they are planned and implemented by the teacher; they encourage active participation beyond teacher explanation and teacher-pupil discussion. Having in mind the affective, behavioral, cognitive, and content objectives to be achieved by the study, the teacher creates the readiness experience which will provide incentive for moving toward their achievement. Knowledge of many types of readiness experiences makes it possible for teachers to select the activity most appropriate to the chosen content.

Dramatic Play

Dramatic play is a readiness experience which is particularly successful in crystallizing pupils' interests and needs and revealing their present understanding of content to be explored. Dramatic play involves pupils in playing roles which may or may not be familiar to them and encourages them to interpret the roles as they presently see them. The situation may be based on a real event or circumstance or a situation which the teacher may describe. Children plan with the teacher how to stage the drama—the setting, the characters, and the events. Those not playing roles serve as observers and are encouraged to note questions they may wish to ask following the enactment. The teacher also records misconceptions that may be used as leads to questions and problems. In the debriefing period, pupils and teachers cooperatively identify problems they perceive and possibly make some hypotheses about likely solutions.

Dramatic Play 1

The teacher recalled a recent emergency which had made it necessary to cancel school the following day. Sometime during the night, steam pipes in several classrooms had exploded, spraying the areas with oil and water. When the teachers arrived the next morning, the building was a shambles. The principal did his best to get the news out to pupils by radio, television, and telephone, but, in spite of his efforts, many children arrived at school, not having heard the word in time.

Capitalizing on the incident to launch a study of communication in the community, the teacher encouraged pupils to play out what happened. They identified the roles to be played—teachers, pupils, parents, principal, announcers—and the scenes. After the role playing, the teacher commented, "I've been taking a few notes on what happened in your play. I'm wondering about the newspaper announcement; did anyone feel puzzled about how the news reached the paper in time for the morning edition? And what about the night watchman—how did he know what had happened inside the classrooms? Why didn't some of the children hear the radio? Did you make that clear? And how did the police get the word? Did what you saw in the play make you wonder about how our community would communicate in other kinds of emergencies? Would it be important to find out how emergency communication works? What things should we find out?"

Such an experience might have been used to introduce other studies: What would happen if schools were closed permanently? How does our community supply heat and light to its citizens? The lead-in and follow-up questions would be different, of course, but dramatic play would provide the vehicle.

●━○━●━○━●━○━●━○━●━○━●━○━●━○━●━○━●━○━●━○━●━○━●━○━●━○━●━━●

Dramatic Play 2

A heavy snowstorm in a northern American city completely immobilized transportation for two days. School was dismissed, and persons were urged to remain at home. The newspaper headlines were tremendous. Recognizing an opportunity to use the incident to build readiness for a study of transportation, the teacher described some situations for groups of pupils to role play.

1. You and your parents are caught at the airport when the storm begins. Since you are waiting for a visitor, you hesitate to leave the airport. Before long the announcement is made that the plane you are expecting has been routed to a different city. What will you do?

2. You are a group of children who are usually transported home from school by bus. When the storm begins, no one expects it to be a big one. By the time the principal decides on an early dismissal, the bus drivers say that they cannot reach the school safely. What will you and your teacher do?

3. You and your family usually do your grocery shopping on Saturday. By that time, the food supplies in your home are pretty well used up, except for some things in the deep freezers. Bread, butter, milk, fresh fruits, and vegetables are completely gone. Your father says that taking the car to the market is impossible. What will you do?

4. You are a storekeeper and checkout clerk. You plan to open your store the morning after the storm, but you are worried because the big trucks which usually bring in supplies for the weekend sales haven't come yet. Friday and Saturday are the busiest times at the store. What will you do?

Following the role playing, the teacher opens the discussion by asking, "What problem was common to all these situations? How easily did these people solve their problems? What happened in your make-believe situation when the snow storm came? How did you solve your problems? What do these experiences tell us about the need for transportation in our community? Could we investigate this useful service to find out more about *why transportation is important in our city?* What questions will we need to ask in order to gather the data we need?"

You will have no difficulty in translating this type of readiness experience to many other studies—emergencies in any kind of service. Communication, power, food shortages, and health care are other examples.

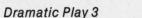

Dramatic Play 3

Pupils are divided into four groups. Each group is asked to play out for the rest of the class the family situation described on the slip of paper they receive.

1. You are a Jewish family in New York that has been reading about the advantages of moving to Israel. In the family group you are discussing the material and trying to decide whether or not you will make the move.
2. You are a Jewish family that has decided to move to Israel. You would like some of your friends and relatives to accompany you, but they are not easily convinced. Your family is arguing with them about the move.
3. You are a Jewish family living in Russia. You would like to move to Israel, but the government is making it very difficult for families like you to leave. Your departure is likely to be dangerous. The family is planning strategies and trying to plan what can be taken on the journey.
4. You are a Jewish family that has recently arrived in Israel from New York. Friends have taken you into their home temporarily. The family is planning how you will live, what kinds of jobs you are willing to do, how you feel about the move you have made.[1]

When the family scenes have been played, the teacher launches the debriefing. What problems did you have in playing your roles? Did you have all the information you needed? Israel is very much in the news these days; did your newspaper reading help you? How could we find out more about this country which has attracted so much attention in recent years? What do we need to know?

This set of role-playing scenes can be tailored easily to engender interest in other cultures; when pupils try to play roles which represent cultures different from their own, they quickly face the problem created by lack of accurate information; hence, they are stimulated to find out.

---

[1] Maxine Dunfee and Claudia Crump, *Teaching for Social Values in Social Studies* (Washington, D.C.: Association for Childhood Education International, 1974), p. 31.

━•━

Dramatic Play 4

During current events sharing time, pupils became interested in the news story of a local young woman who had decided to become a race-car driver, the first woman racer in their community. The article noted that many people were surprised when they heard about this career choice, and several asked how her parents reacted. The teacher, seeing an opportunity to study an aspect of sex roles, proposed that pupils play out a possible discussion when the young woman tells her parents about her career decision. Children broke into groups of three, with father, mother, and daughter role cards drawn from these possible ones in various combinations.

Father

1. You work on a factory assembly line and make good wages. Several young women have recently become very efficient workers on the same assembly line.
2. You are a lawyer and employ several well-paid young women as secretaries.
3. You are a high school teacher who earns a good salary and has considerable influence in your community.

Mother

1. You stay at home and pride yourself on your baking ability, having won several contests. You have involved your daughter in your homemaking activities.
2. Now that your daughter is completing high school, you are thinking of taking a job in the city water department.
3. You are a buyer for a large department store and enjoy the business trips you take at home and abroad.

Daughter

1. You are usually very obedient and try hard to please your parents. Their opinions easily sway your own. Your parents have taken you to several colleges they would like you to consider.
2. You are uncertain about your chosen career but have been talking to a favorite uncle about his work, which seems very exciting to you. You made good grades in high school but have no interest in college.
3. You have always been an independent person and have always liked working with machines. You love sports and have entered several sports contests with your high school classmates.

In the debriefing which follows the discussion, the teacher asks, "What is the problem? Why do the individuals feel the way they do? What is important to each of them? Why do you think the daughter chose the career she did? Why weren't all the mothers and fathers agreed that the choice was a good one? Can you think of other areas of our daily lives where girls and boys are expected to play certain roles and not to be involved in others? How could we find out *why women are not always free to make choices?* Are you interested in *what is being done about this problem?*"

The teacher might have moved the discussion in quite a different direction by asking, "Do you think people choose their work for the same reasons as the young woman in our news items, or for other reasons? How could we find out why people choose the kinds of work they do?"

Simulation Games and Simulations

Simulation games and simulations, which bear some relationship to dramatic play and role playing, have become increasingly popular as ways of involving pupils in a segment of the physical and cultural environment which the activity carefully describes. Both may be used as readiness experiences, designed to arouse interest in a content area and to raise problems for study. In such use, the games and simulations do not develop the content but serve as stimuli to further investigation. Their use as initiatory activities depends upon their relationship to concepts, understandings, and generalizations to be developed; the elements of the affective domain they touch upon; and the exemplary real-life behaviors they encourage. Their effectiveness as readiness experiences is also measured by the opportunities they afford for stimulating inquiry through the debriefing and follow-up discussion.

In simulation games pupils are assigned preplanned roles and must operate within the setting according to the rules (which are as much like the real world as possible). Usually children's success in coping with the problems that are posed and in making the appropriate decisions is measured by a game score. Unfortunately simulation games for young pupils are rare; those that are available are usually recommended for upper elementary pupils of considerable maturity. Following is a representative list of simulation games and the problems which might be raised for investigation as a result of the interest and concern they uncover. All of these games may be played by class-size groups; all but the last two can be played in relatively short periods of time, one to three hours.

Simulation Games

Down with the King (Herder and Herder, New York), suitable for fifth grade and older pupils, provides an uncomplicated demonstration of how people try to overthrow their king, played by the teacher.

Problems which might be raised by pupils as a result of play: What makes a revolution? Why was there a revolution in our country? Why are there revolutions in the world today?

The Game of Together (Family Pastimes, Ontario, Canada), suitable for elementary school pupils, is designed to teach cooperation in solving human problems, such as stealing and hunger.

Problems which might be raised by pupils as a result of play: How does cooperation help people solve problems? How do organizations in our community help people solve their problems? How does competition create problems for people?

Powderhorn (Simile II, LaJolla, California), suitable for grades five to eight, is designed to demonstrate the impact of power on people's behavior and generates decisions about how to prevent one group from gaining all the power.

Problems which might be raised by pupils as a result of play: Why do governments make laws? How does government prevent one group from gaining control? Why do people revolt?

Where Do We Live? (Scott, Foresman and Company, Glenview, Illinois), suitable for primary grades, includes seventeen activities in three different categories: introducing pupils to elements of the environment, making maps, and planning a community. Cooperation and consideration for others are emphasized.

Problems which might be raised by pupils as a result of play: How have people changed the environment as they tried to meet their needs? How do people choose the places in which they decide to live? How are new communities built? How are old communities rebuilt?

Dig (Interact, Lakeside, California), suitable for middle school and older pupils but adaptable for grades five or six, requires each of two teams to create a civilization, bury suitable artifacts, excavate and restore the civilization of the other team. Requires fifteen to thirty hours.

Problems which might be raised by pupils as a result of play: How have we learned about the past? How do archaeologists work? How will people of the future find out about our society today?

Discovery (Interact, Lakeside, California), suitable for grades 4–6, is designed to build understandings about building a successful colony. Requires ten to fifteen hours.

Problems which might be raised by pupils as a result of play: How did early settlers in our country establish their colonies? Why did people come to America to settle? Why did the first groups who settled our country have problems?

Less formal simulations eliminate the game aspect but do set forth specifically the setting and the roles to be played. (In this respect, however, they differ from role playing and dramatic play, which allow pupils to interpret the problem situation in their own way.) As in the case of games, the debriefing period is useful in guiding pupils to identify unanswered questions which encourage future inquiry.

Simulation 1

To open up problems of poverty in large cities and around the world, each child is given a brown paper bag which he is instructed not to open until the signal is given. The teacher explains that in each bag are materials with which the pupil is to construct a beautiful or interesting art object. No other materials may be used; none may be shared. The articles will be judged for creativity and interest by the art teacher or by the class members if preferred.

The paper bags contain at least three levels of economic resources, although more variation is quite possible. A few of the paper bags are empty; one-third of them contain a wide variety of materials—paper, cloth, wire, felt pens, thumb tacks, and similar items; all others contain only construction paper, scissors, and pencil. The completed art objects are displayed.

The teacher opens up the discussion. What happened in the situation we have just experienced? How did you feel when you opened your paper bag? Why did you feel the way you did? Can you think of any situations in real life that are something like this one? What do people do when they have limited resources for completing a task? How could we find out about poverty in our world today? If each of us represented a country and its resources, how would we feel toward the others?

The range of problems might be extensive, including such inquiries as these: What is it like to be poor? How does our community help meet the needs of poor people? What is the responsibility of those who have resources? How does poverty in other lands affect us?

Simulation 2

To stimulate interest in careers, the teacher decides to involve pupils in an assembly line simulation. Children are divided into groups of four. Each group is given the following materials.

1. Pair of scissors
2. Glue or paste
3. Many copies of an envelope to cut and fold

   Each group is directed to do the following:

1. Cut out envelopes on solid lines.
2. Fold on dotted lines.
3. Paste the flaps.
4. Package in fives with a binding strip.

When time is called, each team counts its finished products. In the debriefing period, the pupils discuss several questions: How did your group carry out its work? Was your method effective? Why or why not? How did you feel if you were working on an assembly line? Would you have preferred to work alone? Do you know people who work on assembly lines? Why do you think they chose that kind of work? Do people always choose work which they prefer? How can we find out more about this matter?

Note that this simulation may be used to raise problems in other areas dealing with why we have factories, how production differs from long ago, how unions try to serve workers, etc.

Inquiry Sessions

Inquiry sessions also provide excellent entrees to further study of selected content. They are designed to pique the curiosity of pupils through the elements of surprise, disbelief, or doubt. They may be drawn from everyday life or they may be contrived in the form of discrepant events that call attention to inconsistencies and awaken interest. They may involve pupils in manipulation of artifacts, exploring current events, role playing, and discussion, depending upon the stimulus used.

Inquiry Session 1

A pioneer family has decided to move to Illinois to start a new home. They are trying to decide which of their possessions they will take with them, knowing that they cannot take all the things that mean so much to them. Here is a list of some of the items they hope to take, but they are prepared to leave some of them behind if necessary. Select the items that might be left. Choose first the least useful, then the next least useful. Be ready to defend your choices.

heirloom mirror	wool wheel	loom
flaxbrake	flax seed	cradle
carders	gun	plow
iron spider	axe	clothing
trenchers	awl	jerky

As pupils make the suggested decisions, they may discover that they need much more information. They are on the way to investigating a challenging problem: *Why were pioneers eager to move west when it meant giving up many of the things they were used to?* Pupils begin to hypothesize and to identify informational questions they need to answer.

This inquiry session can be adapted to a variety of locales and historical periods: moving from a farm to the city, moving to another country, making a settlement on an unknown frontier.

Inquiry Session 2

On a display table are placed a group of objects indigenous to a country or region: manufactured items, agricultural products, cultural items, and natural resources. The teacher encourages examination of the items with this question in mind: What hypotheses can you state about this place and its people on the basis of the objects you see here?

The pupils begin to make statements like these: Some of these items are made of steel or have steel wire in them; there are probably iron mines in this country and people who earn their living working in the mines. If both apples and sugar are grown in the country, it must be a large country with different kinds of climate. In this display we see both factory-made and handmade articles; we think the country is becoming more and more modern. When the list is completed for the time being, the teacher inquires, "What questions do we need to ask in order to verify your guesses? Yes, we will need to know the name of the country, and then what?" A larger problem begins to emerge: *How do the products of a country reveal its characteristics?*

This problem, of course, assumes considerable maturity on the part of pupils, but the same technique may be used to introduce any particular region, country, or culture which has been chosen for study.

Inquiry Session 3

On the floor, in the middle of the circle of children, the teacher empties a large bag of litter with the comment that these things were gathered on the way in from the street to the classroom. The teacher begins, "What can you discover about what I have brought in? Do anything you wish with it—we'll wash our hands thoroughly as soon as we finish; handle it, sort it, list it, label it. How do you feel about what you have been doing? What big problem does it suggest? Do you have any ideas about what to do about it?" The discussion culminates in stating a problem for investigation: *How can the litter problem on our school ground be eliminated?*

With some shift in the questions posed by the teacher, the focus of this session is easily broadened to larger pollution concerns to be studied by older pupils.

Inquiry Session 4

Pupils are given a collage of advertisements which show sex bias (stereotyped roles assigned to men and women). For example, the ads show a woman cleaning a dirty oven; a wife serving a meal to her husband; a man cutting meat in a butcher shop; a boy giving flowers to a girl; a woman pushing the shopping cart, accompanied by a man, and similar scenes.

The teacher sparks discussion by asking, "What roles are men and women playing in these ads? How do you feel about these scenes? What conclusions can you draw about the persons who drew the ads? Do you think that these conclusions are common in our world today? Can you hypothesize about why the ads were developed in this way? Can you propose some ways in which the situation might be altered? Are there questions that would have to be investigated before we could make any proposals about the problem of stereotyping men and women?" The umbrella problem might take one of several forms: *Why does sex stereotyping exist in our society? How does our community discriminate against people because of sex? Why should something be done to eliminate discrimination because of sex?*

In such an inquiry session, the stimulus might just as well be illustrations from books, items from the local newspaper, situations drawn from TV viewing or radio listening, or cartoons. The concern might be racial or minority group discrimination rather than sex stereotyping. The range of possibilities is considerable.

Inquiry Session 5

Pupils are given outline maps of the eastern coast of our country, while one is projected on the wall or screen. The map is a simple line drawing without state boundaries; it has a key to various symbols which show the characteristics of the area.

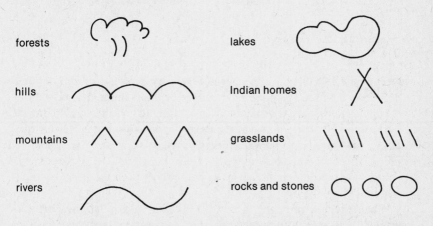

The teacher begins, "We all know that in the very earliest days of our country, only the Indians lived along the eastern edge of America. But we know also that, after America was discovered, people came to look for gold, to worship God as they pleased, build new homes where they could be free, and for other reasons as well.

She continues, saying, "Pretend for awhile that you are looking for a home for your family where you can have a small farm, where the weather will not be too severe, and where you will be safe from the Indians you have heard about. Each table group will be a family. I will be the person arranging the journey for all of you, but I will need your suggestions. Study the map to select the best place for your settlement. Report to me where you wish to go as soon as you have decided, mark it on the projected map, and be ready to defend your choice."

When the family groups have marked the map and explained their reasons, discussion centers around questions like these: What was most important to you in choosing a place to live? Can you think of other people in our history who had this same problem? How do you think they might have reached a decision? What might have prevented them from settling where they wanted to? Has your family ever had such a decision to make? How did you do it? Did it turn out as you expected? Would it be interesting to find out *how people who came to our country decided where to settle?* Would it have something to do with *why they wanted to come to America?* Think about it and be ready tomorrow to see what questions we would need to investigate and how we could go about it.

The applications of this readiness experience are numerous. Explorations of various kinds (past, present, and future), including living on the moon, may be activated by variations of this technique.

Arranged Environments

An arranged environment is often an effective readiness technique, because it capitalizes on children's need for sensory experiences and on their propensity for handling and exploring things about them. Its secret is in its design, calculated to arouse curiosity and direct children's interest toward a specific problem or content area. In the environment pupils find things to do—objects to handle, things to try on, crafts to try, books to examine. Involvement is essential and fairly easy to achieve, if we remember that the environment must be more than something to be casually looked at and passed by.

When the environment is made available to pupils, they are encouraged to move through it leisurely. The exploration experience may go on for as long as pupils are interested and may be continued over several periods. The teacher plans to be free during these periods to take notes of children's comments and questions while avoiding giving too many answers. Then teacher and pupils talk informally about the area of content introduced and eventually record problems and questions they wish to investigate further.

The effective arranged environment meets several criteria. It displays many and varied materials organized to intrigue but not confuse children. It directs their attention to interesting facets of content but does not tell everything children should find out for themselves later. It is organized attractively and accompanied by thought-provoking questions designed to challenge children's thinking.

Arranged Environment 1

Mr. Hubbard's social studies curriculum included a study of Hawaii which he was eager to implement, especially since he enjoyed his visit there. Since he knew that none of his pupils had had firsthand contact with the islands or their people, he decided to use an arranged environment to build some background and stimulate their curiosity. When the children entered the classroom on Monday morning, they found it quite transformed from its usual appearance. On the door was a huge sign: A–L–O–H–A. Inside the air was filled with music.

Near the door on a bulletin board was a large map of the islands next to a world map; on a stand in front of them was a project globe with a chalkboard surface. There was a long, colored string attached to the map of the islands and a question: Can you fasten this string to my location on the globe? On the globe were directions: Use this yellow chalk to draw on me three routes from our town to Honolulu.

On another table were containers of fresh fruit—pineapple, bananas, apples, and black cherries—each piece with a toothpick in it for the tasters. The question on the placard read: Which of these fruits is grown in Hawaii? Do you know why?

On another bulletin board were twenty or more pictures, some showing typical tropical scenes in the islands, others showing typical city scenes in the islands but with no characteristics different from most American cities. The pupils were asked to place a small pineapple sign on each of the pictures they were sure was taken in Hawaii. They were to be ready to defend their choices.

In the corner of the room, some Hawaiian music was being played on the record player. Thrown casually on a chair nearby were a grass skirt and several plastic flower leis. The sign read: LET'S DANCE!

At still another location there was a container holding a collection of small shells and nearby a small hand drill, some fish line, and scissors. Also displayed were several shell leis strung in simple patterns.

A set of slides was arranged for showing in a projector placed before a small screen. The sign read: LOOK ME OVER!

In the reading center there were attractive books, some of them with brightly colored markers in them. In a cookbook the marker read, "Read here if you would like to know how to roast a pig Hawaiian style." Other questions were planned to arouse curiosity: Who is Pele? How do you pronounce Hawaiian words? What does *hula* mean? Where did the islands come from?

After some periods of exploration, discussion began to center on the unique characteristics of the islands pupils had observed and on their amazement that some things seemed just the same as in their own community. To crystallize their thinking, Mr. Hubbard asked, "What guesses can you make to explain why Hawaii is like our community in some ways and so different in others?" As you can observe, this technique is applicable to many locales and cultures.

Sometimes the "arranged environment" is concentrated in a single area—the display table or bulletin board, for example. If this is the choice, then the materials displayed should be extensive and varied to catch the interest of as many pupils as possible, and the area spacious enough to provide for active involvement.

Arranged Environment 2

A local news item has reported progress being made on the restoration of a one-room school which will be used as a learning center by the children of the community schools. Teachers have been asked to build some background and encourage children to raise problems about rural one-room schools before spending a day at the school. The display table is ready for pupil exploration several days before the school visit is to take place. Items are attractively displayed, each with a thought-provoking question.

1. An inkwell and pen: Would you like to use this pen instead of the one you have in your desk? Try it out on the sheet of paper you find here.
2. An old primer: Here is a book used in the school we will visit. Next to it is one of your books. Are they alike in some ways? How are they different?
3. A tin pail with lid: Every child in the school had one of these. Can you guess how it was used?
4. A stout stick: This stick was usually on the teacher's desk. How do you think it was used?
5. A slate: The children in the school used this object many times a day. Can you guess what it is? How would you use it in our school today?

For several days the teacher encourages pupils to try out, or otherwise handle the twenty or so items in the display. Now it is time to pull ideas together. "Were you puzzled about any of the things you saw on

Readiness experiences are designed to arouse pupil interest and encourage problem identification. These children are reliving life in an early day rural school to gather data about questions they raised in an initiatory activity.

the display table? Are you getting curious about the old school we are going to visit? Would it be a good idea to know more about this kind of school before we go? Can we find answers to some of our questions while we are there? Let's list *all the things you want to know about old schools.* Remember to ask some good *why* questions, too, because they are usually more interesting and give us a better chance to use our ideas."

Obviously this readiness experience can be applied to many different studies, not only historical but in the present.

⚫━⚫

Each of the types of readiness experience which has just been described and illustrated has unique facets, while at the same time there are crossover aspects. Role playing, current events, exploration of materials and objects, and discussion appear in one type or another, and all are intended to be involving and curiosity arousing. There are, of course, other ways to build readiness. Many learning experiences with which teachers are already quite familiar—study trips into the community, resource visitors to the classroom, visuals of various kinds, books and other printed materials—may be used as introductory vehicles or combined with other types.

If the teacher chooses to build the readiness experience around one of these activities, caution must be exercised lest the children be bombarded with information which may stifle curiosity and a desire to inquire further. Evaluating the choice in terms of the characteristics of an effective readiness experience may be helpful also in deciding how to approach a new study.

Characteristics of Effective Readiness Experiences

Teachers who use a teacher-directed strategy based on a textbook may feel little need for building readiness beyond the suggestions which accompany the materials they are currently using. On the other hand, there may be merit in stimulating pupil interest prior to introduction of the textbook in order to provide opportunity for pupils to discover for themselves the interesting facets of the content they are about to study. These same observations may also be true of teachers who use guided inquiry based on preplanned materials from publishers or other agencies. The importance of the readiness experience is more easily recognized, perhaps, by teachers who are interested in problem solving, for problem identification is essential to the entire strategy. However, pupil involvement and the awareness which readiness experiences build can be assets in any social studies teaching strategy.

With a variety of readiness activities from which to choose, teachers may be uncertain about making appropriate choices. Intent upon desired outcomes, we may move into content and problem solving too quickly and overlook the advantages of a challenging introduction. Being mindful of the characteristics of effective readiness experiences, we are able to evaluate our proposals.

First, the readiness experience should capture the interest of as many children as possible, generating enthusiastic response to the situation under scrutiny. Interest is manifest in children's facial expression and participation and in discussion. Of course, certain facets of the content or problem will interest some children more than others, and intensity of interest will vary. But the readiness experience is likely to collapse like a punctured balloon if it fails to attract the attention of pupils.

Second, children should be able to identify themselves in the situation in some way. Since one of the purposes of staging the readiness experience is to enable pupils to see the personal values of the experience and of what may follow in social studies instruction, this characteristic is quite crucial. They should be able to relate some of their past experiences to whatever is the focus of attention in the readiness activity. When the teacher hears such expressions as "I remember I tried that and it didn't work," "Our family went there last summer," "Oh, I saw that on TV," or "That isn't the way to do it," this is the evidence that pupils are relating personally to the new experience.

Third, the readiness event should stimulate discussion among the children. It should be widespread, with each child's ideas accepted as worthy of consideration. Interaction flourishes in an atmosphere of give and take as children weigh and react to various things that have happened.

Fourth, the readiness activity should help children to recognize the worthwhileness of the content to which they have been introduced and to discover that there are interesting and useful things to learn about it. In the problem-solving strategy, such recognition leads readily to problem identification, hypothesizing, and proposals for gathering facts.

Problem Identification and Hypothesizing

If the readiness experience has been truly successful in arousing the curiosity and concern of pupils, they are likely to begin almost at once to make proposals about how the study may be continued. They begin to suggest problems that they wish to do something about. These problems often seem more significant to children than problems proposed by an adult or drawn from the textbook, even though their content may be much the same. Children's problems are *theirs,* and that makes all the difference. It does little good to send pupils searching for solutions which they do not see as significant; we cannot be dismayed when pupils ask, "Why do we need to know that?" Furthermore, it is probably useless for children to spend time and energy researching a problem which they are convinced is already solved or that has no apparent solution. They need to see progress toward some satisfying ends.

Not content with setting up problems they want to investigate, pupils usually are eager to speculate about solutions—to make guesses about outcomes—and to do so enthusiastically and with anticipation of something interesting and worthwhile coming out of the plan. They "jump to conclusions"; they begin to make statements which they think explain what they see or to solve the problems generated by their readiness activities. When these statements have been made and refined, they provide a search model for pupils as they take on the task of supporting or rejecting their own ideas. Their hypotheses serve also as a kind of screen through which data may be sifted for relevance and sorted so that effort may be spent in efficient ways. Hypotheses are useful in yet another way; they may be converted to a series of questions for which data may be gathered, though different groups of pupils may choose to work in different ways. When working with the youngest, it is helpful if teachers and pupils study their "guesses" cooperatively to determine appropriate fact-finding questions.

Many primary grade pupils study life on farms and how farmers help us. Assume that a teacher has involved pupils in a study of this content but has planned a readiness experience which leads pupils to focus on a slightly different aspect: How would we have to change our ways of living if there were no longer any farmers? The teacher intends to develop concepts of *basic needs, change,* and *interdependence* as they are explained in these generalizations:

1. People everywhere are concerned with providing food, clothing, and shelter for themselves and their families.
2. Changes come about as people try to improve their ways of living.
3. Persons and groups must depend upon each other in order to meet their needs.

As the readiness experience draws to a close, the teacher suggests, "Suppose that overnight, all farmers decide to move to the city." Hypotheses begin to emerge.

1. Every family will have to raise its own food garden.
2. People will search for wild plants and animals to use for food and clothing.
3. Stores may disappear, because they will have nothing to sell.
4. New kinds of clothing materials and foods will have to be invented.
5. Many people will lose their jobs, because there will be no foods or clothes to sell.
6. Food will be very expensive.
7. People will use more vitamins and other pills.
8. Much land will no longer be used; it may become forest or desert.

These hypotheses are necessarily simply stated by children; to adults they may appear naïve and imply much more in the way of consequences than young pupils could anticipate; nevertheless, they are statements based on experience or knowledge and are offered in good faith as predictions of what would happen in such unusual circumstances as proposed by the problem.

What lies ahead, then, is to help pupils select the hypotheses they wish to pursue and to identify questions which will guide their data gathering. For example, these questions may be used to test one of the hypotheses drawn from the list: *People will start searching for wild plants and animals to use for food and clothing.*

1. What wild foods near our homes and in the woods are good to eat? How are these foods prepared for eating?
2. What wild foods are not good to eat?
3. What plants could be used for weaving? How would they be prepared?
4. What wild animals could supply food or clothing?
5. Are these animals now protected by laws? How could their numbers be increased?
6. What groups of people in the past and in other parts of the world today have lived without large farms and many farmers?

Hypotheses and the related questions are not to be accepted by pupils and teacher without some attention to their usefulness. Together they can study a hypothesis (or set of hypotheses, if the problem area is broad rather than very narrow) and begin to ask criterion questions. Can the hypothesis be tested? The ease with which fact-finding questions can be identified and data located will certainly be a factor in determining the usefulness of the predictions. To be ultimately accepted, the hypotheses should incorporate all the facts of the case, at least at the maturity level of the pupils. Obviously the economic ramifications of the problems used as examples are beyond the comprehension of young children. Nevertheless, the desired concepts previously selected by the teacher can be clearly emphasized. It follows then that acceptable hypotheses will solve the problem as adequately as possible for the present and be free to contradictions, in so far as the children are able to discern them.

In some brainstorming sessions, where pupils are urged to go beyond known data and experience, to go "way out" to see what they can suggest, a number of alternative hypotheses may be proposed in response to a problem. An example follows in which pupils, as a result of their data-gathering experiences, learned that farmers who use machines to harvest their crops use fewer workers than those who do not have such devices.

"What of fruit and vegetable growers?" they ask. Since Congress has passed a law prohibiting employment of migrant workers who are not United States citizens, such growers are having harvesting troubles. "Could they also solve their labor shortage with mechanical devices?"

The pupils review the situations in which farmers use mechanical devices and note that, although vegetables and fruit might be more difficult to harvest than corn or wheat, soybeans or alfalfa, using mechanical devices does not seem impossible.

Drawing on their individual storehouses for conceptual ideas about the use of machines in performing tasks, about harvesting and related phenomena, they inquire into the problem and formulate theories about its solution. The following is a sample.

"In the same way that airplanes are used to spray crops, balls could be dropped from them to knock off fruit like hail knocks it off. . . ."

"But hail bruises fruit, doesn't it? . . ."

"Big nets are dropped from airplanes to capture animals. A net dropped over a tree and tied around the trunk like a laundry bag would catch the fruit. . . ."

"Instead of a net tied *around* the trunk, spread it out on stilts *under* the tree. . . ."

"Or instead of dropping something from an airplane to knock the fruit off the tree, use a machine that shakes the trunk. . . ."

"A corn-picking machine must work something like ice tongs. Use the same idea for picking fruit. . . ."

"But what about the many different sizes of fruits and vegetables there are? Could a machine work at all? . . ."

"Try experimenting with seeds to grow more of the fruit and vegetables the same size and shape. . . ."

"Would using mechanical devices decrease or increase how much it would cost to harvest fruits or vegetables? . . ."

"Such a machine would be very expensive. A little thing like a lawn mower costs a lot of money. . . ."

"But many farmers use the same wheat cutting machine. A big orchard owner could rent the machine to many others. . . ."

"Not if all the fruit ripens at the same time. . . ."[2]

━━━━━━━━━━━━━━━━━━━━━━━━━━━━━━

In such a hypothesizing session there are many alternatives; but at this point, pupils and teachers apply these criteria to each of them: Can it be tested? Will it incorporate all the facts of the case? Will it actually solve the problem? Will the solution be free of contradictions?

The Teacher in the Readiness Experience

As we can see in the foregoing experiences, teachers play a key role in building readiness, encouraging problem identification, and hypothesizing. The stage setting is chosen carefully, not only to meet the needs and interests of the pupils but to generate the enthusiasm and concern prerequisite to embarking on a search for solutions. Teachers, of course, must feel a strong interest in the problem, too; pupils are quick to recognize false enthusiasm or artificiality. On the other hand, teachers should not assume that their own high anticipations will be transferred automatically to pupils; if they do, they may hasten the readiness experience unduly, thus depriving pupils of the opportunity to critically examine an area of concern and to clearly identify the problem.

In the main, the teacher plans *for* children at this stage rather than *with* them, leading them toward desired goals but at all times remaining flexible and adaptable, ready and willing to alter plans and change procedures.

---

[2] "Problem Solving, Inquiry, Discovery?" by Helen Sagl, from *Childhood Education* 43, No. 2 (November, 1966):140–141. Reprinted by permission of Helen Sagl and the Association for Childhood Education International, 3615 Wisconsin Ave., N.W., Washington, D.C. Copyright © 1966 by the Association.

In planning the introductory experiences, the teacher clarifies the purposes they will serve, determining the answers to such questions as these: What is the experience to accomplish? What is the content or problem toward which we are moving? Is the purpose to uncover children's present understandings? Or is it to strengthen interests that have already been expressed? Is arousing curiosity and interest the prime goal? Do children need a panoramic view of the problem and some acquaintance with the content?

Once purposes are defined, the teacher selects a readiness experience which will fulfill them. Special requirements of the experience are noted. If dramatic play is to be used, the situation or story to be enacted is selected and properties made available. In the same way, materials are collected and displayed for an arranged environment. Before embarking on an inquiry session, the teacher gives some thought to procedures and has in mind questions which will stimulate the discussion. Estimates of the time required will make possible more realistic adjustment of the daily schedule to accommodate the activity.

When plans are complete, all materials ready, and necessary arrangements made, the activity unfolds. Using the criteria for an effective readiness experience as bench marks, the teacher keeps the action on its course, directing it toward desired outcomes. Critical thinking is encouraged; value judgments are analyzed. The teacher guides children as they formulate their problems but does not dominate the process nor manipulate their problems to fit some preconceived idea of what they should be. Irrelevant, superficial, or trivial questions are held up to scrutiny and discarded if necessary. Thought-provoking questions and problems are highlighted, problems that are significant to pupils and vital to the content under study.

Indispensable to building readiness and to the hypothesizing that quite naturally follows is the climate of open inquiry which the teacher creates. Freedom to make guesses, even wild ones, is an absolute requirement; and the freedom must be real, not a pretense. It is sometimes difficult for teachers who are accustomed to controlling discussion rather closely to encourage divergence, to applaud the unusual thought, to accept "way out" suggestions; some teachers feel more comfortable holding the reins securely, pushing more directly and efficiently to a predetermined goal. But unless pupils know that their ideas, if honestly offered, will be accepted warmly (even though held up for critical evaluation later), problem raising and hypothesizing are not likely to be creative or purposeful. Therefore, the teacher's role in helping children to break through reticence to brainstorm, to propose, and to predict, is one of the most crucial ones to be played in the problem-solving process.

Other Points of View

Ahern, John F., and Lucas, Nanci D. *Ideas: A Handbook for Elementary Social Studies.* New York: Harper & Row, 1975, pp. 86–99.
Introductory activities for units of study.

Chapin, June R., and Gross, Richard E. *Teaching Social Studies Skills.* Boston: Little, Brown and Company, 1973.
Chapter 8: Specific Inquiry Skills: Initial Phases.

Irwin, Martha, and Russell, Wilma, "Let's Begin with the Real World." *Childhood Education* 51 (February 1975):187–89.
Ways to use the environment to encourage the pupils' curiosity.

LeBaron, John. "School, Community and Television." *Childhood Education* 51 (February 1975):190–94.
Television as a tool for readiness.

Mallan, John T., and Hersh, Richard. *No G.O.D.s in the Classroom: Inquiry and Elementary Social Studies.* Philadelphia: W.B. Saunders Company, 1972.
Chapter 7: The Use of Primary Activities; Chapter 8: The Use of Intermediate Activities.

Ryan, Frank L. *Exemplars for the New Social Studies.* Englewood Cliffs, New Jersey: Prentice-Hall, 1971.
Chapter 2: Strategies—Involvement and Inquiry.

Ryan, Frank L., and Ellis, Arthur K. *Instructional Implications of Inquiry.* Englewood Cliffs, New Jersey: Prentice-Hall, 1974.
Chapter 2: Stating a Problem and Hypothesizing.

Thomas, R. Murray, and Brubaker, Dale L. *Decisions in Teaching Elementary Social Studies.* Belmont, California: Wadsworth, 1971.
Chapter 8: Active Simulation.

Seif, Elliott. *Teaching Significant Social Studies in the Elementary School.* Chicago: Rand McNally, 1977.
Chapter 2: pp. 65–75 (Activities for Raising Questions Increasing Involvement).

Four
Planning for Social Studies Instruction

Planning to implement goals for social studies instruction is a continual process, which begins when the school selects curriculum guidelines, chooses textbooks and other materials, and recommends particular teaching strategies. Planning continues through teachers' preplanning and carries on through the week-by-week and day-to-day planning which children and teachers cooperatively undertake.

We may hypothesize that the amount and kind of planning varies with the teacher's teaching style. In the teacher-centered classroom, planning will be done carefully in advance and may be closely related to the specific suggestions and directions accompanying a selected textbook or curriculum guide. In the pupil-centered, open classroom, teachers plan in terms of interest centers designed to stimulate individuals or small groups. Such centers foster exploration of various areas of content chosen by the teacher or suggested by the students. While the activity in the open classroom may seem casual, it is likely that considerable planning has preceded the children's activity.

Assuming, however, that teachers prize flexibility and creativity in the pursuit of social studies goals, we may find those who wish to personalize some or all of their social studies program to relate it more closely to the needs and interests of their children and community. Those who are following a predesigned program may wish to depart from it to deal with some particular problem of which children are becoming aware; others may be seeking ways to move toward a problem-solving strategy in which they may involve pupils more actively in planning. In any case, most teachers will find it useful on occasion to make both long- and short-range plans which are not prescribed for them by an outside agency or program.

Resource Units as Long-range Plans

The long-range plan in social studies usually takes the form of a resource unit. A series of resource units often comprises the social studies curriculum guide in the school. Such guides may have been prepared by curriculum specialists, supervisors, and committees of teachers in a variety of working groups. In other school situations, teachers are free to develop content of their choice in the form of resource units which may be added to or used as alternatives to the suggested curriculum. In any case, knowledge of the nature of such units and of their construction makes it possible for teachers to contribute to curriculum building with skill and understanding.

Functions of the Resource Unit Model

The resource unit is a teacher's guide to planning and action. In effect, it is a blueprint of suggestions and resources for developing a theme, problem, topic, or body of content. All resource units, regardless of form or structure, include statements of objectives, readiness or initiatory experiences, content outlines, direct experiences, related skills, summarizing experiences, evaluation techniques, and instructional materials.

The resource unit provides an overview of an area of study, enabling teachers to become acquainted with purposes, content, and learning experiences and their interrelationships. Whether they construct the plans themselves or interpret the work of others, they have an opportunity to think through the study with their own pupils in mind. With the availability of this overview, teachers can encourage cooperative planning with considerable security and confidence, encouraging pupils to pursue the channels most vital to them and to discover new areas of concern as they move forward.

The resource unit is intended as a reservoir of ideas into which teacher and pupils may dip as they explore the possibilities of problem solving in a particular area. Most resource units contain many more suggestions than any one group of pupils could probably engage in; and it is quite possible that cooperative planning will uncover ideas for data gathering superior to those suggested in the resource unit. For creative teachers and pupils, the resource unit is truly only a point of departure; as such, it has value.

It must be noted also that a number of nationally supported special social studies programs recently developed do not rely on the resource unit as the principal tool to be put into the hands of the teacher. Instead, carefully developed text materials and teachers' guides outline the content and methods recommended for implementing the program. While several new programs emphasize methods of inquiry, pupils and teachers are not generally engaged in cooperatively identifying problems for study or in planning how to research the problems.

Resource units take varied forms, depending upon the point of view of those who develop them and the emphasis given to various elements of the long-range plan. The most useful resource units, however, are those that are arranged so that relationships among purposes, experiences, and materials can be readily ascertained. To see these relationships clearly, the teacher may find helpful the following sketch of unit components, briefly described in the left-hand column and illustrated in the right with excerpts from a unit plan.

Justification

In the Justification, the relationship of the area of study to criteria for selection is thoroughly explored. Is the study a natural outgrowth of a real-life situation? Does it open up significant problems? Can it satisfy the present needs and interests of pupils? Are new interests likely to grow out of the study? Is the study well suited to the nature of the elementary school child and practical from other points of view?

Of special importance in the justification is the identification of high-order generalizations which can be illustrated by the study. These generalizations are the basis for many of the relationships developed throughout the study.

Why Does Prejudice Create Problems in American Life?

The study of prejudice in American life is easily justified, for the problems it creates are evident everywhere. Children are very much aware of prejudice in their school and community and in the world they see in films and on television. As they discuss what they have heard and seen, they discover what prejudice is and how it affects those they know. They ask, "How can we change peoples' feelings and actions?" They may develop new interests in the past and in various cultures, races, and religions. New instructional materials help them develop concepts of interdependence, cooperation, democracy, and cultural diversity. The community itself is a storehouse of resource persons of varied ethnic backgrounds who can provide useful data. A study of prejudice can be an effective tool in eliminating discrimination in everyday life.

Generalization II: Democracy is based on belief in the integrity and dignity of the individual and in equality of opportunity.

* * *

* * *

* * *

Generalization IV: People of all races, religions, and cultures contribute to cultural heritage.

* * *

* * *

Objectives

The resource unit includes objectives which may be stated in various ways. The accompanying resource unit identifies three types; numerals show the relationship of each specific objective to the corresponding generalization cited previously.

An understanding is a low-level generalization which pupils may infer from data and which is closely related to the pupils' own hypotheses.

An attitude is the readiness to respond, which is the result of an internalization of an understanding.

A behavior is the action which pupils may be expected to exhibit now or in the future as a result of the ideas and attitudes they have acquired.

Understanding II: Since democracy assumes that every citizen is entitled to equal rights and opportunities, in our country there is no place for prejudice and discrimination.

Understanding IV: Many of the good things our country enjoys have come from its minority groups.

     *   *   *   *

Attitude II: Respect for each person as a human being. Awareness of the injustices that exist.

Attitude IV: Respect for cultural differences. Awareness of the contributions of minorities.

Behavior II: Makes friends with persons of other groups. Defends the rights of other persons.

Behavior IV: Participates in the cultural activities of many different groups. Helps others know about the cultural contributions of minorities.

Readiness Suggestions

Resource unit suggestions for readiness experiences are designed to arouse children's interest and to encourage them to raise problems for study and hypothesize about solutions.

Why Does Prejudice Create Problems In American Life? (continued)

Dramatic play. The teacher selects two stories, "No Trespassing" and "Second Prize," which pose problems of discrimination, and encourages pupils to play out solutions.[1]

Contrived situation. The teacher may create a situation in which pupils experience the hurt and frustration associated with discrimination. For example, "Only children with brown hair may go to the playground."

Using the arts. Music and poetry of minority groups may be used in various ways to arouse interest. For example, songs sung by Black Americans today, "We're Movin' On Up" and "We Shall Overcome," suggest events and feelings that may stimulate the raising of questions.

Arranged environment. The teacher assembles a variety of materials which pupils may explore and examine. Thought-provoking questions accompany books, pictures, and realia—artistic products of minority groups, samples of favorite foods, household items that reveal cultural influences, clothing, jewelry, and the like.

[1] Fannie R. Shaftel and George Shaftel, *Role Playing for Social Values*, (Englewood Cliffs, New Jersey: Prentice-Hall, Inc., 1957), pp. 351–360, 368–374.

Questions and Problems

The problems identified in the readiness period serve as the vehicles for achieving the objectives of the study. For the guidance of the teacher, resource units sometimes include a list of possible, significant problems and questions. Pupils are not limited to these particular problems and questions, phrased in these ways.

The Roman numerals of the examples indicate the relationship of each to generalizations listed previously.

Content Outline

Resource units frequently, although not always, include an outline of the specific learnings and related facts essential to the development of each understanding.

The content outline provides a skeleton of knowledge useful in testing hypotheses, although obviously these hypotheses may go beyond the basic content outline, since it is not possible to anticipate all the proposals pupils may make. Content for Understanding II only is included in the example.

II. Why is discrimination undemocratic?
A. What is discrimination?
B. What do democratic ideals say about discrimination?

IV. Why are minority groups an important part of our culture?
A. How has our culture been enriched by the contributions of Afro-Americans?
B. How have people from minority groups helped all Americans live better?

* * * * *

Since democracy assumes that every citizen is entitled to equal rights and opportunities, in our country there is no place for prejudice and discrimination.
A. *Discrimination is showing favoritism toward a particular group or person.*
1. Discrimination is the result of prejudice.
2. Prejudice and discrimination are found in all parts of the world.
3. Discrimination in America is not a recent problem.
4. Prejudice and discrimination are the result of many factors.

Why Does Prejudice Create Problems in American Life? (continued)

B. Discrimination against minority groups is contrary to the beliefs on which our country was founded.
   1. Our basic documents—the Declaration of Independence and the Constitution (especially the Bill of Rights)—state these beliefs and rights clearly.
   2. The thirteenth, fourteenth, fifteenth, and nineteenth amendments provide for equality without discrimination.
   3. Recent civil rights laws forbid discrimination in housing, schools, voting, and public facilities.

The charts for data gathering and related experiences appear on pp. 94–97.

Data-gathering and Related Experiences

The resource unit includes suggestions for experiences which enable pupils to gather the data they need. Usually some type of chart is employed to make clear the relationships of data-gathering experiences to problems and to understandings. The charts may suggest also related skills and creative activities.

Summarizing Experiences

The resource unit may or may not include ideas for summarizing experiences designed to assist pupils in pulling together their learnings in an organized way. In these experiences special emphasis is given to the understandings which are the focus of the study.

Dramatizations

Understanding II: Groups of children play out incidents showing discrimination: a competent person of a minority group loses a job to a less able person; a minority group child is socially snubbed in entering a classroom, etc.

Understanding IV: Family groups play out a scene in which they are suddenly deprived of things that have been contributed by minority groups—music of various kinds, traffic signals, books, blood plasma, etc.

Scrapbooks

Understanding II: The selection of freedom documents which guarantee rights to everyone are marked to show significant ideas.

Understanding IV: A series of pictures or drawings represents the products and inventions of famous minority group persons.

Dioramas or Murals

Understanding II: Each scene in the series shows discrimination based on different reasons.

Understanding IV: Scenes show the life and activities of Martin Luther King or other famous persons.

93

Problem II A: What is discrimination?

Data-Gathering Experiences that Solve Problems

Reading Experiences	*Direct Experiences*
Pupils choose books which show how discrimination created problems for people in the stories. *Melindy's Happy Summer* by Faulkner, *New Boy in School* by Justus, and *The Empty Schoolhouse* by Carlson are typical. *Purpose:* To recognize and share examples of discrimination.	Teacher simulates a discrimination situation in which one group of pupils is given special privileges while others are not; then the situation is reversed. *Purpose:* To help pupils feel what it is like to be discriminated against.
	Pupils view the film *The Toymaker* (McGraw-Hill) and discuss reasons why some people may not like those who differ from them. *Purpose:* To discover what happens when unimportant differences are emphasized.
Pupils recall and reread well-known tales in which discrimination is shown and overcome. *Cinderella, The Ugly Duckling,* and *Rudolph, the Red-Nosed Reindeer* are examples. *Purpose:* To gain skill in recognizing discrimination.	
	Pupils invite to class a minority group member who is willing to talk about what it is like to be discriminated against. *Purpose:* To share feelings with a victim of prejudice.
	Mature pupils sit in on a meeting of the local human relationships commission to hear a discussion of community problems. *Purpose:* To discover how discrimination creates problems in the community.

Understanding II: Since democracy assumes that every citizen is entitled to equal rights and opportunities, in a country like ours there is no place for prejudice and discrimination.

Experiences that Reinforce and Enrich Learning

Related Skills	*Creative Activities*
Pupils use story-telling skills to relate incidents of discrimination from their reading.	Pupils may dramatize incidents from the stories they read and show other ways in which the problems might have been solved.
Pupils use listening and observing skills as they view the film.	
	Pupils may create and illustrate stories in which discrimination is overcome by cooperative action.
Pupils perfect skills in questioning their resource visitor.	
Pupils use planning skills as they prepare for their field trip.	
Pupils practice reporting skills in taking back to class the data from their visit.	Pupils may use stick puppets to enact examples of discrimination which are common in their community.

Problem IV D: How have Afro-Americans contributed to aspects of life other than the arts?

Data-Gathering Experiences that Solve Problems

Reading Experiences	*Direct Experiences*
Pupils form interest groups to explore the contributions of Afro-Americans to various areas of life. They search for data in such books as *Great Negroes, Past and Present* by Adams; *Famous American Negroes* by Hughes; and *The International Library of Negro Life and History* and compile a chart of famous names in each area and their contributions. *Purpose:* To demonstrate the breadth of contribution by Afro-Americans.	Pupils make a time line of well-known Afro-Americans and what they did. *Purpose:* To gain perspective on Afro-American contributions in relationship to other significant events in American history.
	Pupils interview a Black athlete, business executive, or politician, asking how they became successful in their work. *Purpose:* To emphasize that many people who succeed must put forth great personal effort.
	Pupils see the films *The House on Cedar Hill* (Artisan) and *The Jackie Robinson Story* (Films, Inc.). *Purpose:* To gather data on how famous persons were able to rise above discrimination.
Pupils arrange a bulletin board collection of news items about Afro-Americans in the areas they have been studying. From time to time they add new ones. *Purpose:* To emphasize the continuing contributions of Afro-Americans.	

Understanding IV: Many good things our country enjoys have come from people of minority groups; Afro-Americans are a good example.

Experiences that Reinforce and Enrich Learning

Related Skills

Pupils review how to locate data quickly in reference books of various kinds.

Pupils use mathematics skills as they work on their time line.

Pupils use writing skills in preparing their booklets of biography.

Pupils plan the questions they use in the interview and review the characteristics of a good interview.

Pupils use skills of listening and observing as they view the films.

Pupils use principles of good organization in preparing their display of news items for the bulletin board.

Creative Activities

Each interest group may present a skit based on incidents in the life of one of the persons they studied.

Pupils may create and illustrate a book of famous Afro-Americans.

Pupils make plans to celebrate birthdays of some famous Afro-Americans.

Pupils create a decorative border and title for their bulletin board.

Evaluation

The resource unit includes suggestions for evaluating pupil progress toward objectives of the study. Various techniques may be described. In these samples, Roman numerals refer to objectives.

Observation. The teacher has some opportunities to observe the behaviors of pupils as they carry on their daily activities in and out of school.

Discussion. The teacher may assess pupil attitudes when pupils have an opportunity to discuss questions designed to bring out opinions and values.

Behavior II: Do pupils treat their classmates as equals regardless of differences? Do pupils greet sincerely visitors and newcomers from other groups?

Behavior IV: Do pupils participate in occasions when the music and literature of other groups is being shared? Do pupils attend performances in which minority group persons are the artists?

* * * *

* * *

Attitude II: What difference does it make whether or not all people have equal rights? Are there some people who do not deserve justice and fair play? Defend your opinion.

Attitude IV: How did you feel about the jazz music we heard in music class? Would things have been better if minority groups had not come to America? Defend your idea.

Resource Unit Construction

Whether or not the resource unit will continue to be widely used in social studies planning, no one can predict. The teacher who knows how to develop such a plan has taken an important step toward problem solving as a teaching strategy in social studies. Teachers, both experienced and inexperienced, who have engaged in resource unit construction, have reacted positively and have revealed considerable change in attitudes toward social studies and teaching performance. Greater awareness of the relationship between objectives and data-gathering experiences, use of a broader spectrum of resources, and more involvement in cooperative planning have characterized the behavior of teachers following their active participation in building the kind of long-range plan the resource unit represents.

The steps in producing the resource unit can be clearly defined and ordered. The following outline, given in considerable detail, has been used successfully by many teachers. It is included here to assist those who are likely to be undertaking such a task.

1. Select a significant area of study for a group of children. Justify the selection using these questions as criteria:
   Is the area of study a natural outgrowth of a real-life situation?
   Will it reveal significant problems to be solved and hypotheses to be tested?
   Does it have potential for helping pupils move toward the goals of social studies instruction?
   What present needs and interests can be satisfied?
   What previous contacts with the area have the children had?
   What new interests may be developed?
   Is the study appropriate for the developmental level of the pupils?
   Is the choice a practical one?

2. Survey instructional resources and compile a bibliography, including materials for both teachers and pupils.

3. Consider ways to develop readiness for the study and select the best, using these questions as guides:
   Does the readiness experience grow out of a real-life experience?
   Is it the most suitable for the study?
   Will it draw upon the past experiences of the pupils?
   Will it capture the interest of pupils and involve them actively?
   Will it lead to problem raising and hypothesizing?

4. List, in children's language, a variety of thought-provoking questions that may grow out of the readiness experience and that will serve as the focus of the study.

5. (Optional). Using the materials collected, select and record in outline form information that will answer questions, provide data for testing hypotheses, and solve problems.

6. Identify the objectives of the study, selecting the high-order generalizations to which they will contribute and the related understandings, attitudes and values, behaviors, and skills.

7. Select the reading experiences that will develop understandings basic to the study. Include experiences that will build background information, provide data for answering questions and testing hypotheses, and information for carrying out activities and projects.

8. Consider the format which will be used for recording not only reading experiences, but the direct and related experiences to be incorporated into the resource unit. Charts are often used to make relationships clear between objectives and data-gathering experiences. The charts on previous pages are one way in which these may be recorded.

9. Describe the community experiences that will be needed, including steps to be taken in planning the experience and the purpose of each.

10. Identify the construction and processing experiences and the experiences with other educational media which will make a purposeful contribution to the area of study, indicating the particular materials needed and the purpose of each data-gathering activity.

11. Analyze the data-gathering experiences included in the plan to discover the opportunities for teaching or practicing the skills needed to carry out these experiences.

12. Analyze the data-gathering experiences to discover the opportunities for expressing ideas creatively. Select experiences in art, music, creative writing, and dramatics which naturally grow out of data-gathering experiences and which reinforce and enrich the study.

13. Identify and describe briefly the experiences which will summarize the study, keeping in mind the understandings, attitudes and values, behaviors, and skills which are the objectives of the study. If more than one experience would effectively summarize the study, include the alternatives.

14. Review the purposes of the study. Select evaluation techniques that may be used to determine pupils' growth toward these objectives. List opportunities for cooperative evaluation, including questions which will guide pupils in their review and evaluation of the experiences they have planned and implemented.

    List opportunities for teacher evaluation that may arise during the study, including checklists and rating scales that may be useful.

List techniques to be used at the close of the study to assess the pupils' growth toward the objectives of the study. Include discussion, interview guides, and suggestions for observation of pupil behavior.

Include examples of (*a*) test items which may be used to assess the acquisition of significant information and understandings and (*b*) problem situations which may reveal pupils' attitudes and behaviors.

Lesson Plans as Short-range Plans

Preplanning, represented by the resource unit or directions to the teacher which may accompany text materials or other program guides, is but a prelude to specific planning for each day as the area of study unfolds. The short-range plan, typically the lesson plan, is the vehicle through which the suggestions of the long-range plan, altered or augmented in planning with children, take form in the classroom. The challenging planning period, the exciting inquiry session, the lively discussion hour are the concrete realization of projections made by pupils and teacher. The experienced teacher sets the stage for the lesson, involves pupils in its development, and successfully achieves its purpose. All this does not come about by chance. Lesson planning contributes considerably to profitable learning experiences in social studies.

Lesson Plan Model

Lesson plans take a variety of forms, but, regardless of their makeup or arrangement, they are likely to include the following components.

1. *Objective:* The objective of the lesson is derived from the overall objectives of the area of study but is more specific to the particular problem being investigated at the moment. Today there is interest in stating the lesson objective in behavioral terms—in other words, a statement of what pupils, given the experience of the lesson, will be able to do.
2. *Materials:* The lesson plan identifies all materials and equipment needed in the lesson. Thinking through the requirements of the lesson is good insurance against delays and disorganization.
3. *Approach:* The lesson plan gives special attention to the introduction to the lesson. The approach sets the stage for the lesson, creating interest in the coming experience. When appropriate, it provides a transition from previous experiences.
4. *Procedures:* The lesson plan lists the steps by which teacher and pupils will achieve the lesson objective. Depending upon the type of lesson,

pupils may be planning an experience, gathering and compiling data, or summarizing data in order to formulate understandings. The plan usually includes questions the teacher will use to stimulate discussion.

5. *Evaluation:* The lesson plan suggests the evidence that will determine the pupils' progress toward the objective and the means by which the evidence will be secured.

6. *Related Learnings:* Every lesson provides opportunities for learnings which are not specific to the lesson objective but nevertheless worth noting.

The lesson plans which follow show how this format is used. The first plan describes a data-sharing experience. The second is a readiness experience designed to encourage exploration of an historical period. The third involves young pupils in a discussion of rules.

Lesson Plan 1

Objective: Given an opportunity to gather data about how simple communication devices work and how each is used, the pupil states understandings based on this information.

Materials: Each group has its own equipment for demonstration.

Approach: Recall the question: How do we communicate over distance? Review why the construction experiences were undertaken. Recall the planning session and check each group's preparation.

Procedures:

1. Ask one of the groups to report; assist when necessary; note misconceptions, points to be clarified later.

2. After the report, ask pupils such questions as these: Why do you think this group chose its study? How did the demonstration help you to understand newspaper communication over distance? What have you concluded about the work and time required to publish a newspaper?

3. Discuss the strengths and weaknesses of the report; ask, "What did the group do to make the report interesting? Are there some things that other groups should try to do in their reports?"

4. Follow with other reports in similar way.

5. Raise such questions as these: How did these reports help us to understand better how people communicate over distance? How did these simple devices differ from more complex devices used to com-

municate over distance? What can you say about how simple or difficult these operations are? What would happen today if there were no ways to communicate with people in other places?

6. From responses to these questions, record the understandings which pupils state: Communication over distance is a complex process. Many people are necessary to keep the communication systems in order. One kind of communication is often dependent upon other kinds.

Evaluation:

1. Each pupil describes in writing one of the communication devices demonstrated in the reports.
2. Each pupil describes in writing how the reports helped to provide data on the problem: How do we communicate over distance?
3. Each pupil writes a summary statement related to the problem.

Related Learnings: The pupil has an opportunity to practice organizing data, reporting, demonstrating, and answering questions. Speaking clearly, listening attentively, and asking questions are other skills used.

Lesson Plan 2

Objective: Given a set of copies of colonial coins to examine, the pupil shows interest in finding out about them by stating some hypotheses about where they came from.

Materials: A set of copies of colonial coins; chart paper and pen.

Approach: Let's pretend that you are living when the Declaration of Independence is about to be written in 1776. You are one of the delegates who will decide what is to be done in Philadelphia. You have just arrived at the meeting hall and have discovered that you have forgotten the writing materials you will need. You rush out to a little shop nearby to get what you need. How will you pay for your purchases?

Procedures:

1. Encourage pupils to play out and share their ideas about what they would do.
2. Distribute the set of coins; suggest that they study them carefully. Do not answer questions or supply information about the coins.
3. Ask pupils to hypothesize about where the coins might have come from. Ask them to record in writing their guesses about each coin and to be ready to give reasons for their ideas.

4. Suggest sharing ideas and recording the data on the chart.

5. Then ask, "As you look at our chart, what statements can you make about these coins? How could we find out whether or not you are right about your hypotheses?"

Evaluation: To determine the level of children's thinking, study children's written hypotheses and the reasons they give in discussion. Consider the interest shown in the coins to determine next steps.

Related Learnings: Pupils have opportunities to use mathematics skills in studying the coins and determining their values.

Lesson Plan 3

Objective: Given situations to enact with puppets, the pupil will be able to identify reasons for having rules.

Materials: Puppets.

Approach: How many rules have you followed since you got out of bed this morning? Were these rules useful ones? What would have happened without these rules?

Procedures:

1. Ask who would like to use the puppets to play out what might happen if some person does not follow a rule or law.

2. Select the cast and props. Several groups may play out different situations.

3. When each scene has been played, discuss why the rule was broken. What happened when the rule was broken? Was the rule a reasonable one?

4. Ask the rule-breakers why they broke the rule and how they felt about it. Ask other players how they felt when rules were broken.

5. Include in the discussion the problem of rules that seem unfair and what should be done about them.

6. Encourage pupils to make some statements about why we have rules.

Evaluation: Ask each pupil to list reasons why we have rules in our school; each pupil should be able to give at least three reasons.

Related Learnings: Pupils will have opportunities to manipulate puppets, dramatize their ideas, and participate in meaningful discussion.

Functions of the Lesson Plan

The experienced teacher is well aware of the importance of the lesson plan and recognizes the relationship between thorough planning and successful teaching. The lesson plan serves several rather obvious functions, mentioned here only briefly.

The lesson plan is a useful vehicle for preplanning—obliging the teacher to consider how lesson objectives may best be achieved and to give attention to necessary materials. Such preplanning gives the teacher, especially the inexperienced one, the confidence to plan cooperatively with pupils and to guide their data gathering and problem solving to a profitable conclusion.

The lesson plan is the blueprint for the lesson. Having thought through the lesson prior to its staging, the teacher has an overview of its development and its outcomes. Although the plan may be altered in the course of its implementation, it is nevertheless a good base of operations.

The lesson plan fails in its functions, however, if it becomes a prescription which cannot be changed or if the teacher fails to take advantage of the proposals children make or the ideas they share. For this reason, once the lesson plan is completed, it is wise to anticipate the points at which changes may be necessary or where flexibility may be desirable.

What has been said here about lesson planning is not intended to imply that all social studies lessons are of the closed-inquiry type used as examples or that all teachers compose plans in such detail as those given. Furthermore, experienced teachers have their own styles of lesson planning; inexperienced teachers usually find some definite structure helpful in putting the plan into action.

Cooperative Planning in Social Studies

Teachers who are seeking to move toward more purposeful experiences which will have significance for pupils and which will involve them more actively in their learning find that cooperative planning is a good way to bring the teacher's and pupils' purposes together and to generate enthusiastic concern about a problem or topic. All adults have participated in activities which they were directed to undertake and in others which they helped to plan. Unusually there is a difference in the initiative and effort which both children and grown-ups exhibit in these two types of situations, other things being equal, of course. Would you be willing to hypothesize about which experiences—leader prescribed or cooperatively planned—would hold attention and encourage commitment to a higher level?

Cooperative planning in the early stages of a study helps pupils crystallize their purposes. These purposes, as we have seen, are often stated as questions, sometimes as problems, and often as hypotheses to be tested. Planning sessions which follow a readiness activity give needed direction to a search for data. Later planning sessions involve pupils in organizing data-gathering activities and in making decisions about how to assemble and record what they have found out. The problem-solving strategy, by its very nature, offers special opportunities for freedom and innovation in planning with pupils.

Initial Sessions

When pupils become excited about an area of content, planning is readily undertaken. In fact, teachers sometimes have to encourage pupils not to rush headlong into plans without taking time to evaluate suggestions for appropriateness and practicality. On the other hand, the free range of ideas is encouraged, and brainstorming is a common phenomenon in these initial planning sessions. The planning session develops in different ways, in different classrooms, and with different content. Some groups begin by organizing their questions and problems for study. Note the concern for efficient handling of their inquiries.

Planning Session 1

Mrs. Johnson: Yesterday we found that we had many questions about the water main break and the ways in which the news reached us. In fact, we used all our chalkboard space to record them.

Jack: Can we add more questions? I've already thought of something else we should investigate.

Mrs. Johnson: Of course. But just now, let's look at the list we wrote yesterday. Do you think we're ready to make plans for securing the data we need?

Susan: We'll have to find a place to start.

Anne: There are questions about so many different things. Can't we do something about that?

Donald: And we jump around from one thing to another and then back again. The questions are really mixed up.

Jack: Maybe some of the questions can be put together. That'll leave more room for new questions later.

Mrs. Johnson: Let's try to organize the list, then, to make it easier to work with. I'll write the new list on this newsprint, and we can check off the old list as we decide what to do with each question. Shall we try first to put together questions that belong together?

Susan: We have three questions that are almost alike: *How does the telephone work? How do we send telegrams? How do we communicate by letter?* Couldn't we just make them into one question: *How do we communicate with people at a distance?*

Maria: That's a good idea. Why don't we do that whenever we can.

Mrs. Johnson: Do you all agree? Are there other questions that can be put together?

Andy: Those about radio, television, and newspapers could be included in one question: *How do we communicate with large groups of people?*

Carlos: What about these two: *What inconveniences are created when news is not received? What happens when communication breaks down?* Wouldn't just one of them do? They mean the same. I like the second one better.

Wayne: And to help find out about all the different workers, we could ask, *Why does communication require the work of so many people?* One question can take the place of several that way.

Dick: There are some questions, though, that just belong by themselves, and we ought to keep them on the list.

Mrs. Johnson: What do you have in mind, Dick?

Dick: Well, there's that one about what kinds of communication should be used for different purposes. That really ought to be on the list, because during the water-main break lots of people had to decide quickly which was the best way to communicate with someone else.

Groups that move into hypothesizing during the readiness experience may be encouraged in the planning session to analyze these hypotheses into their various components so that appropriate data for testing them may be sought. In the illustration that follows, note how the trend of the planning differs from the previous example.

Planning Session 2

A group of fifth grade pupils in suburban Chicago had just come to an agreement that, in their opinion, Chicago's greatest problem for those living outside the inner city was the inefficiency of the transportation system and the increasing traffic on the public thoroughfares. The children had drawn not only upon their own experience but on the daily experience of their parents, especially the fathers, who commuted daily downtown to their work, leaving early to avoid the traffic and arriving home late because they had been unable to avoid it in the evening. Pupils were encouraged and stimulated by their teacher to speculate about how the traffic and transportation problem might be solved. Their "brainstorming" took the form of proposals for eliminating the present chaos. The following were among the ideas submitted:

1. Pass a law that every passenger car that goes from the suburbs to work in the downtown area must carry a full load of passengers.
2. Install moving highways which flow only toward the city at certain hours of the morning and flow outward at work-closing time.
3. Provide jet packs and landing areas for all workers who must commute into the city and return at the end of the day.
4. Require passenger automobiles to be removed from the streets to garages during the work day and provide continuously moving vehicles that converge on the city in the morning and move outward in the evening.

The list was a very long one, more than thirty proposals; from among them the pupils selected several that from their own limited experience seemed practical. In the planning session pupils stated their suggestions as hypotheses and began to analyze each to determine the limits implied by the proposal and the specific types of data needed to test it. To illustrate, here is the breakdown for the first of the hypotheses, with the necessary delimitations and data required, as pupils saw them in the planning sessions.

The hypothesis: Passing a law that every passenger car carrying a worker from the suburbs to the city proper must carry a full load of workers will reduce the traffic volume at rush hours at a given traffic checkpoint.

Decisions necessary to set limits for the investigation: The exact boundaries of the suburban area to be used; the definition of terms: *passenger car, full load, city proper, rush hours;* the selection of the traffic checkpoint.

Data needed to test the hypothesis: What hours are considered to be the rush hours? How many cars pass the checkpoint in a given amount of time during the rush hours? How many cars at the checkpoint carry only one passenger? How many passenger cars in the suburban area make daily trips to work in the city proper? How many persons does each of these cars usually carry to work? What is the potential full load for each of these cars? To what extent would the law be likely to reduce traffic at the checkpoint? How could such a law be passed and enforced? To whom would the law be objectionable? For what reasons?

When encouraged by teachers, pupils usually move easily into making plans of action. They suggest many activities that may be valuable in accomplishing their purposes. From all these sources of data, they make choices and come to some agreement about first steps. Children may ask themselves, "Which of these experiences will produce accurate information? Which can be accomplished in the time we have? Which can be carried on by individuals, by small groups, or by the whole class?" As discussion continues and decisions are made, the plan of action takes form. It may be a step-by-step outline of the next day's activities or it may be wider in scope, encompassing proposals for a wide series of experiences directed toward data gathering. Following is a plan of action drawn up during a cooperative planning session, accompanied by brief descriptions of the experiences as they were developed later in the classroom. Can you think of other ways in which pupils might have secured appropriate data?

Planning Session 3

The middle-school children had identified a rather complex problem as the focus of their study: Why do good human relationships in a democracy depend upon communication? The teacher suggested that they organize their suggestions for data gathering into a plan of action. What they did to implement their plan later is also shown here.

1. *We can read to find out how people of different groups learn to work together.* Pupils read such books as *High-Rise Secret* by Lenski, *The House at 12 Rose Street* by Brodsky, *The Swimming Pool* by Cobb, *Easy Does It* by Wier, and *All-American* by Tunis. They

recorded types of situations in which people of various backgrounds faced problems and eventually learned to communicate.

2. *We can locate films that deal with problems of communication among groups of people and view them for ideas.* Pupils saw such films as *Brotherhood of Man* and *The Toymaker* (McGraw-Hill), recording evidence that differences are more often imagined than real.

3. *We can study communication problems in the United Nations.* Pupils interviewed a local reporter who had served as his newspaper's representative during a session of the United Nations. They investigated the provisions made for instantaneous translations during sessions. They collected newspaper articles about current discussion and controversy in the world organization.

4. *We can study local conflict situations to see what part communication plays.* Pupils collected accounts of racial problems in the community and studied them to see whether or not problems of communication were apparent. They sat in on a meeting of the local human relations commission to hear a discussion of ways in which persons of different races were trying to improve their communication. They discovered that people sometimes misunderstand because they cannot communicate.

5. *We can get acquainted with persons from other groups in the community.* Pupils planned occasions in which they could meet persons of minority groups not represented in their school. They invited resource persons to discuss problems of communication among groups. They planned an exchange school day with a class whose background differed from theirs. They discovered that knowing someone usually improves communication.

6. *We can find out how various groups express their ideas through their art and music.* Pupils shared poetry, literature, arts, and music from various cultural groups. They invited local artists to perform typical artistic works and to interpret their meaning.

Such plans of action, though they are necessarily not highly specific at their inception, serve useful functions. They require pupils to analyze their problems and questions and to examine alternatives critically. While the plan of action is not intended to be unalterable, it does provide a framework within which children can develop specific plans as their study unfolds.

Later Sessions

Not only does cooperative planning promote a vigorous and creative introduction to pupil investigation, it also encourages the exploration of ways to gather data for testing hypotheses and solving problems. As we have seen, pupils suggest various sources of information and plan to implement their plan of action; they plan special ways of working individually or in groups to collect data. As they move from one experience to another, new problems arise; these then become the focus of further planning.

When relevant information has been secured from reliable sources, cooperative planning includes plans for the organization, sharing, and evaluation of all collected data. Pupils participate in planning their reading experiences, their field trips, their interviewing of resource persons. They come together from time to time to evaluate the adequacy of their recording schemes and to note progress in collecting data. When data about any aspect of their problem have been assembled and discussed, pupils resume planning to determine whether or not they are ready to move on to other phases of their study.

After pupils have accepted certain of their hypotheses, they make plans to test these decisions. Some decisions are simple to test in everyday situations because observation can show whether a proposed solution is workable. For example, one group of pupils hypothesized that the school ground was badly littered because there were too few trash containers at strategic points. When the data they collected seemed to confirm the hypothesis, they set up plans for installing the trash cans at places indicated by their data. The results were easily observed.

Children find sometimes that because of conditions beyond their control they cannot make plans to put their ideas into actual practice. For example, children's proposal to reduce rush hour traffic in urban areas, previously described, was found to be not only practical but also promising; and yet pupils recognized that they could do little to effect the proposed change. In this case, however, their efforts were partially rewarded when they were invited to discuss their study with a city government official. Whenever possible, of course, pupils plan to test their problem solutions in the real world, for every successful application encourages them to attack the next problem with vigor and enthusiasm.

The Teacher in Cooperative Planning

We have emphasized the role of the pupils in cooperative planning, because they are so often left out, particularly in the teacher-centered classrooms. However, when children help plan, the role of teachers is even more crucial, for they are responsible ultimately for guiding children's learning in appropriate directions. If teachers believe in the values of planning, they will open up as many opportunities as possible in the day-to-day unfolding of social studies experiences. These opportunities are especially rich and numerous in a problem-solving strategy.

Do you have doubts about the wisdom of involving pupils in planning? If you do, you are probably not alone, for some teachers do not feel that such cooperative planning is feasible or significant.

The development of worthwhile planning sessions requires both the teacher's skill and the pupils' efforts. You may need to teach how to plan, if children are accustomed to a high degree of direction in carrying out social studies assignments. Cooperative planning requires a different orientation of teacher to pupils and of children to adult. For children who are new to the idea of planning, the teacher may present a plan, ask for discussion and possible alternatives. Later on, pupils may enter into planning much more fully as they share the tasks of suggesting, evaluating, and deciding.

In preparation for the planning session which grows out of the readiness activities, teachers evaluate in terms of objectives the problems children raised and the hypotheses they stated. The direction of planning is anticipated and possible sources of data are considered. If there is a resource unit or curriculum guide available, it is consulted in preparation for planning with pupils.

Teachers also anticipate that children's problems may need to be reformulated, reorganized, and hypotheses sharpened or limited. They try to foresee the kinds of data-gathering activity appropriate for children. Having given some thought to these facets, they are better able to guide pupils in their evaluation of alternatives in the search for information. Being the most knowledgeable resource persons at hand, teachers will naturally be the ones to whom pupils turn as they begin to exhaust their own ideas for plans. Pupils also depend upon their teachers in testing the feasibility of their plans, recognizing the adult's wider experience in the community and broader knowledge of possible activities.

As children plan, the teacher considers the experience in light of several useful criteria. Are pupils identifying the kinds of information they need? Are they drawing upon past experiences for ideas about how to secure data? Are they taking time to consider alternative courses of action and to examine their proposals critically? In addition to these criteria is the teacher's concern for the extent and character of the pupils' participation. Recognizing that involvement is good insurance against superficial and stereotyped response, the teacher takes special care to bring as many

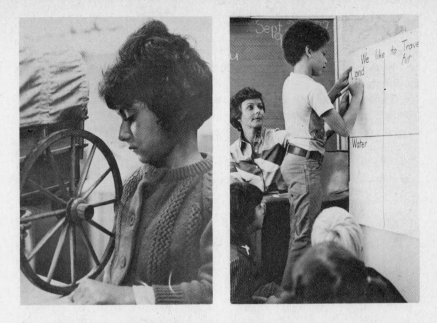

Teacher preplanning and cooperative planning combine to involve pupils in experiences appropriate to their needs and concerns and to meet long-range social studies goals. The children in these scenes are engaged with their teacher in planning a social studies investigation.

pupils as possible into the planning, avoiding the possibility that planning may be dominated by a few or that naturally reticent children may stay on the sidelines.

Through careful preplanning, both long-range represented by the resource unit and short-range as in lesson planning, the teacher sets the stage for pupil planning. Through cooperative effort, pupils may improve the quality of their search in both group and individual endeavors. Planning makes possible the development of the study, as pupils define problems, search for data, and evaluate findings in terms of objectives.

Other Points of View

Ellis, Arthur K. *Teaching and Learning Elementary School Studies*. Boston: Allyn and Bacon, 1977.
Chapter 2: Planning for Instruction.

Fraenkel, Jack R. *Helping Students Think and Value: Strategies for Teaching the Social Studies*. Englewood Cliffs, New Jersey: Prentice-Hall, 1973.
Chapter 8: Planning (Putting Objectives, Subject Matter, Learning Activities, Teaching Strategies, and Evaluative Devices Together).

Jarolimek, John. *Social Studies in Elementary Education*. 5th ed. New York: Macmillan, 1977.
Chapter 2: Planning for Teaching the Social Studies.

Michaelis, John U. *Social Studies for Children in a Democracy*. 6th ed. Englewood Cliffs, New Jersey: Prentice-Hall, 1976.
Chapter 3: Planning Units of Instruction.

Oliner, Pearl M. *Teaching Elementary Social Studies: A Rational and Humanistic Approach*. New York: Harcourt, Brace, Jovanovich, 1976.
Chapter 10: Unit and Lesson Plans.

Preston, Ralph C., and Herman, Wayne L., Jr. *Teaching Social Studies in the Elementary School*. 4th ed. New York: Holt, Rinehart & Winston, 1974.
Chapter 7: The Unit: What It Is and How to Plan It.

Seif, Elliott. *Teaching Significant Social Studies in the Elementary School*. Chicago: Rand McNally, 1977.
Chapter 9: Organizing a Significant Social Studies Program.

Welton, David A., and Mallan, John T. *Children and Their World: Teaching Elementary Social Studies*. Chicago: Rand McNally, 1976.
Chapter 14: Planning: Units and Lessons.

Investigating Problem Areas from the Real World

Whether or not pupils are involved in a predesigned social studies program or in a series of investigations which they cooperatively plan with their teachers, it is not possible for them to put aside consideration of problems which arise in the real world. Television and newspapers bring to their attention a wide range of events and problems with which citizens are concerned; the daily life of the community poses many unanswered questions for both young and old. It is not too early in the elementary school years to encourage investigations of these dilemmas which are appropriate to children's interests and maturity. Such problems may become the major thrust of the social studies curriculum or they may complement the ongoing studies prescribed by textbook or curriculum guide.

Although teachers may be hesitant about encouraging the selection of real problems from today or the past, they may test their choices with these questions: Is the problem socially significant now and likely to be so in the future? Does it stimulate inquiry and problem solving? Does it illustrate generalizations with which pupils have had previous contact or which they will find useful in explaining happenings and situations in the future? Does it encourage the identification of socially desirable values? Does it lead to skills and actions which characterize responsible citizens?

While it may be presumptuous to identify problem areas from the real world in an exclusive way, we can survey several significant ones for this discussion, clarifying objectives and possible sources and avenues of investigation. These suggestions may open up other directions for the pupils' search. They will be helpful also to teachers who need to become more knowledgeable about areas into which pupils will be delving.

The Environment

The critical nature of our environmental problems calls for serious educational effort. Daily these problems touch the lives of pupils and arouse their interest and concern. When their awareness of events and circumstances leads to inquiry and problem solving, pupils are more likely to take action to improve the environment rather than ignore its deterioration.

Objectives

Basic to pupil action are the meanings children derive from the data collected and ordered during their study of the environment. What are some of the big ideas which pupils may infer from their data? Among them are these:

1. As the environment becomes more littered, it may be increasingly difficult for people to meet their basic needs well.
2. Because survival depends on an adequate supply of energy, air, and water, people must bear serious responsibility for protecting these resources.
3. Increasing population and its demands for more and more industrial goods have produced a great threat to our supply of water and other natural resources and created serious problems of waste disposal.
4. Because it is not possible for one individual alone to solve major problems of pollution, cooperative effort and governmental action are essential.
5. In spite of the enormity of our environmental problems, there are specific actions each individual can take in alleviating pollution and saving energy.

Knowledge alone, as implied in the achievement of these ideas, is, however, not enough. Attitudes and values which will predispose pupils to action must be generated. What attitudes are worth developing? Surely among the essential ones are a keen awareness of the detrimental affects of littering, a determination to use resources wisely, an eagerness to improve the environment wherever possible, and a desire to take positive steps to prevent further pollution and waste.

What actions in the environment are achievable by each pupil, now and in the future? Consider the results if all citizens were to exhibit these behaviors:

1. Disposing of all litter in proper containers in the proper way.
2. Taking advantage of recycling plans and avoiding nondegradable products.
3. Avoiding polluting lakes and streams when camping, boating, or hiking.
4. Avoiding polluting the air with trash burning, excessive exhaust fumes, and spraying.

5. Cooperating with neighbors and other community persons in efforts to improve the environment and conserve energy.

6. Promoting and participating in campaigns to reduce pollution.

What kinds of problems are identified by pupils? Their inquiries are often monumental. Why do people spoil their environment? How can we make them stop? Why is littering getting worse? Why do cities pour waste into lakes and rivers? How can polluted water and air be made safe again? Will we really wear gas masks some day? How can people be persuaded to stop pollution? What can each of us do to make our energy supply last longer?

Data Sources

Pupils will naturally draw upon the local environment for data to answer questions and provide solutions to problems. Unfortunately examples of all aspects of pollution and unwise use of natural resources can be found in almost every community. The firsthand investigations pupils make put them in the role of citizens concerned with human welfare. From their local findings, pupils can hypothesize to wider fronts, drawing data from less concrete sources to confirm or reject their thoughtful guesses. While materials for children are not overly plentiful, some are appearing; environment-conscious teachers and pupils can find some sources of data among materials primarily intended for adult citizens—magazines, newspapers, radio, and television.

How pupils use available data sources in their inquiry into environmental problems is illustrated in the following.

Data Sources: The Environment

Collect and organize data from local industries: amount of energy used daily, disposal of wastes into water supply, measures being taken to reduce pollution, etc.

Map the community, marking the industries and other facilities which contribute to air pollution.

Visit a variety of businesses in the community, each small group being responsible for noting and recording evidences of air pollution.

Study the water system of the community to learn how it is purified and what pollution problems the community faces.

Study maps of the sewage disposal system in the community, comparing it with approved plans developed by experts.

Take a field trip to the local sanitation disposal facility to see how refuse is disposed of.

Survey home uses of energy and note opportunities to conserve.

Investigate the costs of insulating homes of various sizes.

Try out alternative ways of getting to school without using gasoline.

Study a local stream or lake to determine kinds and amount of pollution: litter present in the area, substances in the water.

Visit a polluted water-recreation area, interview the rangers, observe people who use the area; use the data as the basis for planning relief measures.

Gather samples of water from various community sources and analyze their content.

Record the water used at home, compile the data, and determine ways in which water may be conserved.

Keep a record of instances of air pollution in the home; make a composite chart of these sources.

Investigate waste disposal problems at home and assemble data on poor practices.

Photograph community areas where litter has created unsightly views.

Map homes, school grounds, or neighborhood, marking areas of pollution.

Survey the neighborhood, interviewing people about their uses of outdoor incinerators, their spraying practices, and their tree-planting plans.

Survey the supermarket to discover what products could be sold without containers.

Collect and classify litter from a specified area and determine which is and which is not degradable.

Interview a person from the local or state air pollution control board to find out the most serious causes of air pollution and legal steps that are being taken to remove the causes.

Determine the agencies, industries, and legislative bodies that are likely to have some influence on air pollution control and persons to whom they may write their concerns.

Take note of and record public-service TV and radio messages on air pollution and energy conservation and create similar messages which can be submitted for broadcast.

Investigate the operation of a gas mask, try it on, speculate about the possibility that such equipment could become common.

Observe the operation of equipment designed to test the emission from auto exhaust to determine degrees of pollution.

Clip newspaper articles which describe environmental problems in other communities; record locations on the map, using a key to indicate the type of problem; compare with the local situation.

The World of Work

Community resources are particularly useful in developing various facets of career education, a current effort to introduce children to the world of work in more meaningful ways than we did in the past with our studies of community helpers. Young pupils, especially those in the primary grades, traditionally have been taught about the work of fire fighters, postal workers, doctors, and police, with the emphasis on what they did to help us. Older children seldom touched upon the work of the local community —nor, in fact, on the essential work done by people of the world.

Recently, however, there has been considerable concern about children's attitudes toward work and their lack of contact with it in a realistic way. They are being encouraged to think about work and workers in relation to themselves: How does it feel to be a fire fighter? How do store clerks feel about their work? Would I like to be a carpenter, a gas station manager, or a teacher? What would be good about the job? What might be unpleasant about it?

As pupils progress through the elementary school, they should experience several stages of career awareness. The very youngest are interested in themselves; the goal of career education is to help them find out who they are as individuals. In other words, they answer the question, Who am I? Awareness of self and the building of self-image are the goals of early development in career education.

The second stage of career education emphasizes the world of work and introduces children to many kinds of work. It encourages pupils to see for themselves many workers at their jobs, to find out how these workers feel about their jobs, to consider whether any of these jobs might appeal to them, and to discover the life-style which accompanies these jobs. Awareness of the world of work is the goal in this stage, with pupils asking, "Would I like that kind of work? How would I feel? Does the worker like this job—why or why not?"

The third stage involves pupils in looking realistically at the career opportunities that might be open for them. Here they are concerned about the specifics: opportunities, demands, advantages, services performed, and training required. Awareness of personal career opportunities is the focal point at this level; later comes emphasis upon career choices, not in elementary school.

Objectives

What are the understandings which pupils may develop as they investigate problems appropriate to these stages of career development?

1. Each person is an individual with strengths and weaknesses, likes and dislikes.
2. It is important for people to think well of themselves and of the work they are doing.
3. We could not meet our daily needs adequately if it were not for the many different kinds of workers who help us.
4. All honest work is worthy of our interest and respect.
5. When people feel good about their work, they are more likely to overlook its disadvantages.
6. The amount of money to be earned in a job is not always the most important thing to be considered when choosing it.
7. People choose their work for many different reasons.
8. Some persons are engaged in careers which they did not choose freely.
9. If people can "try out" a career before choosing it, their decision is likely to be more realistic than if they do not have such an opportunity.
10. There are many kinds of work which need to be done, even though they are not attractive or well paid.
11. A person should investigate many kinds of jobs in a career cluster before making a choice.
12. Our world would be very different if there were no workers to help us and to help each other.

Although career education looks to the future, the pupils' behavior in the world at hand should reflect their growing awareness of their own potential and of the world of work and its many opportunities.

1. Expressing appreciation to workers who help them.
2. Cooperating with the workers they meet in their daily activities—school personnel, bus drivers, store clerks, librarians, and others.
3. Taking an interest in observing workers at their jobs—at school, in the community, on the trips they take.
4. At home and in the community, trying different kinds of work tasks which are appropriate for their maturity level.
5. Demonstrating effective interpersonal skills.
6. Taking pride in doing a good job.

Data Sources

There are many sources of data in the local community which will lead pupils to discover answers to their question, What do they do?

Data Sources: The World of Work

"Shadow" various workers and participate as much as possible in their activities.

Accompany fathers or mothers or other relatives to their jobs and observe closely what they do.

Keep a record of their work experiences at home, checking those they enjoy and those they do not enjoy.

Interview workers to find out how they feel about their jobs.

Make things produced by workers—foods, models, gardens—to see what these production tasks are like.

Experiment with tools or equipment to find out what it feels like to be a particular worker.

Read things workers have to read; bank deposit slips, travel schedules, sales slips, telephone directories, etc.

Show significant work experiences of a particular worker on a life rope—a rope or cord on which are strung a series of cards. Each card lists an event in a person's work experience.

Make collages of workers showing various facets of their work.

Collect newspaper accounts of workers to discover their accomplishments.

Survey a work site, such as the city hall, to list all the kinds of workers located there; survey the school neighborhood for all the kinds of work being done.

Study various workers as portrayed on television to discover the goods or services they produce.

Ask adults to finish the statement, "Success is . . ." and compare the responses to determine the values that motivate people to work.

Take pictures or slides of workers for bulletin boards or classification experiences, comparing jobs, environments, training, advantages, and disadvantages.

Interview those who receive services and ask them how they would get along without those services.

Divide a circle into fractional parts to show how a worker spends the day; compare circles for various workers.

Check want ads to see what careers are in demand.

Look for cartoons that show the worker and decide what characteristics of the job are being emphasized.

Study the yellow pages of the telephone directory to find out about kinds of work in the community.

On a walk through the neighborhood list all the types of work being done; in the classroom identify the noticeably pleasant and unpleasant features of each.

━━━━━━━━━━━━━━━━━━━━━━━━━━━━━━━━━━

Here's how an enterprising teacher of young children provided sources of data about careers in which pupils had expressed an interest.

━━━━━━━━━━━━━━━━━━━━━━━━━━━━━━━━━━

Exploring the World of Work

Mrs. Lewiston gave considerable thought to possible sources of data for her first grade pupils who were interested in kinds of work they might like to do when they grew up. Since their reading skills were limited, she decided to set up some rather simple learning centers for each of the careers the pupils mentioned as ones they would like to know more about. Each learning center contained typical materials and equipment, a large sign with the name of the worker, some very simple directions of things to do, and the available related storybooks.[1] In the planning sessions, pupils decided to try as many centers as possible during the week, to think about whether or not they might like the job they were examining, and to be ready to share their feelings about each one at the end of the week. There were ten centers in all; new ones would follow a week later.

Musician's Center: Rhythm instruments, xylophone, autoharp, tonette, and musical bells to try out old tunes or to make new ones.

Plumber's Center: Plumbing fixtures to be taken apart and reassembled.

Artist's Center: Variety of art materials to be used in drawing and crafts.

Carpenter's Center: Pieces of wood and tools for building things.

Banker's Center: Blank checks, banks, toy money to be counted and recorded.

Storekeeper's Center: Counter and shelves, cartons and cans for buying and selling.

Cook's Center: Ingredients and directions for making simple foods—soups, puddings, cookies.

Actor's Center: Puppets and costumes to try on and suggestions for playing out stories.

Gardener's Center: Containers, soil, and seeds for starting new plants, tools for cultivating.

---

[1] *Early Careers Series* (Minneapolis, Minnesota: Lerner Publications Company, 1974) includes easy-to-read books and study prints on an array of careers, with additional subjects being produced.

Repair Center: Simple household items—flashlights, clocks, cameras, pictures in frames, and mechanical pencils—to be taken apart and put together again.

Our American Heritage

The study of history has been a part of the elementary social studies curriculum for a long time, but few teachers feel great satisfaction with their efforts or the results achieved by their pupils. Research has pointed out why it is difficult for pupils to grasp concepts of time; it is clear that a sense of chronology develops rather later in the elementary school years and that children's sense of time develops best when teachers make some conscious effort to assist them in seeing relationships between the present and the past.[2] Then, too, it is not easy for children, or adults for that matter, to feel a part of events long since passed into "limbo"; youngsters are usually unable to distinguish between fact and fiction; consequently, a story drawn from history may seem little different from a make-believe one. Nevertheless, there is considerable evidence that pupils can develop concepts of time at an earlier age and that they already possess some competencies in handling ideas from the past.[3]

Objectives

Again, it is well to look for those large ideas, or understandings, about the relationships of past and present toward which elementary school children can make some progress. Among them surely are the following:

1. All the things that have happened in the past can be arranged in a sequence that helps us see how they are related to us in time.
2. The space of time in which people have lived is a very short part of the time since the earth began.
3. The world and its people are continually changing; history records these changes.
4. We often can understand the present better if we understand how it was shaped and influenced by the events of the past.
5. Through all time, people have sought to satisfy their needs for food, clothing, and shelter by exploring unknown regions of the world.

---

[2] Val E. Arnsdorf, "An Investigation of the Teaching of Chronology in the Sixth Grade," *Journal of Experimental Education* 27, no. 3 (March 1961):307–313.

[3] J.D. McAulay, "What Understandings Do Second Grade Children Have of Time Relationships?" *Journal of Educational Research* 54, no. 8 (April 1961):312–314.

6. Among the historical leaders are the people whose ideas and inventions improved the welfare of the people among whom they lived.

7. We are a part of living history as we observe and take part in the events of each day and year.

Can pupils become curious about the past? What kinds of questions may voice this curiosity? Why should we, they ask, care about what happened a long time ago? What was it really like back then? Why are some people famous and some are not? How did this problem we are studying begin? Why do we celebrate special days? How do historians gather data? Why are people always trying to explore new places? What if things never changed? What if this event had never happened? What if it had turned out in a different way?

To ask what children will do, what actions they will take in the real world as a result of the development of such historical perspectives and attitudes, is to suggest that all knowledge must be of a practical nature. There are many who feel that the study of history need not result in accomplishment of behavioral objectives; that it is an intellectual activity valuable for its own sake; that somehow competency in the study of history will subtly, if not outwardly, change the behavior of the learner. Whether or not these ideas are justified, it is possible to identify some behaviors which will reveal the pupils' success in grasping significant historical relationships, in handling historical content, and in applying the knowledge to the here and now. These behaviors include:

1. Whenever they are examining a current problem, asking and seeking to find out how it all began.

2. When reading or hearing about an historical event, asking why it happened.

3. Putting events in proper chronological order when it is important to be able to do so.

4. Explaining how one historical event may have grown out of another.

5. Choosing history as part of their interest and recreational reading.

6. Following current news and discussing it with others.

7. Explaining the events and ideas behind special holiday observances.

8. Associating famous persons with the deeds that made them famous and explaining why they are remembered.

Data Sources

What sources of data will pupils use to make the past live again and to satisfy the inquiries they seek to make? Obviously, they may find help in the community, not only investigations into its past, but artifacts and realia. Community resource surveys should have identified whatever may be available. Beyond these, the study of history calls for a recreation of ways of living and human events through sight and sound if pupils are to uncover accurate and authentic data.

Data Sources: Our American Heritage

View a film such as "The Pioneer Blacksmith" (Indiana University Audio-Visual Center) to discover the relationship between the level of technology of an era and the kinds of work done by its people. Students can also identify the steps in a process that is becoming rare.

View a film such as "New England Sea Community" (Indiana University Audio-Visual Center) to uncover how a particular kind of work (whaling) influenced the life of a community.

View a filmstrip such as "Legacy of Honor" (National Education Association) to gather historical data for the construction of a time line about Black Americans.

View museum dioramas to check the authenticity of the illustrations (drawings) in the references they are using.

Project a small but detailed working drawing of a Conestoga wagon to compare it with commonly held ideas about covered wagons.

Listen carefully to a recording of the voice of a famous person, such as John F. Kennedy, to speculate why personality is important.

Visit a reconstruction or a restoration to gather data about a particular set of problems and to compare them with printed and visual details found in other sources.

Listen to a tape made from a television report of an historic event, such as the first moon walk, to consider what facts are likely to be considered most significant in the future.

Listen to an authentic dramatization on record such as "Paul Revere and the Minute Men" (Enrichment Records) to gather data about how people of the time viewed the event.

Observe a film such as "Pioneer Spinning" (Indiana University Audio-Visual Center) to learn how to use a spinning wheel which has been brought into the classroom.

Collect pictures of old tools and equipment and match them with modern equivalents to discover how such items have changed and how they have changed ways of doing things.

Make a file of pioneer recipes—johnny cake, parched corn, hominy, pumpkin leather—to hypothesize about ways in which these foods were related to the environment in which they were used.

Make a file of directions for simple home crafts and products—making soap, weaving, churning butter, drying foods, knitting clothing, retting flax—to compare them with corresponding activities today.

Trace on a large map the most used routes for westward movement in America and compare them with most used highways today; draw conclusions about similarities and differences.

Compare a television series such as "Little House on the Prairie" with historical facts gathered from nonfiction sources.

Listen to recordings of songs from history such as "The Rich Old Lady," "The Erie Canal," "Down the River," or "The Chisholm Trail," to gather information about the feelings and aspirations of people of other times.[4]

Compare old photographs of the downtown area of the community with more modern views to find out how the area has changed.

Political and Civic Life

Pupils who develop habits of inquiring about problems of concern to them and develop ideas and values compatible with the ideas of a democratic society are making progress toward responsible citizenship. Concern for the environment, awareness of the gifts of the past, desire to foster good relationships with others, interest in the world of work—all are characteristic of effective citizens. The elementary years, however, are not too early to involve pupils directly in the investigation of what it means to be a member of a democratic society. While many of the data-gathering experiences are more appropriate for pupils in the intermediate than in the primary years, some of the suggestions which follow may be simplified for young children by enterprising and concerned teachers. Political socialization and citizen education should begin whenever there is opportunity.

Objectives

What understandings about political and civic life are appropriate for the elementary school child? Here is at least a partial list.

1. America is a democracy based on rules and laws, rights and duties established by or implied by the Constitution.

2. Because many responsibilities for government are given to elected officials, all citizens should exercise the right to vote for these persons.

---

[4] Investigate *Celebrate America,* a set of twenty cassette tapes with scripts of songs from twenty periods of American history from colonial days to World War II (Santa Ana, California: Doubleday Multimedia, 1975).

3. In order to engage in discussion of community and national issues and to vote intelligently, citizens need to be well informed.

4. Decision making depends upon skill in gathering accurate information, freedom to examine issues, and the ability to draw valid conclusions from data.

5. Cooperative effort to improve group living is characteristic of a democratic society.

6. Even though a citizen is only one person, there are ways in which individuals can influence political decisions.

7. Even though individuals, organizations, and nations do not always live up to the values and ideals of democracy, these ideals serve as goals for their behavior.

8. We can learn something of the democratic process through the ways in which we plan and work in our homes, neighborhoods, and classrooms.

How will we know whether or not children are experiencing the impact of these ideas? The attitudes and values they exhibit in what they say and do will provide the evidence we are looking for: respect for the worth of each individual, belief in democratic ways of working, belief in the importance of cooperative effort, concern for the welfare of others, willingness to participate in community action projects, interest in the activities of government, and an appreciation of the responsibilities of citizens. Are there behaviors which will attest to the pupils' political socialization?

1. Insistence on using the democratic process when making decisions in the home and at school.

2. Participation in choosing their leaders in teams, clubs, and other group activities.

3. Use of the problem-solving process skillfully when attacking a real problem.

4. Bringing to the classroom for discussion the issues they meet in the community and in the news.

5. Influencing the decisions of others by marshalling good arguments and communicating them.

6. Urging eligible persons to vote in every election, and making decisions about how they would vote if they were old enough.

7. Defending the rights of others, especially those of minorities and women.

8. Cooperating in worthwhile community action projects and campaigns.

9. Observing rules and laws and urging others to do so; working through appropriate channels to change unfair laws.

Significant social studies content is closely related to the everyday concerns of the present and the future. These young children are studying problems of air, land, and water pollution through experiences appropriate to their maturity level.

10. Protesting injustice and undemocratic procedures in school and community.

What kinds of questions and problems may spur pupils to investigate the political and civic life of the community? Circumstances and events will determine what these may be, but we can predict some of them: Why do many people fail to vote? What does it mean to be democratic? How does the government of our city decide things? What can citizens do to make the community a better place in which to live? How would our daily lives be different if there were no laws? How are the rights of citizens protected? How can families and schools be more democratic? How can we help everyone enjoy the privilege of being free? How can people persuade their government to make changes? Important, even profound, questions!

Data Sources

Sources of data which pupils can use in this problem area are somewhat limited. Very little data appear in books at the elementary level, although recently textbooks are giving more attention to political and civic concerns. Instead, pupils can draw upon accounts of local events, news reports from beyond the community, surveys of opinion about citizen behavior, observations of community groups in action, and interviews with officials and other citizens.

Pupils' data-gathering experiences often will put them in the role of the citizen. The following are examples.

Data Sources: Political and Civic Life

Identify rules they must obey at home, at school, and in the community, perhaps role playing what would happen if everyone ignored a given rule.

List the decisions they participate in (at home and at school) and identify other situations in which adults make decisions for children; analyze the differences in the situations and consider possible reasons for these differences.

Survey parents to determine what decisions the family regularly makes in a cooperative manner; chart the results and note likenesses and variations.

Cooperatively design rules needed in the classroom and plan for enforcement to discover the problems involved in self-government.

To gather data about how democracy works, organize the classroom democratically, electing officials, identifying responsibilities and opportunities for decision making.

From members of various service groups, gather data about the kinds of behavior they consider positive and productive in the group and those they consider negative and unproductive. Use the data to establish some practice group sessions.

Discover how the class changes under strict leadership when all pupil participation in decision making and freedom to move about are suspended for a specified period of time.

Interview school officials to find out how tax money is spent for education; convert the data to some visual form for sharing—a circle graph, for example.

Take part in a serious and needed classroom or school election; discuss issues and outcomes.

Participate in a community campaign to get people to vote in a particular election.

Debate a current problem. For example, should tax money be spent to build a community swimming pool, when pools are available in nearby state parks?

Observe sessions of the town council when an appropriate problem is being discussed to note the council members' ways of working and making decisions.

Examine the purpose of organizations to which pupils belong—Boy Scouts or Girl Scouts, for example—to see whether or not they emphasize citizenship.

Survey community opinion regarding a current problem (one appropriate for the pupils' interest and maturity); for example, building a new animal shelter or controlling bicycle traffic on busy streets.

Design a playground needed in a new housing development; present or send the plan to the city planning commission and ask for a response.

With adult assistance, at a safe distance, observe and keep a record of violations of speed limits and littering on particular highways for a specified period of time; draw some conclusions about observance of these laws.

Explore the biographies of citizens who have made special contributions to the realization of democratic ideas; gather data about their goals and the problems they overcame to achieve them.

Collect news items which communicate to citizens the decisions which government is making; classify items according to level of government and types of decisions being made.

Study a government order, such as the ban on artificial sweeteners, to determine the pros and cons of such a ruling.

Write a politician for data about a particular problem under study or to urge that a certain action be taken.

To record reactions to the type of service rendered and the manner in which it was given, interview community members who have had contact with the police, the fire department, or other service personnel during emergencies.

To illustrate how citizens can help in gathering data needed in improving a public service, assist in home surveys of fire hazards, using an official report form or one planned by the class group.

◆━◇━◆━◇━◆━◇━◆━◇━◆━◇━◆━◇━◆━◇━◆━◇━◆━◇━◆━◇━◆━◇━◆━◇━◆

Controversial Issues

As children raise problems and ask questions, they inevitably pose questions of a controversial nature. There is no way in open inquiry to avoid such issues, nor is it wise to do so if democratic principles of thinking and discussion are to be encouraged. On the other hand, teachers sometimes feel that they are restricted in the handling of problems that are open to controversy, and some actually seek to avoid involvement. When several hundred teachers in the elementary schools of one state were asked if controversial issues were a part of the social studies curriculum, about 80 percent indicated that they did not discuss such questions in their classrooms. [5] Of the remaining teachers who did consider these issues with their pupils, most were teachers in the fifth and sixth grades.

Teachers in this study gave a variety of reasons for their inattention to controversial issues: lack of competence in dealing with the questions, fear of rebuke from patrons or school board, a feeling that the curriculum is already too crowded, and insecurity in keeping the discussion under control.

Whatever the reasons (and the teaching of controversial issues appears to be controversial), it is necessary to ask how boys and girls can learn to gather data and to make decisions based on that data if a social studies program ignores the live questions of the day, many of which will be identified quite naturally as pupils pursue significant problems. It must be said, of course, that the issues introduced or encouraged ought to be within the maturity level of the pupils, should touch their lives in some real way, should be ones on which adequate data are available, and should be those which can be justified in terms of their appropriateness and relevance. When such investigations are undertaken, parents and administrators can be informed, so that they will understand what is happening, visit if they desire, and explain to others should questions be raised.

Data gathering is particularly critical in the study of controversial issues. Children's judgments will be based on the sources of data and their quality; these sources must be impressive enough to counterbalance emotional undertones likely to surround issues upon which people may

---

[5] J.D. McAulay, "Controversial Issues in the Social Studies," *Education* 86 (September 1965):27–30.

strongly disagree. While criteria like the following may well apply to the selection of data sources for inquiry in general, they are especially worth attending to in areas of controversy:

1. The source of data should be firsthand whenever it is possible; information that passes through another medium is open to distortion.
2. A single source of data is usually inadequate as the basis for making a judgment on a controversial point.
3. The source of data should be objective and neutral, without bias or effort to propagandize; it should be free of emotion; sources of data that do not meet the criteria must be used with full awareness of their shortcomings.
4. Opinions must be recognized as opinions rather than taken as facts.
5. Data should be free from hidden meanings and in a form which pupils can interpret objectively.
6. The data from one source should be verified by other sources.

In dealing with controversial questions, it is critical also that the data represent all sides of the problem and all points of view. The teacher must be on guard in this matter, since pupils may not have the maturity to recognize the shades of opinion that exist and to sense when all sides of a problem have been examined. The teacher, of course, may have a personal stand on a matter, and when asked, can state that position; but a major responsibility is to help pupils marshal facts representing all facets of the issue so that they have sound bases for making judgments. Through the data-gathering process, pupils are encouraged to keep an open mind and to be willing to change their own positions if the facts warrant.

Data Gathering on a Current Issue

An imminent and warmly contested election in a community became a controversial issue in the sixth grade of one school. Two mayoral candidates—one, the incumbent; the other, a former mayor—were vigorously pressing their campaigns. They discussed community planning and zoning, use of federal funds for community development, the influence of business and industrial expansion, the need for improved recreational facilities, and public transportation. Since both candidates were well known and had community service records of considerable proportions, each had many supporters. Because the pupils were looking at the role of government in everyday life, the election was of immediate interest to them. As pupils reflected arguments that were going on in the community, and especially at home, emotions began to run rather high. Many of the resulting classroom arguments seemed based on heresay, unsupported evidence, or opinion.

The teacher decided to channel pupils' interest into an in-depth study of the local election. Pupils raised the questions they thought were important and began to search for data. Pupils agreed that citizens ought to base their voting on evidence that would point to the candidates' intentions concerning each of the urgent community problems. Recognizing the importance of seeing all sides of the various issues, the pupils decided, after identifying the major issues, to gather data about each candidate's stand. They used interviews with each, tape recordings of their major speeches, their views as reported in the press and approved by the candidates, résumés of what each had done about the problems while he had been in office, and party platforms. They recorded their findings on the following chart:

Issues	Incumbent		Former Mayor	
	Position	Action Taken	Position	Action Taken

Using the chart as a basis for discussion put the controversy on quite a different foundation. There is no record of whether or not pupils changed personal opinions or altered judgments on the issues, but they were receiving valuable experience in marshalling facts upon all sides of a question before making decisions.

Global Perspectives

The world and its problems are very much a part of the daily lives of most school children, who, through the medium of television, observe the events and the people that make the news. Children are aware, even though they may not understand, that people in the world are continually struggling to get along with each other and with themselves. Everywhere on the globe there are tensions, quarrels, and battles. The missing ingredients to a more peaceful world may be an understanding of why others do what they do, a determination to minimize differences in order to foster that understanding, and an awareness of our interdependence.

Certainly available research about the conceptions children have of foreigners is no cause for complacency or satisfaction with the way children think about the world.[6] It seems clear that stereotyped thinking is the rule, cultivated by the emphasis put upon differences among people; the comparison of other groups with one's own, usually to the disadvantage of the other group; the lack of firsthand experiences with foreigners; and the great influence of the mass media. Developing global perspectives appears to be an urgent need.

Objectives

What understandings should pupils begin to develop in the elementary school? These are surely on any list.

1. Everyone in the world is interdependent; what happens in one part of the world will have impact on the rest of the world because of cultural, historical, and economic ties.

2. People of the world all face problems of survival, of providing for their basic needs in a situation of expanding population and diminishing resources.

3. People of the world vary in their ways of doing things, because they were brought up to perceive, think, feel, and act in accordance with their own culture.

4. People are motivated by the things they value; the things that people hold dear differ from group to group.

5. The principles of democracy are not always interpreted or understood by other people as we interpret them.

6. People love their countries and their own languages; consequently when others are critical of them, they may react strongly.

7. Each of the peoples of the world has contributed and continues to contribute to world culture; each group of people has borrowed ideas from other groups and has incorporated them into its own ways of living.

8. The more isolated people are, the less likely they are to change.

---

[6]Wallace E. Lambert and Otto Klineberg, *Children's Views of Foreign Peoples* (New York: Appleton-Century-Crofts, 1967).

9. Nations of the world who have limited resources may find it difficult to accept the fact that other nations have much wealth; consequently their behavior may reflect this feeling.

10. We have many links with other people of the earth; these links are evident everywhere.

Will these ideas make any difference in the lives of children? If these understandings are strong enough to generate attitudes of empathy, compassion, patience, and aversion to inaction, the pupils' behavior toward the world and its people may be changed. What kinds of behavior may be accepted as evidence of changes in pupils?

1. Seeking out people from other countries and enjoying them as friends.

2. Avoiding use of common stereotypes.

3. Cautioning others who are speaking of people in degrading or belittling ways.

4. Following the happenings in other countries through news media.

5. Eagerly accepting opportunities to travel to other places.

6. Listening thoughtfully to ideas with which they do not agree.

7. Treating others with kindness and respect, strangers as well as friends.

8. Comparing and questioning printed information about other countries when the data are not in agreement.

9. Participating in service activities.

10. Enjoying the arts of other peoples without making unfavorable criticisms and comparisons.

11. Participating in the holidays and festivals of others when they have such an opportunity.

12. Learning a second language.

What kinds of problems will lead pupils to want to know more about their world? They may ask, "Why are so many people of the world hungry? Why can't people settle their differences peacefully? Why are we so concerned about what happens in the Far East? The Middle East? Why do nations sometimes hate those who try to help them? Why don't all people have democratic forms of government? What would happen if our country could no longer import things from other countries?"

Data Sources

When pupils are studying other places and people, they are essentially trying to create and make real the environments and cultures with which they do not have firsthand association. While the local community may offer some resources, they are not as readily available as in, for example, the study of the ecology. Children must go beyond their community in order to recreate the setting and the people they wish to understand better. Whatever they observe, touch, or listen to should be as truly representative as possible; they will be looking for reality.

If all pupils could live abroad for a time, the problem of building understanding might be considerably reduced, but at present only those who have traveled have a glimpse of what life is like in another part of the world. To recreate the world with the data they secure, pupils turn to artifacts, realia, and cultural products, supplemented by authentic visuals. These items from the real world have very special contributions to make to the children's learning. Because children like to touch and feel, to handle and to try on, objects are unusually appealing. Objects are also excellent motivating devices to raise questions for investigation: they make reading more meaningful; they illustrate concepts pupils meet in their investigation; they facilitate contrast and comparison.

Sometimes pupils seek reality through reproducing objects—dolls, dwellings, tools, dress, foods—in as authentic a way as possible. They engage in several aspects of inquiry, clarifying the nature of the materials needed (Are they from the environment? If so, what does that fact mean?), putting into concrete form the steps in the processing or constructing (Did they do it all by hand? By machine?), and comparing the product with an original.

Many of the realia which help make other people real may be found as a result of the community survey mentioned earlier. Travelers, former residents of another country, museums, and school collections are common sources. Children become aware, of course, that when objects are taken from their natural setting, they become distorted in that they lose some of their reality; consequently, pupils must recreate the setting through visuals. In constructing and processing, similarly, pupils must know exactly how their process or product differs from the original; only in this way can the data they gather from the experience be truly legitimate.

How will pupils gather data about the world from the realia, artifacts, products, and reproductions of other cultures?

Data Sources: Global Perspectives

Use the art products of a country to explore the idea that only people of one's own country can produce beautiful, well-made items.

Collect paintings from a country to illustrate how environment influences the creative work of an artist.

Learn the patriotic songs of a country to discover how they reflect the country's history.

Perform dances from various countries to discover their unique elements and the things they have in common.

Study folk songs to find out how they reflect the problems and daily life of the people.

Study a doll collection to discover how native dress relates to environment and how costumes from one group reflect the influence of another.

Study present-day fashions to discover the influence of other cultures and the use of foreign-produced clothing.

Correspond with children in other parts of the country and the world, exchanging ideas about daily life, school, etc.

"Adopt" another school, exchanging letters, art work, stories, and photographs.

Finance CARE packages; support Junior Red Cross; engage in UNICEF collections.

Collect clothing, money, food, and school supplies for children or adults who are in need.

Visit markets and restaurants specializing in foods from other countries, relating these products to the natural environment and culture of the country.

Make foods representative of various countries to note similarities and differences. Try to account for differences in terms of culture and environment.

Begin the study of another language to get a feeling for the difficulties of communication.

Engage in weaving, pottery-making, carving, and similar crafts representative of other people to discover the skills required.

Search for architectural examples of influence from other peoples in order to understand the idea of cultural diffusion.

Survey rooms in the home or the classroom to discover what items have come from other countries; record these data on a world map.

Make a content analysis of the classroom newspaper over a period of several weeks and tabulate the number of stories from various parts of the globe; monitor radio and television in the same way to discover global links.

Take a walking tour of the business area of the town to record the evidences of ties with the world—names, shops, products, etc.

Keep a record of foreign cars seen on the streets or check parking lots regularly for a period of time to find out the origin of the vehicles.

View selected television programs to gather and compare data about life in various parts of the world.

Analyze one's own language to discover the influence of other languages.

Search the community for persons who have firsthand knowledge of life abroad and who may model or demonstrate realia.

Teaching about other countries in the elementary school often has been superficial and stereotyped; children have come through such studies with feelings of superiority rather than empathy, with data about exotic differences rather than human likenesses, and with a collection of facts about discrete countries rather than a sense of a common humanity. The in-depth study can counteract these weaknesses as it encourages careful data gathering from varied sources and the formulating of generalizations which help to explain the world's peoples. Finding interesting and different avenues of exploration may provide new ways to look at the world and to discover what it means to be part of a global family. How one teacher sought to develop an out-of-the-ordinary approach is described in the following scene.

Developing Global Perspectives 1

In-depth studies were a continuing experience for Mrs. Dorsett's third grade, for her pupils seldom wanted to do just a little with a social studies idea. In the first grade they had learned much about family life in Mexico, because of their interest in several Latino children who had come to the community to harvest tomatoes. In the second grade their teacher had introduced them to Japan, because he had spent a summer there; the pupils investigated every aspect of life in Japan that was within their level of understanding. Remembering these adventures into other cultures, they asked Mrs. Dorsett where they would be "travelling" in the third grade.

Mrs. Dorsett didn't respond immediately, but a while later she said, "Sometimes we spend time digging deep into one country or another and forget that the whole world is full of interesting people. I wonder if we could investigate some bit of living that might happen everywhere in the world? Most of us like games very much. Do you suppose that if we travel around the world we will find games wherever we go? Will they be like the ones we play? Why might they be different? Will there be other kinds of sports? Will the games people play tell us something about them? Let's put our hypotheses on the chalkboard and then we can plan a way to begin."

Any number of possibilities exist for unique in-depth studies of world peoples, studies designed to depart from the country-by-country investigation which is more common. Do these questions suggest interesting avenues?

1. How do people of the world use music to show what they value?
2. Why do people everywhere engage in games and sports?
3. How do the holidays people celebrate show what is important to them?
4. How do pastries in different places tell us about the people?
5. How are the superstitions of people around the world alike or different?
6. How do myths and legends help us to know something about the people of the world?
7. Why do hats and other head coverings around the world come in different shapes and materials?
8. Why do children everywhere like to have pets?

Current affairs and circumstances are also excellent entrees for in-depth studies of the world for older pupils, as they seek data to explain events and conditions about which they are reading and hearing. Teachers encourage investigation of those within pupils' maturity range. Here are some examples.

1. Why is the world's need for oil creating tension among nations?
2. How are new methods of farming helping people of the world to produce more adequate supplies of food?
3. Why is it dangerous to be completely dependent for an important resource or product?
4. Why is America sometimes not well liked in the world?
5. How can bridges of friendship be built between our country and others?
6. How do organizations like United Nations and Peace Corps assist nations that have serious health problems?

7. Why is it difficult for many countries to provide adequate supplies of milk for their children?

8. Why are some countries, but not others, included for study in our social studies textbook?

Developing Global Perspectives 2

When Mr. Raoul introduced his pupils to their new social studies textbook, he suggested that they take a little time to look it over and then try to hypothesize about why the authors had chosen its particular content.

The textbook was one of a new series emphasizing the social science disciplines, but Mr. Raoul didn't mention that professional information to the children. Instead he hoped to arouse their curiosity about its content. The textbook included information and ideas about ancient Greece, Confucian China, medieval France, India, the Middle East, Nigeria, Brazil, and the Soviet Union. After encouraging pupils' comments about the format and illustrations of the book and welcoming other observations they were making, he asked, "I'm wondering whether or not you were at all puzzled about the selection of countries which the authors made? What criteria do you think they may have used?"

After children had mentioned such obvious things as representation from different parts of the world, different periods of life in the past, and the possible interest of the authors in certain places and what they thought might be important for children to know, Mr. Raoul asked whether or not the countries are important in the world today and whether or not that might be a useful criteria for choosing places to study. There was considerable interest in his speculation and some arguments from children who thought studying countries in the long ago was not very useful today and from others who thought it unfair to choose just one country from a continent. Other pupils had ideas to support inclusion of one or more of the countries in the textbook, but there was no agreement about their importance.

Mr. Raoul proposed some data gathering to resolve the differences of opinion. He suggested that individuals or groups begin the collection of current items from newspapers and magazines about each of the countries in their list. It would be necessary for the class to plan how the collection would be made, organized, and filed as the semester went on. On a regular basis, perhaps in a special current events time, items would be shared and discussed. More importantly, the items would update the textbook as various countries were investigated.

In their planning, the pupils set up some tentative questions to guide their use of the file for a particular country.

1. Are news items and magazine articles about the country appearing regularly today?
2. What kinds of situations or events are being recorded?
3. How do these reports relate to the background information which the textbook gives us?
4. How does the textbook help to explain what is happening in the country or its region?
5. Can we hypothesize or draw any conclusions about why people in these countries or regions feel or act as they do?
6. On the basis of our discussion, would we include this country in a textbook we might write?

Developing Global Perspectives 3

When Ms. Ferguson's pupils were studying the United Nations, and especially about hunger problems in the world, the teacher realized from their comments that they had very little understanding of the meaning of hunger or of the uneven distribution of food among the countries they were talking about.

"How many of you have ever been hungry?" she asked. The pupils shared instances where they had missed a meal or had run out of food for a short time.

She continued, "None of us has been really hungry for long periods of time, but we know from the data we have collected already that some countries have much more food than others and that in some lands there is never enough food to go around. Let's try an experiment to discover these differences. I have a loaf of bread here that represents the amount of food available for the whole world to eat in a day. I am going to divide you into groups representing continents. The size of the group will tell you which continents have many people to feed and which ones have fewer people. The number of slices your group receives will tell you how much of the world's food your continent has available. The person to whom I give the slices of bread may give some to others in the continent group or leave them out, for we know that food is not divided equally among people.

"When all the continent groups have their food supply, look around to see the differences. Then you must eat every crumb and not waste one bit. As you eat the bread, think about what has happened and how your continent feels about the situation. On the chalkboard are the continent groups and their food supply. We'll share ideas and questions when you have finished."

The information on the chalkboard read like this: Africa, two persons, one slice of bread; Asia, ten persons, three slices; Europe, three persons, four slices; Latin America, one person, one slice; North America, one person, three slices.

━━━━━━━━━━━━━━━━━━━━━━━━━━━━━━━━━━━

Whatever the nature of the social studies program which is being developed in the school, there can be no escaping the intrusion of problems drawn from many of the areas included in this chapter or from other concerns in community and in the world. Teacher-directed learning and guided inquiry strategies can certainly direct pupils' attention to past events and current factors as they relate to the predetermined curriculum. Where greater freedom is possible, significant problem areas from the real world have their own potential for challenging children to assume citizenship roles as planners, investigators, and decision makers.

Other Points of View

Buggey, JoAnne. "Citizenship and Community Involvement: Primary Grades." *Social Education* 40 (March 1976):160–63.

Ellis, Arthur K. *Teaching and Learning Elementary Social Studies.* Boston: Allyn Bacon, 1977.
Chapter 11: Research Methods.

Kenworthy, Leonard S. *Social Studies for the Seventies.* Toronto: Xerox Corporation, 1973.
Chapters 16 to 23 suggest data sources and experiences for learning about families, communities, our country, and the world.

Logacz, Gregory; Laurich, Suzanne; and Hummel, Elaine. "Career Development: Applications to the Elementary Classroom." *Social Education* 39 (May 1975): 313–15.

Oliner, Pearl M. *Teaching Elementary Social Studies: A Rational and Humanistic Approach.* New York: Harcourt, Brace, Jovanovich, 1976.
Chapter 7: Instructional Resources.

Ploghoft, Milton E., and Shuster, Albert H. *Social Science Education in the Elementary School.* Columbus, Ohio: Charles E. Merrill, 1976.
Chapter 9: Career Education: A Social Concern; Chapter 10: Multicultural and Intergroup Education.

Preston, Ralph C., and Herman, Wayne L., Jr. *Teaching Social Studies in the Elementary School.* 4th ed. New York: Holt, Rinehart & Winston, 1974.
Part IV: Using the Social Sciences in Teaching.

Ragan, William Burk, and McAulay, John D. *Social Studies for Today's Children.* 2nd ed. New York: Appleton-Century-Crofts, 1973.
Chapter 5: Introducing Children to Current Social Studies Problems.

Ryan, Frank L., and Ellis, Arthur K. *Instructional Implications of Inquiry.* Englewood Cliffs, New Jersey: Prentice-Hall, 1974.
Chapter 4: Selecting Data Sources.

Seif, Elliott. *Teaching Significant Social Studies in the Elementary School.* Chicago: Rand McNally, 1977.
Chapter 6: What Is an Economic, Consumer, and Career Education? Chapter 7: What Is an Environmental Education? Chapter 8: What Is a Political and Citizenship Education?

Selecting Sources, Gathering and Processing Data in Social Studies

As decisions are cooperatively made about the problem areas pupils will investigate and the specific information they will be seeking in order to test their hypotheses, teachers become more and more aware of the elementary research skills children need to master. These skills include the wise selection of relevant and accurate data sources, the collection of facts and information through a variety of data-gathering activities, and the data processing which will help them organize and record the data they uncover. These skills function advantageously as children are encouraged, through whatever strategy the teacher may be using, to search for solutions to problems and for answers to thought-provoking questions. The energetic quest for appropriate data is at the heart of the inquiry process and fosters a desire to know which has continuing significance.

Selection of Data Sources

The careful search for and selection of data sources are not only requisite to problem solving in social studies but also have long-range carry-over to situations in the real world in which needed data are not readily available. Social problems that arise outside the school seldom can be attacked without a preliminary survey of resources.

Problem solving within the social studies program emphasizes purposeful data gathering, sparked by the pupils' deep interest in a problem and their motivation to research it. The readiness experience and the cooperative planning sessions crystallize interest and involve pupils actively in setting up plans. Hypothesizing further whets their appetite for investigation as they look forward to accepting or rejecting each of their propositions.

When pupils know the general direction of their inquiry, they begin the identification of possible data sources. Both teacher and pupils bear responsibility for implementing this stage. Children draw upon their past experiences in suggesting sources of data: places they have been, resource people they know, books and other materials they have seen at home or in the library, television or radio programs they have listened to. The teacher suggests other possibilities based on preliminary investigation in the preplanning period.

When sources have been gathered, the task of sorting them follows. Teacher and children survey printed materials, examining the contents for relevance. They test each of the other resources against their problems and hypotheses, selecting those that have promise and laying aside others. They critically consider community resources for availability and richness of data, marking those they wish to retain for further consideration.

At this point, pupils look at their selected sources more closely, locating specific information through application of various location skills; listening, viewing and sorting out needed facts; visiting, interviewing and asking for data. Pupils are encouraged to evaluate each source of data as carefully as their maturity allows. They should be concerned about the authenticity of their data and its accuracy. No teacher needs to be reminded of the pitfalls that exist in drawing conclusions from unreliable data, generalizing on too few facts, or failing to gather data to represent all facets of a problem. Even young children can be encouraged to ask, "Who is writing or speaking? What does the person know about the subject? Where did he get his information?" Older children may go further: "Why do these sources of information differ? How up-to-date is this material? Do we have to look more critically at the facts?"

Also of importance currently is the evidence of bias in textbooks and trade books which describe the characteristics, history, and life-styles of racial and other cultural groups. While there is evidence that bias is being eliminated from school materials as time goes on, pupils need to become aware that the problem is real. Whenever they are reading accounts about such stereotyped groups, they should be cautioned to be on the alert for phrases that degrade, misconstrue, or misrepresent. They need to ask, "Is this material free from racial and sex bias? Who wrote the account? Is the writer qualified to write about this group? How do such groups react to this person's descriptions?" Selecting data sources offers many opportunities for children to discover that not all sources are equally reliable and acceptable. It encourages them to think critically about the kinds of data sources they may be called·upon to use in the future and to anticipate new sources of data which they will have to evaluate, accept, or reject.

Here is how one teacher encouraged pupils to examine their social studies textbook for accuracy and freedom from bias.

Selecting Data Sources

The class was talking about poverty in India.

"Children," Mrs. Silva's voice broke into the conversation, "sometimes I hear you support your ideas or opinions by saying, 'The textbook says so,' and you are generally very positive about your statements. I am wondering how you can be so sure that your textbook has all the data you might need or that it is always correct in what it includes. Have you ever thought about this? After all, a textbook is just what some person is saying."

"Well, it must be true or we wouldn't be studying it; would we? There wouldn't be much sense in using a book if the information is not correct." Jane was a little indignant, but other pupils took up the challenge, commenting on the fact that the book was several years old and they knew nothing about the authors.

"What if they didn't really like the people or the country or hadn't even been there?"

"How could we confirm or reject the data about the various countries included in the text?" their teacher asked. "Any ideas?"

"One thing we could do is to compare our book with other textbooks, or with the encyclopedia," a student answered.

Another added, "Or better yet, we could ask someone who knows the country well to criticize it for us."

Mrs. Silva encouraged them. "I think we could make a plan to do something about this problem, so we'll know how safe it is to say, 'It's true, because the book said so.'"

And so they decided. They would select five countries from the textbook for which they could find the following data sources: a community person who had lived in the country for at least a year, or preferably a native; two recent textbooks; two nonfiction books recommended as good sources by the librarian; an encyclopedia; and an up-to-date film.

They planned to concentrate on the following aspects of the culture: ways of living in rural areas; customs, traditions, and values; serious current problems. The data would be organized so that they could draw some conclusions about the textbook's accuracy and freedom from bias and try to determine how much they could depend on it when they wanted to support their ideas by saying, "The textbook says. . . ."

Data Gathering

To facilitate the collection of data, the teacher identifies the fact-finding skills which will be required as pupils use various sources of information. Skills in direct observation; interviewing and surveying in the community, and in using other nonprint sources will loom large in importance. Equally useful and necessary will be the skills in locating, comprehending, and interpreting data in print form, both verbal and graphic. Purposeful search without control of skills is difficult if not impossible; furthermore, the need to know is the best possible motivation for acquiring skills not already in the pupils' repertoire.

Nonprint Sources

Community resources play a major role in providing data for a wide variety of current problems. These sources have special value because firsthand data have an apparent relevance and authenticity; pupils feel that they are in a community laboratory where they may discover how things work and how problems are created and solved. Furthermore, the use of community sources of data strengthens the relationships between pupils and adults as they look together at a local problem, exchange information and ideas. These relationships also help to build bridges of understanding which have significance for pupils' future involvement in the community as they grow to adulthood.

Although teachers find community sources of data very useful, they often feel inadequate to guide pupils to such sources, perhaps because they are unacquainted broadly in the community or have failed to develop interests in that direction; others feel restricted by school policies. Teachers may appreciate the results of a community survey in which resources are identified, described, and recorded in a file which may be used whenever data are needed. A well-planned and executed survey, recorded, and augmented as new sources become known, adds considerably to the data-gathering power of pupils.[1]

Data search in the community requires a variety of skills for which instruction may be needed: how to observe and how to record observed data, how to plan and carry out field trips and interviews, how to build questionnaires and conduct surveys. As children plan their search and identify the data they are seeking, they may set up practice sessions in which they role play how they will achieve their purposes. They give attention to speaking and listening skills and think ahead of ways to process their data. Out of their experiences in planning and implementing their search for data, they develop some practical guidelines.

1. A preview of the experience—the place to be visited, the neighborhood to be surveyed, the resource person to be interviewed—is helpful in deciding upon the techniques to be used.
2. Well-chosen questions are good insurance for fruitful data gathering.

---

[1] For directions for such a survey see Maxine Dunfee and Helen Sagl, *Social Studies through Problem Solving* (New York: Holt, Rinehart & Winston, 1966), pp. 135–38.

Children use a wide variety of community sources in gathering, recording, and reporting data related to the problems they are exploring. These pupils and their teacher are using the local greenhouse as a data source about tropical environments.

3. It is usually wise to alert those who will be interviewed or observed to the purpose of the experience and the questions and problems on which data is to be secured.
4. Courtesy and thoughtfulness in interviewing, surveying, and visiting will win the cooperation of those from whom information is being sought.
5. An efficient way to record information quickly is desirable.
6. It may be necessary to confirm community data with information from other sources.
7. Planned debriefing following the experience provides for pooling of data, for interpretation, and for consideration of appropriate methods of processing.

When firsthand experiences in the community are not available or relevant, pupils turn to other data sources. If problems they are investigating take youthful investigators back in time or to environments far removed from their community, direct observation, interviewing, and surveying may be inadequate techniques. Then pupils must depend upon vicarious experience provided through various instructional media.

While, as we shall see later, print sources are prime sources of data, nonprint sources, being more concrete, are especially well liked by pupils. No doubt they are strongly influenced in this direction by their ready access to radio, television, and theater; and for children who do not read well, such sources are essential.

Films, filmstrips, slides, and picture sets are excellent sources of data when pupils need to recreate the past, investigate environments beyond the local community, or view a process as it develops. Because pupils see so many programs which are intended for entertainment only, it may be necessary to teach them how to gather data from visual sources—how to observe and listen thoughtfully with their questions in mind and how to record information as it is discovered.

Recordings provide pupils with sources of data which often are not available in any other way. They bring a rich storehouse of music, folktale, and dance from every corner of the world, as well as transcriptions of programs and on-the-spot recordings of current events. Successful data gathering from such sources hinges upon pupils' ability to listen attentively and to extract data related to the problems they are investigating.

Realia—objects, devices, artifacts, or tools—are excellent nonprint sources of data which pupils examine enthusiastically and from which they can gather data both through observing and touching. Realia are found in children's homes, in the homes of other community members, or in organized displays and museums. When pupils are trying to discover information about real people, articles of clothing, pottery, tools, equipment, and food produce data that are concrete and authentic. Children's success in using such sources of data depends somewhat on their ability to relate the realia to the environments from which they were taken and to avoid overgeneralizing without confirming data from other sources.

As children learn to use these varied nonprint sources which complement their community data-gathering experiences, teachers guide them to recognize these facilitating points:

1. Selection of visual and auditory sources is more efficient if they can be previewed.
2. Preliminary decisions about how to record hoped-for data will simplify the data-gathering task.
3. On-target listening and observing are possible only when purposes are clear.
4. Operating equipment properly and handling materials carefully are required if data gathering is to proceed smoothly.
5. Allowing time to study a given source adequately—seeing a film a second time, for example—helps to insure thoroughness in data collection.
6. Sharing with other pupils data gleaned from a source provides confirmation and avoids misinterpretation.

Gathering Data from Nonprint Sources

While the children in a fifth grade were studying reasons why people emigrated from their homelands to America in colonial days, pupils became interested in discovering whether or not people today move from their own countries to another for the same or for different reasons.

In their search for data they came across the results of an international poll which asked the question, "If you were free to go, would you like to settle in another country?" The report gave the responses of almost ten thousand persons in seven countries. For example, in Uruguay, 41 percent would emigrate if they could; in Great Britain, 39 percent; in Canada, 15 percent; in Australia, 13 percent; in Spain, 13 percent; in the United States, 10 percent.

Although the poll did not give reasons why people were interested in emigrating, it aroused the curiosity of the pupils so much that they decided to build on the idea with a survey of their own. They constructed a simple questionnaire in four parts:

1. If you were free to go, would you like to settle in another country?
2. To what country would you go?

3. Why would you like to move to the country you named in question 2?

4. If you *had* to move away from America, where would you choose to go?

When the questionnaire was completed, they decided on the neighborhood areas to be surveyed. They agreed upon the explanation they would give when presenting the questionnaire and rehearsed what they would do and say. Finally they made a preliminary sketch of the chart on which they would compile their data, planned how they would compare their data with the original poll and how they would relate their findings to their study of immigration in colonial days.

Print Sources

Complementary to the variety of nonprint data sources are the many reading materials which provide information on most of the problems which interest pupils. Reading will become an increasingly practical approach to data gathering as pupils master the skills in its use.

Reading extends children's experiences beyond realia, pictures, recordings, and community activities, enlarging their view of the real world of the present and of the past. At times, reading becomes a substitute for sources of data which are out of reach. In fact, as children grow older, they can rely more and more on the printed word, provided that they have built up a store of impressions and concepts based on reality which they can bring to their reading to render it meaningful.

In some of their data-gathering efforts pupils will make use of the more traditional reading materials, textbooks sometimes providing a useful overview of information or a helpful summary of data. Encyclopedias will be a ready reference on a great array of topics. Pupils should be encouraged, however, to go beyond both these sources for more current data and for in-depth treatment. In considerable favor as sources that offer detail with human interest slants are unit books, produced in sets by several publishers.[2]

Trade books open up whole new vistas from which data may be collected by enterprising pupils. Young ecologists, for example, choose such books as *Jeff and Mr. James' Pond* (Lothrop), *The Only Earth We Have* (Macmillan), *Who Will Wash the River?* (Coward-McCann), and *Shadow Over the Land* (Seabury). Life-styles of other people are detailed in books

---

[2] For example, Cities of the World (Rand), Colonial American Craftsman (Watts), First Book (Watts), True Book (Children's Press), Let's Find Out (Watts), and A Book to Begin On (Holt).

like these: *The Paper Flower Tree* for life in Thailand (Harcourt), *Follow the Reindeer* for life in Lapland (Patheon), and for the Indian-American, *Along Sandy Trails* (Viking). History comes alive in *Finding Out about the Past* (Random), *To Be a Slave* (Dial), *Westward the Nation in Song, Dance, and Story* (Franklin), *The Schoolmasters* (Watts), and *They Built a City,* about the beginnings of Washington, D.C. (Scribner's). Happily the list is almost endless.[3]

Current problems, of course, will appear in print only in newspapers, periodicals, yearbooks, and similar up-to-date records and reports. With modern copy techniques and permission to copy it is possible to reproduce material from these sources for pupils who have the ability to do the required reading. Other pupils can use such items with assistance from the teacher. Fortunately school newspapers graded for each of the levels in the school are usually abreast of important problems and bring them to the attention of pupils in vocabulary they understand. Periodicals for children also provide current data sources, like *Ranger Rick* (National Wildlife Federation), *National Geographic World* (National Geographic Society), *Cricket* (Open Court Publishing Company), and *Ebony Jr.* (Johnson Publishing Company).

Finding data from the printed word poses few problems for children making normal progress at their age level or for those superior readers who find adult materials no particular hurdle. Teachers are often surprised and delighted to find that a keen interest in a real problem stimulates children to pore over reading materials no one would have thought them capable of reading. Even original sources from the past are eagerly examined and read by intermediate grade pupils with the assistance of teachers. There is also some research evidence that elementary school pupils can use primary source material as authentic data sources.[4] Note what happened in one classroom.

Gathering Data from Print Sources

"What I don't understand," complained ten-year-old David to Mr. Buell, his social studies teacher, "is why people would leave their homes to look for gold in California, when they couldn't be sure they would ever get there."

---

[3] For further selections, see *Bibliography of Books for Children* (Washington, D.C.: Association for Childhood Education International), periodically revised.

[4] Maxine Dunfee, "An Evaluation of Social Studies Source Materials by Fifth and Sixth Grade Children" (Ph.d. diss., Indiana University, 1949).

Sharon continued the complaints: "Why doesn't our textbook tell us more about the people themselves and what they were thinking and hoping for? It just says that the journey west was long and dangerous, but we could guess *that* from all the old movies we've seen. Wouldn't it be good if we could find out how ordinary people felt about what they were doing? I'd like to know what it was really like."

"How could we find that out? Where would we look? Do you suppose these people recorded their thoughts as they went along? Who might have observed them and written down what they saw and heard?" responded Mr. Buell.

Charles had an idea. "Somebody must have kept a diary or wrote letters home. We could find some of these things at the big library downtown, I'm pretty sure. It would be exiciting to try to find something written right when people were trying to reach the gold. I'd be willing to look, if some others will help me," he volunteered.

Mr Buell was enthusiastic, because up to this moment he hadn't thought about the possibility of using original sources. "You've hit upon a splendid idea, one that is worth trying to work out. If a committee wants to go first, I'll arrange with your parents to take you after school on Thursday; that's a day that's pretty free of clubs and other after-school activities. All right with you, Charles? Let me know who else will go." The more he thought about it, the better he liked the idea. He alerted the librarian and met with almost instant success.

The librarian was ready to help. "I'm sure we can locate materials pupils will be able to read. There were a number of travelers who recorded their experiences in simple and interesting ways. I'll start looking right away."

The librarian's search and the committee's exploration of possible sources resulted in some very relevant accounts which yielded a richness of detail not found in the textbooks. Pupils were delighted and were soon caught up in the excitement of reading materials more than one hundred years old, discovering real people and their emotions. Two of their favorites were these:

On reaching the willows, no amount of digging produced a drop of water; so after trying several places, both up and down the dry bed of a stream, we were obliged to put up with dry camp. The poor horses, as usual in such a plight, looked the picture of misery after their dusty march, and seemed to ask with their eyes, "Why are we forgotten?" We chained up the mules with extra care, and let them kick away to their hearts' content, and make the night hideous from their seventy dry throats.[5]

*   *   *   *   *

---

[5] William S Bell, *New Tracks in North America* (New York: Scribner, Walford and Company, 1870), p. 267.

When a few miles from Black Rock Spring, I came to a wagon, standing in the road, in which was seated a young woman, with a child. The little boy was crying for water, and the poor mother, with the tears running down her cheeks, was trying to pacify the little sufferer.

"Where is your husband?" I inquired, on going up.

"He has gone on with the cattle," she replied, "and to try to get us some water, but I think we shall die before he comes back. It seems as if I could not endure it much longer."

"Keep up a stout heart," I returned, "a few more miles will bring us in, and we shall be safe. I have a little water left: I am strong and can walk in—you are welcome to it."

"God bless you—God bless you," said she, grasping the flask eagerly. "Here my child—here is water!" and before she had tasted a drop herself, she gave her child nearly all, which was but little more than a teacupful. Even in distress and misery, a mother's love is for her children, rather than for herself.[6]

Data sources for the less successful reader pose problems, however, even though it is usually possible to locate some that do not require reading. When most of the pupils in the group are researching a problem in books and other printed sources, poor readers do not enjoy being left out of the search. Furthermore, we need to emphasize with all pupils that reading is a useful tool for securing information.

If books of easier reading level are not available for data gathering and if current printed matter is too difficult, the teacher may rewrite accounts in simpler language and sentence structure or write original materials. In Chapter 8 there is an account of the history of maps which a teacher wrote just for children who could not read more advanced data sources. When teachers do prepare materials for the less able readers, they have excellent chances to introduce pupils to certain concepts and particular data pupils need. They may also lay a foundation in basic understandings and vocabulary that facilitates progression into more difficult printed sources.

Reading Skills in Data Gathering

Teachers play a primary role in making sure that all pupils have in hand the skills needed in gathering data from print sources: skills in locating information, in reading with comprehension, and in interpreting maps, graphs, and charts.

---

[6]Alonzo Delano, *Life on the Plains* (Buffalo: Miller, Orton and Mulligan, 1854), pp. 184–85.

Skill in locating information is important for young investigators who are using print sources. Through planned skill development and through functional use of the skill, children acquire learnings (such as these) useful now and in the future:

1. Although the table of contents of a publication lists only titles of large divisions in the order in which they appear in the reading, an index lists many topics in alphabetical order.

2. Locating items in an index requires an understanding of alphabetical order, the use of key words, and the interpretation of special symbols indicating illustrations, cross references, and the like.

3. Some references depend upon alphabetical order for arrangement of content: dictionaries which assist with meaning, pronunciation, and spelling; encyclopedias which contain summaries of content on a wide range of topics.

4. Certain references specialize in a specific kind of information: atlases contain maps and tables of data about geographical features; a fact almanac contains a great array of data, much of it in tabular form; the library card catalogue is an efficient guide to books in a variety of categories.

5. Each type of reference material requires particular skills on the part of the searcher; data gathering can be considerably more efficient if these skills are well in hand.

6. Location skills must also include skills in finding exact information needed, once the appropriate reference section has been identified; using headings and subtopics, skimming for the information desired; and focusing upon the parts that are to be read in detail.

Skill in comprehending reading materials is also crucial in data gathering. Into service now is drawn the facility pupils have acquired in the developmental reading program, with the teacher making sure that children are reading at their ability levels. Developed ahead of time is the new vocabulary pupils may meet in their reading, and emphasis is placed on the importance of reading pictures as well as words. Pupils are encouraged to read rapidly to get the general idea and then to reread for specific details if the material seems useful. To develop skills in comprehension, the teacher may provide detailed study guides that help pupils identify and focus upon important information related to the problems and questions being studied. Pupils discover that some important ideas help them handle the comprehension task:

1. Many writers put the main ideas of each paragraph in a topic sentence at the beginning of a paragraph or in a summary statement at the end; some writers leave the summarizing up to the reader.

2. Various paragraphs in a piece of writing serve different purposes: to introduce, to inform, to illustrate, to generalize.

3. The same data may appear in different forms: descriptive data may be translated into graphic form; picture data may be converted to verbal form; tabular data of certain kinds may also be recorded on graphs or maps.

4. Recording details read in some logical way helps to recall them later in discussion. Historical data can be put into chronological order; data about a process can be put into sequence; comparisons call for likenesses and differences; problems and questions often suggest a useful organization of information.

Skill in reading and interpreting maps aids in the search for data along many avenues of inquiry. The skill can be directly taught because of the standardization of maps and map symbols. So essential is that skill not only to inquiry and problem solving but also to intelligent understanding of the real world, that techniques for its development have been outlined in considerable detail in Chapter 8.

Skill in reading and interpreting graphs and charts opens up many sources of data, although the usefulness of these graphics may not be readily apparent to children. Because pupils do not seem to turn naturally to these representations, seeming to prefer pictorial sources instead, they need to be encouraged to use them.

In their search for data, pupils can find graphs quite helpful. Even pupils in elementary grades can learn to interpret graphs, to make comparisons, and to draw conclusions. The picture graph is easiest for young children to interpret. In it, a small picture is used to represent a fixed quantity of something, and the number of symbols appearing in each row of the graph represents the total for that category. Pupils can move easily from the picture graph to the bar graph, which, like the picture graph, is an effective way to show comparisons. On the bar graph, quantities are indicated by bars of varying lengths in either horizontal or vertical positions. The line graph is better suited to the abilities of older children. Its representation is not so clear cut as that of the bar graph and its content usually more abstract. For data that deal with the parts of a whole, the circle graph seems the most popular. As pupils learn how to use graphs, they acquire some basic ideas about the medium:

1. Graphs are a very efficient way to show relationships among ideas that are expressed in quantities.
2. Each kind of graph is best suited to particular kinds of data.
3. Each well-constructed graph shows its title, its vertical and horizontal axes (if not a circle graph), its symbols clearly explained, and its source of data.
4. It is possible to misinterpret a graph, to "see" a relationship where one does not exist; i.e., to see cause-and-effect relationship where there is no causation.
5. Verbal data are sometimes more understandable when converted to graphic form.

When pupils use charts and diagrams, they are working with representations that are more visual and less statistical than graphs. Like graphs, however, they contain verbal data as well as visual data; the emphasis is on the relationships shown visually. The chart or diagram is a rather natural way to explain something; it is a tool that almost everyone uses at times to explain something; one may say, "Here, let me draw you a picture." What is meant usually is a schematic drawing or chart rather than an artistic product. Social studies materials include a variety of charts and diagrams, which pupils learn to interpret as they gather data.

The narrative chart shows events or developments in sequence, as in Figure 6-1.

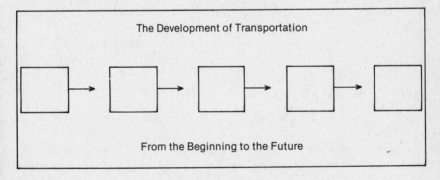

The Development of Transportation

From the Beginning to the Future

Figure 6–1. Narrative chart.

Tables like Figure 6-2 present numerical data in organized form for ready access.

Persons Eligible for Voting in Our Community			
Election Year	Eligible Voters	Number Voting	Percent Voting
1960 1964 1968 1972 1976	2,934	1,790	61

Figure 6–2. Table.

The classification chart, as in Figure 6–3, arranges information in a systematic way according to particular categories.

A Comparison of Foreign Schools				
Country	Day Length	Year Length	Subjects	Games and Sports

Figure 6–3. Classification chart.

The process chart, like the one in Figure 6–4, shows changes that occur as a product or plan develops from its beginning to the end. Arrows lead the reader through the process.

Pupils also use organizational charts as sources of data; the chart in Figure 6–5 would be an example.

The skills required in chart reading may be developed as pupils search for data. Through inquiry approaches, teachers and children study the chart to discover the author's purpose, the method of showing the data, and the intended relationships. Since charts differ far more widely

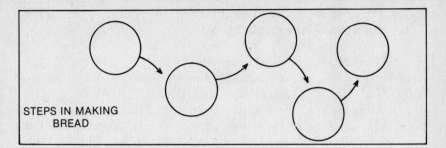

STEPS IN MAKING
BREAD

Figure 6–4. Process chart.

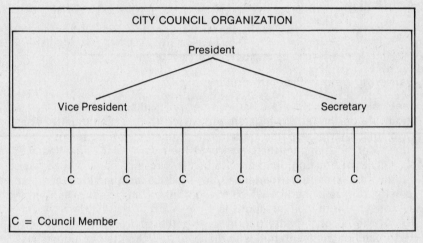

CITY COUNCIL ORGANIZATION

President

Vice President   Secretary

C   C   C   C   C   C

C = Council Member

Figure 6–5. Organizational chart.

than graphs in their format, it seems more profitable to analyze them in relation to an identified problem. As pupils work with charts and diagrams of various kinds, they are able to formulate some generalizations from their experiences.

1. Each chart has to be studied on its own merits in terms of the author's purpose.

2. There are various types of charts, each particularly useful for certain kinds of information.

3. Some charts may combine the characteristics of more than one type; for example, a table also may be a classification chart.

4. There is no standard way to show data on a chart as there is, for example, in a bar graph.

5. A summary statement based on chart data can be made if the author has created the chart successfully.

   Skill in selecting and using both nonprint and print sources of data is complemented by a host of other skills drawn from language arts, mathematics, and science. In fact, problem solving makes possible the integration of many facets of the elementary school curriculum, primarily because the study of any real problem cuts across various aspects of life and is seldom confined only to social studies considerations. All these skills function realistically as pupils engage in inquiry. Some of the ways in which skills facilitate pupil investigation are illustrated in the classroom vignettes which follow.

Gathering Data in Problem Solving

The first grade pupils are using a variety of skills as they gather data about life on the farm compared with living in their community. They have invited two resource persons, a farmer and an assembly line supervisor, to compare their work and their ways of living—hours of work, type of housing, land and its use, sources of power. In carrying out the data-gathering experience, they practice the questions they plan to ask, draw up a chart on which to record the comparisons, and listen purposefully with their questions in mind.

   In the second grade, pupils have gathered from the community items used by pioneer families to discover how the life of pioneers was different from their own. In implementing their plan, skills have been put to work: asking questions to secure data from the owners, using the dictionary to be sure of spellings, reading reference books to check the accuracy of their data about each item.

   In another second grade, pupils are investigating the problem: Why do children all around the world play games? Just now they are viewing several short films of family life in various parts of the world to gather data about recreational activities. In preparation for the viewing they have reviewed how to take simple notes on various activities, how to categorize them, and how to build a comparison chart.

   How to use leisure time well is the problem engaging the third grade. They are planning to visit the library to compile a list of leisure-time books they can recommend to others. In preparation for their visit, the librarian has taught them the skills they will need: how to use a simple card catalog, how to locate books on the shelves, how to use the table of contents, and how to determine the appropriateness of the content.

The fourth grade has been asking, "Why do we have to pay taxes?" They are studying local newspaper information about the current school budget, which is presented in graphs and tables. Since a new type of graph is used—the circle graph showing percentages—the pupils have used a mathematics period earlier in the day to improve their skill in interpreting the graph. They have discovered also that they need to know how to read figures in the millions of dollars if they are to gather the data they need.

Fifth grade pupils are in the process of finding out how inventions have changed their lives. They are examining a dozen social studies textbooks to find out what inventions are included and tabulating the frequency of mention. They plan to investigate further those most often included. They have reviewed the use of the index to facilitate their data collection and have decided on the kind of frequency table they will use.

Contributions of Afro-Americans are the current interest of the sixth graders. They have decided to survey the members of their family to find out how much they know about famous Black Americans. In preparation for the survey, they have studied various types of questionnaires and several methods of organizing survey data.

In the upper grades, children are trying to find out why population control is an issue today. They are planning to study population growth figures for the past one hundred years to clarify the problems of increasing population. The teacher has taught pupils how to use an information almanac and to read the tables it contains. Similar information in graphic form in a recent periodical has sparked a review of different types of graphs and how to read them.

When well-developed skills make possible competent data gathering, a major step in problem solving has been accomplished. While guiding the process, the teacher recognizes the importance of encouraging pupils to be independent in their search. Pupils will continue to make decisions on problems of concern to them throughout their lives; whether or not they are satisfied with incomplete, biased, inaccurate data will depend much upon their experiences as problems solvers in the school setting. There will be no teacher to direct their efforts later on, to caution them, to suggest wider horizons of information. Our hope is that skills mastered in the school years will persist.

Data Processing

When pupils engage enthusiastically in data gathering, their efforts usually are rewarded with quantities of data. How to record and communicate the data surfaces as an operational problem to be dealt with, for such data seldom come in an organized form. Casual collection and careless relay of questionable or incomplete information are time consuming and wasteful of their energy. At a time when data processing has reached refined levels in many fields of adult endeavor, it is appropriate to look critically at the pupils' efforts to sort out and put in order the data they have accumulated. Only under such conditions can pupils develop skills in recording and reporting which make summarizing and generalizing possible.

Efficient data recording contributes significantly to problem solving. A well-thought-out scheme for organization makes data readily available for discussion and sharing, saving time in presentation and avoiding unnecessary repetition. As pupils relate information to a problem or hypothesis, they are aided by data recorded in some way suited to the content. Historical problems may emphasize chronology, noted persons, steps in the development of a process or idea. Geographical data may be descriptive of places or regions, of ways in which people adapt to environment, with pupils organizing data for comparison and contrast. Pupils acting as young sociologists arrange data about people in terms of tools, food, communication, shelter, family life, religion, and the like. Without a scheme for organization, data may remain a chaotic mass of detail.

Furthermore, well-ordered data can be more easily inspected to determine whether or not all aspects of the problem or hypothesis have been dealt with and whether or not there are inadequate or conflicting data. Helping children recognize the incompleteness of their information is wise; to facilitate this inspection, data must be recorded in orderly fashion. Similarly, the criterion of relevance is much more easily applied; data which is not related to the problem can be as much an impediment to problem solving as incomplete or inaccurate information.

Still another reason for devising methods of organizing data is that it gives focus to group discussion, making it possible for contributors to pool what they know directly to the point, to avoid straying from the problem, and to perceive easily how the data relates to it.

Finally, the organization of data makes generalizing possible. The teacher helps children see the pattern of relationships among the data, as they consider what the data mean and how they contribute to the testing of hypotheses.

Several factors determine the data recording and organizing techniques which pupils are encouraged to use. Obviously the maturity of children must be taken into account when teacher and pupils plan the best way to make a record of the information they are obtaining. In the early years the teacher may act as scribe, while pupils suggest the content of the record. Through this joint effort young pupils learn techniques which later on they may use independently. With maturity, pupils employ more sophisticated ways to record data and add other adult skills to their repertoire.

Of course the nature of the problem dictates somewhat the method of data recording. Certain information-seeking questions (What fruits are grown in Hawaii? Which of our natural resources cannot be replaced?) lend themselves to simple note taking. Other information-seeking questions (What kinds of work does Congress do? Why does California have a warm climate?) are made to order for outlining. Time lines, graphs, and maps can be developed to show certain quantitative or areal data. Illustrations are effective in recording data on field trips. Most thought-provoking questions (Why are we giving economic aid to South America? Why were pioneers so dependent on their environment?) require preliminary identification of informational questions before reasons and cause-and-effect relationships can be recorded. A cluster of related informational questions often suggests the utility of a retrieval chart for organizing data in a form which makes generalizing possible.

Note Taking and Outlining

Note taking to record information is useful in all simple research reading in social studies. Young children cannot take extensive notes, but they can assist the teacher in recording key words to remind them of points to make in discussion. Older children can record more detail but also must learn to do it efficiently. Any recording scheme which reduces the time pupils have for investigation can become a handicap and seriously impede the data-gathering process. When pupils are encouraged to take brief notes of the most important facts, they learn to enter into discussion without depending upon notes for details; during their reading they are taught to select and hold in mind the most telling points rather than record everything they read.

Outlining also helps pupils organize information from a variety of sources. They may use their information-seeking questions as the main topics in outline form, adding subpoints as they search out relevant facts and ideas. For example, pupils investigating the problems of environmental pollution developed an outline like this one, using their fact-finding questions as topics and words, phrases, or clauses to complete each section.

I. What kinds of litter are most common in our community?
   A. Paper and packaging

B. Tin and aluminum cans
C. Abandoned cars
II. How does our city government provide for litter disposal?
A. Incinerators for burnable trash
B. Landfill for other solid waste
C. Glass recycling plant
D. Weekly garbage and semi-annual large trash pickup

Children learn the skills of outlining in part through imitation as they assist the teacher in organizing problems and questions identified in the readiness sessions. At times the teacher plans direct instruction to develop these skills. Pupils learn how to select the major divisions of the outline, the meaning of subpoints and how to record them, and how to use the outline in discussion and reporting. A standard form throughout a school avoids confusion as pupils move from class to class.

Records in Graphic Forms

Recording in graphic form is sometimes better suited to data than note taking or outlining, especially if areal or quantitative data are being gathered or if certain kinds of relationships are to be illustrated. For example, on a neighborhood map which pupils sketch, they record spots where trees should be planted; on a map of the local region, locate dairy farms; on a map of a farm they have visited, show crops grown; indicate on a community map recreation facilities nearest the school. In the sketch maps, scale and proportion are not so important as the representation of the data in communicable form. If more accurate locations seem necessary, community and regional maps are usually available.

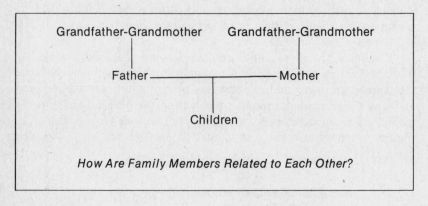

How Are Family Members Related to Each Other?

Figure 6–6. Family relationships.

In organizing other data in graphic form, pupils use the skills they have acquired previously in learning to read and interpret these representations. Figures 6–6, 6–7, and 6–8 are some charts which individuals and small groups in a primary class prepared for their discussion of family life.

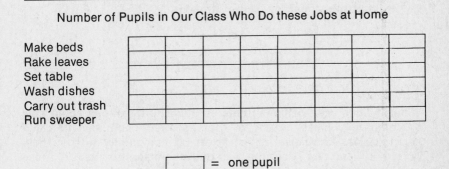

Number of Pupils in Our Class Who Do these Jobs at Home

Make beds
Rake leaves
Set table
Wash dishes
Carry out trash
Run sweeper

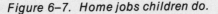

= one pupil

Figure 6–7. Home jobs children do.

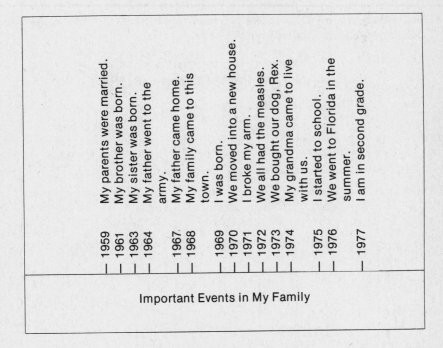

Important Events in My Family

Figure 6–8. Family time line.

Retrieval Charts

Retrieval charts are a practical way to organize data when a set of questions or problems is being applied to various persons, places, or things. The chart has two axes, one representing the questions being investigated, the other, the things to which the questions are being related. Note how retrieval charts functioned in these classrooms.

Organizing Data on a Retrieval Chart 1

Primary pupils were gathering data pertinent to questions about how the community meets needs for food, shelter, communication and transportation. They also asked, "How do community workers help each other?" and "Why does the work of the community change?" These questions examined the idea of interdependence and illustrated the concept of change. They developed a retrieval chart on which to record data for discussion and summary. Their data were well organized when they began to pool ideas on their original questions and later when the teacher asked, "Why would it be difficult for each of us to meet these needs alone? What is likely to happen when any of these workers decides to leave without warning?"

How Community Workers Meet Community Needs				
Needs	Workers	Jobs	Changes	Other Workers Needed
Food	farmers dairy farmers grocers	grow crops produce milk sell foods	new ways to plant and harvest	machinists carpenters
Shelter				
Moving About				
Communi- cation				

Organizing Data on a Retrieval Chart 2

Pupils in the fourth grade were gathering data related to the problem: Why is each region of our country dependent upon other regions? The teacher had encouraged this approach to the regional study to avoid treating each region as a separate entity, each with its own distinctive characteristics. The pupils had decided as the first step in their plan of action to set up a list of information-seeking questions about the regions and then ask a small group of pupils to be responsible for examining a region in order to collect facts for the chart to be used later in discussion and summary.

Region	Climate	Soil	Farm Products	Natural Resources	Unique Contributions
Our Region					
Northwest					
Southeast					
New England					
Southwest					

The completed chart presented a more extensive array of data than pupils could carry in mind without the use of some aid to recall. It was an effective aid to discussion when the teacher asked, "Why does each region of our country have to depend upon other regions for some of the things it needs? How are products and climate of a region related? How would a region be changed if its climate and soil were altered? What would happen to us if one of the regions no longer existed? What would be the result if all regions were alike? What important ideas about how the regions of our country fit together can we discover from studying the chart?"

Organizing Data on a Retrieval Chart 3

A retrieval chart requiring more mature handling of data was executed by a sixth grade class investigating the problem, Why is protection of questions—What caused the problem? What is the present state of the problem? What has been done to try to solve the problem? What must be done in the future?—made up the horizontal axis of the chart; various aspects of the environment—soil depletion and erosion, forest and wildlife destruction, water and air pollution, neglect of human resources—were the vertical axis components. After pupils had reviewed the facts about environmental problems, they were ready to move to questions that would lead them to see relationships, to evaluate progress already made, to propose courses of action, and to predict outcomes. The teacher asked, "How does destroying one aspect of the environment affect other aspects? Why is it impossible to ignore these problems? How can our proposals for the future be evaluated? If we were to remake this chart a year from now, how might it be different?"

Individual and Group Reports

Once data are located, gathered, and organized, pupils may decide to share them through special reports, particularly if the projects and explorations were undertaken by individuals and small groups working somewhat on their own. These reports, if well done, serve a variety of functions. If the report catches the interest and attention of the learners, it provides excellent leads to questioning and discussion. It is also a vehicle for fitting together data from many sources, offering the opportunity for cooperative planning and decision making as children think through their presentations. Skills in reporting also have continuing value as pupils grow into adulthood.

Planning Reports

The success of reporting begins even before research actually gets under way. Through teacher-pupil planning, children arrive at the answers to these questions:

1. What is the purpose of each of the reports we are planning?
2. How will each report contribute to the testing of the hypotheses we have set up?
3. What data will be needed for each report?
4. What are the best sources for these data?
5. How will the groups organize for work?

6. Where will each group work?

7. When will the reports be completed?

Using their skills in research reading and other types of data gathering, small groups proceed with their plans. At some suitable point during their work periods, pupils begin to think about how they will report their information and relate it to the problem being studied. The teacher may help by talking over, and illustrating if necessary, a variety of report forms. Oral reports can become panel discussions, debates, mock interviews, quiz programs, pretend radio and television programs. Eye-catching "chalk talks," "flannel board talks," and talks illustrated with slides or transparencies are fun to make and watch. Drawings, charts, graphs, and maps make points more emphatically. Drama plays a part, too, with dialogues, role playing, and puppet shows high on the list of most-liked report forms. If the teacher broadens children's knowledge of reporting possibilities, pupils can better select a method of presentation suited to the kind of data they plan to share.

At this stage of the enterprise it may be prudent also to review with children how groups plan for reporting. Suggestions listened to and evaluated; ideas tried out, accepted, or rejected; attention to fitting the method of reporting to the kind of data—these are important facets of small group planning. Once a decision has been made as to the technique, definite planning for individual responsibilities can be completed. If the class talks over these points together, small groups and individuals can proceed more efficiently. Pupils may waste valuable time in arriving at operational decisions if they are uncertain about how to carry on or if they do not know how to plan in an orderly way.

When the reporting groups, having collected necessary data, decide to move ahead with plans for their reports, they have several decisions which must be made before work on the final report can begin. Selecting the important points or ideas to be presented is a logical first step. When these are agreed upon, it is time to choose the method for making these ideas clear to others. Other decisions will follow: Will the group report be given by one person or by several? How will the report be introduced and concluded? What illustrations, realia, or properties are necessary? What room arrangement will be required? How much rehearsal time will be needed?

Preparation and Sharing of Reports

During the work periods, the teacher functions as a resource person, suggesting appropriate techniques, helping groups solve problems and make decisions, providing time for rehearsal, and thinking ahead to the time when reports will be given.

When all are ready, how to listen and question are reviewed and general guidelines for management of the reporting period will be co-operatively planned. Most important of all, pupils are reminded of the purposes for which the reports were undertaken.

During the presentation of reports, teachers try to guard against extended reporting, when children are likely to become bored, suggesting subtly how reports may be brought to a close before audience interest is lost. They encourage discussion of each report so that its purpose and main ideas are emphasized.

Cooperative evaluation of pupils' reports can do much to improve their quality. Together teacher and pupils review the reporting effort, talking over such questions as these: Did the reports accomplish the purposes we had for them? Was the information accurate and related to the hypotheses or problems being investigated? Were they given in interesting ways? Were they well planned? How could the reports have been improved? Further discussion will emphasize the concepts and understandings to be drawn from the content, as we shall see later in this chapter.

Rather than a series of reports over several days, the teacher may prefer to integrate the reports through an ongoing discussion of the problem to which they are related. Note how this integration was accomplished with a group of children exploring problems of communication in democracy. Note also how the teacher helped children draw conclusions from their experiences.

━━━━━━━━━━━━━━━━━━━━━━━━━━━━━━━━━━

Reporting Data: Class Discussion

Mrs. Steinbrook: I hope you have been thinking about the discussion we planned for today. Leon, will you read the problem?

Leon: *Why is communication needed in a democratic country?* It's a big problem, but we couldn't have democracy if it wasn't for communication.

Mrs. Steinbrook: Well, we have some groups gathering data about this problem. What did your group do, Allen?

Allen: We interviewed the mayor to find out how communication worked in our city government. Here's our chart showing all the ideas we got at City Hall. After we interviewed the mayor, he asked one of his secretaries to take us around to the other offices. We went early Saturday morning, so they weren't too busy to

	talk to us. Before we left, though, the telephones were ringing everywhere. Anyway, here's our report. You can see that the city government uses every kind of communication we had on our very first reading chart.
Mrs. Steinbrook:	Your list is impressive; you do know how to work as a group. What did you conclude from your experience?
Ruth:	I think I can tell that, because I went with Allen. We found out that without communication it would be impossible for the city officials to take care of all the problems that come up and impossible for them to make any plans for the future.
Mrs. Steinbrook:	Any other evidence? Janet, what did your group do?
Janet:	We made a list of the clubs and organizations which the kids in our class belong to. Then we asked a representative of each one to list as many ways as possible in which the group used communication. The bulletin board at the back of the room tells what we found out. Most of you have looked at it already. The pictures down the center show the means of communication most often used, and the arrows point to each of the community groups that uses that means of communication. Do you know what we decided? That we probably wouldn't have any clubs or organizations in the community if communication was difficult. Even getting people together for meetings would be almost impossible.
Mrs. Steinbrook:	Very good. Now who else has data for us? Is this tape recording from your group, Robert? What did you folks do?
Robert:	We took our tapes with us to call on six people we thought would help us with our problem. We asked each of them to answer the question we're working on. We asked Peter's brother who is home on leave from the army; Frank's father at the television studio; Susan's mother because she works hard in the PTA; Pat's father who is a reporter for the newspaper; Mr. Rogers, who is our state senator, he lives near me; and we won't tell you who the last one is—see if you know the voice. Shall we play the tape now?
Mrs. Steinbrook:	(A few minutes later.) The tape was a very good way to report; it's nice to have the voices and the exact words. Were these people in agreement on our problem or not? . . . There certainly seems to be evidence that democracy depends upon communication; all these people gave us good examples. Now, is there one more? Ronnie?

Ronnie: Yes, ours is the newspaper collection on the reading table. We tried to do something that seemed kind of hard, so Mrs. Steinbrook gave us a hand. When we were talking things over with her, she thought we might try to find articles in the newspaper that show how people learn what their government is doing; these articles have blue circles around them. Then some of us thought we could look further for articles which show how people feel about what is happening. These have red circles around them. The headlines aren't too hard, even if the rest of the article is.

Mrs. Steinbrook: Children, what do you think we'll discover by the work this group did? . . . Yes, all those red and blue pencil marks show that there is much information going from one group to another to inform them about what is going on. Of course, we know that newspapers are not the only way to keep communication going.

Leon: Couldn't the government just make up its own mind about what to do without asking us or even telling us?

Martha: We chose them; they ought to ask us. It isn't democracy otherwise. But my dad says we've got a long way to go.

Peter: There's another thing, too. In a democracy people can't choose a government if they don't know anything about it. Newspapers and television and books and magazines have a lot of information in them; only people don't always pay attention to it. I've heard people say you can't believe any of it anyway. We need to work on that problem before we finish this communication study.

As we read the discussion Mrs. Steinbrook and the pupils were engaged in, we can readily see that this lesson period was not a series of unrelated and isolated reports of routinely gathered facts. Can you see how the teacher lifted children's thinking to generalize on their data-gathering experience to some larger ideas, some understandings about communication in democracy?

What happens to the data pupils gather and process is a vitally important step in probem solving or in any report effort pupils may make. Developing concepts, drawing conclusions, generalizing, and making application to new situations and problems are real-life skills of continuing usefulness and applicability.

Other Points of View

Armstrong, David G., and Savage, Tom V., Jr. "A Framework for Utilizing the Community for Social Learning in Grades 4 to 6." *Social Education* 40 (March 1976):164–67.

Carpenter, Helen McCracken, ed. *Skill Development in Social Studies.* Washington, D.C.: National Council for the Social Studies, 1963.

Chapter 4: Locating and Gathering Information; Chapter 5: Organizing and Evaluating Information; Chapter 11: Interpreting Materials Presented in Graphic Form.

Chapin, June R., and Gross, Richard E. *Teaching Social Studies Skills.* Boston: Little, Brown and Company, 1973.

Chapter 9: Specific Inquiry Skills: Data Collection, Data Analysis, and Hypothesis Testing.

Ellis, Arthur K. *Teaching and Learning Elementary Social Studies.* Boston: Allyn and Bacon, 1977.

Chapter 11: Research Methods.

Martorella, Peter H. *Elementary Social Studies as a Learning System.* New York: Harper & Row, 1976.

Chapter 10: Analytical Tools for Research.

Ryan, Frank L., and Ellis, Arthur K. *Instructional Implications of Inquiry.* Englewood Cliffs, New Jersey: Prentice-Hall, 1974.

Chapter 4: Selecting Data Sources; Chapter 5: Gathering Data; Chapter 6: Processing Data.

Developing Concepts,
Drawing Conclusions,
and Generalizing

Seven

With an array of processed data before them, children are ready to move into the most significant stage of their investigations. Regardless of the teaching strategy employed by the teacher, this stage is one in which pupils can put facts and information together in such a way that larger ideas—concepts, conclusions, understandings, and generalizations— emerge. For pupils this stage can be a satisfying experience, for they see their efforts at fact-gathering moving toward larger ideas. For teachers this stage is equally rewarding, for they can observe pupil progress toward the predetermined goals of social studies instruction.

Importance of Generalizing

Generalizing, however, has significance which pupils may not readily appreciate. Each well-supported generalization gives pupils a tool which they can use in hypothesizing about solutions to new problems and in making inferences from new data. If the generalizing stage is omitted, pupils may reach a kind of dead end where they are satisfied with facts and do little more with them. In the example which follows, children have worked diligently to fulfill their assigned responsibilities, but you may be the judge of whether or not they have gone beyond facts and information to some larger ideas.

Concluding a Study 1

The sixth grade pupils have been at work in committees for the past month, preparing reports on various countries which they identified as significant in current world news. Each committee chose one country and has been busy with maps, books, artifacts, resource persons, films, and other visuals.

When the question of reporting and sharing was raised, one of the young persons who had traveled abroad suggested a fair in which each committee would present its country in a shop or booth format. Everyone agreed.

When fair day came, guests moved about the stations, examining materials, charts, and maps arranged by the group in charge. Children

180

took turns explaining to visitors, while other members of each group visited the various booths in the fair.

Now the guests have departed, and the pupils are congratulating themselves on its success. The teacher is saying, "I think you can feel very good about your fair; your materials were interesting, and you seemed to have the information well in hand. And I think your guests and classmates enjoyed it, too. Tomorrow we will have time to clear everything away and make some plans for our next study."

Without attending the fair or listening to the pupils, we probably should not evaluate their experience. There is evidence, however, that pupils were not encouraged to go beyond the facts which they had reported, even though they had done so in very interesting ways, pleasing both to themselves and their guests. Let's suppose that the teacher's comments following the fair had been of a different nature.

Concluding a Study 2

"Now that we have visited all the countries represented in our fair, I wonder if we can fit all these facts together in some sorts of patterns? For example, we have been talking all along about *interdependence* among people. Did you find evidence of it among or within these countries? . . . What about the idea of *environment?* Did it make very much difference in what went on in the countries you studied? . . . Or *change?* Is this concept operating in the parts of the world you looked at? . . . Now, can each committee make some general statements about life in your country? . . . What are the similarities and the differences? . . . Why aren't all countries exactly the same? . . . Is it possible to make some generalizations that might apply to all countries of the world, even those you did not study?"

As pupils give positive examples of concepts of change, interdependence, and environment, they are reinforcing and enlarging their interpretations of these phenomena. As they pull together the facts about each country, they draw conclusions about its culture, its physical environment, and its people. When they look at the array of countries as a whole, noting likenesses and differences, they can make some general statements which may be true of all countries. Here they are at the highest level of generalizing, making statements which can be applied later on to new situations and new problems yet to be encountered.

Concept Development

The generalizing stage in problem solving depends upon pupils' grasp of a wide range of concepts unique to social studies. Steps in the development of concepts have been developed by both Gagné[1] and DeCecco.[2] While there are some variations in their strategies, the two are quite similar. If we put the two together, the procedure looks something like this:

1. Determine what pupils should be able to do as a result of instruction designed to develop the concept.
2. Identify the unique characteristics related to the concept.
3. Show pupils an example (object, picture, or verbal description) of the concept and name it. Repeat with another example.
4. Show pupils an example of what the concept is not and state clearly that it is *not* an example of the concept.
5. Show pupils another example of the concept and another that is not. Identify clearly which is and which is not an example. Repeat with other examples if necessary.
6. Ask pupils to identify examples of the concept from items presented.
7. Ask them to name their own examples or, if appropriate for the age level, ask them to define the concept.

Although the strategy outlined here and drawn from Gagné and DeCecco seems rather structured, in practice what is basic is the general principle of reinforcing the concept by comparing it with negative examples. The design can be varied as the teacher pleases. While the steps work most easily with concepts like *mountain, desert, river, factory,* let's see how the procedure might be used to develop more abstract social studies concepts.

---

[1] Robert M. Gagné, *The Conditions of Learning,* 2nd ed. (New York: Holt, Rinehart & Winston, 1970), pp. 172–88.

[2] John P. DeCecco, *The Psychology of Learning and Instruction* (Englewood Cliffs, New Jersey: Prentice-Hall, 1968), pp. 402–16.

Developing a Concept 1

You and your pupils are investigating the way in which your community provides goods and services for its pupils. Some discussion has arisen about the meaning of *cooperation.* Sharon says that cooperation is doing what you're supposed to do. Rich says it's when people are doing something together. Joe adds, "It's like when people stop fighting and start helping each other."

You think that perhaps role playing may make the concept clearer, that *cooperation* is people working together for a common purpose. With the assistance of several pupils to whom you whisper a few quick instructions, you role play a situation in which your group is talking over plans to repair broken toys for needy children in the community. You then identify the situation as one that shows *cooperation.*

After a very brief consultation with another small group, you role play another positive example, a committee talking over plans for taking part in a community clean-up campaign. Again the concept is identified.

When you ask, "Who can play out a situation which doesn't show cooperation?" you are likely to find some ready actors. After checking to make sure they are on the right course, you encourage them to play the situation, identifying it as a negative example of cooperation. Depending on the interests of the pupils, play out other brief scenes that show what cooperation is and what it is not. By the time all the would-be players have portrayed their ideas, and all the arguments have been settled about the examples (Were they or were they not cooperation?), the concept of cooperation should be fairly clear. Pupils should have little difficulty in verbalizing its meaning.

Developing a Concept 2

Mr. Vierra wishes his pupils to be able to identify natural resources and distinguish them from artificial creations. He has chosen to emphasize these characteristics: natural resources are needed by human beings; they are found in nature; they are not produced by people. He is using these verbal descriptors to develop the concept. He makes these points:

1. Many weeks of dry weather in our part of the state might cause a severe shortage of water in the near future. Water is a natural resource.

2. Mr. Hanson manages a huge forest from which thousands of trees are cut annually to be sold to furniture factories. Trees are a natural resource.

3. There are several new stores being added to our shopping center. Two of them will sell men's and boys' clothing. Clothing is *not* a natural resource.

4. Many houses in the community are built of limestone taken from quarries outside the town. Limestone is a natural resource. From the limestone many beautiful statues and carvings can be made. The statues and carvings are *not* natural resources.

5. Last night's news indicated that factories may close this winter because of a shortage of coal from which electricity is made. Coal is a natural resource; electricity is *not*.

After further examples, if needed, the teacher asks pupils to classify as natural resources or as artificial things a list of items previously prepared. He may decide to ask them to add to the lists if reinforcement seems necessary.

<hr />

You are thinking, no doubt, that there are certainly other ways in which pupils develop concepts. Each child has a unique way of adding to a reservoir of concepts and draws many facets of meaning from daily experiences in the world, from reading, from television, from adult conversation. Sometimes there are misconceptions as well. Certainly some attention to concept development as a formal intention is appropriate. For those who wish to delve into the matter more thoroughly, we would recommend the suggestions of Martorella, who has made concept development one of his very special concerns.[3]

Levels of Generalization

It is sometimes difficult for pupils to distinguish among facts, conclusions, understandings, and generalizations as they try to interpret the data they have gathered and processed. Ryan and Ellis[4] pursue this problem in what they term *levels of inference* and make some very useful suggestions for clarifying the kinds of statements pupils should be encouraged to make about collected data. They identify the three levels in this way: (*a*) making data statements, (*b*) relating the present investigation to previous work, and (*c*) drawing implications.

<hr />

[3] Peter H. Martorella, *Elementary Social Studies as a Learning System* (New York: Harper & Row, 1976).

[4] Frank L. Ryan and Arthur K. Ellis, *Instructional Implications of Inquiry* (Englewood Cliffs, New Jersey: Prentice-Hall, 1974), pp. 125–30.

The first and simplest statements tell the results of the study or the conclusions that can be supported by facts. These statements, or understandings, relate to definite places, times, people, or situations.

━━━━━━━━━━━━━━━━━━━━━━━━━━━━━━━━━━━━

Generalizing: Summary Statements, Conclusions, or Understandings

Life on the frontier during the American Revolution was an investigation that intrigued some fourth grade pupils during the Bicentennial years, because, they said, almost every book paid much more attention to the colonies east of the mountains than they did to people who had gone west. They were wondering what it was like to live in homes which lacked many of the simple necessities of life, to learn to live in a rugged environment, and to live in fear of Indian attacks.

Based on the data they had gathered from books, films, artifacts from the museum, and postcards of historic frontier villages like Boonesborough, Fort Harrod, and Vincennes, they were able to support a number of statements. Susan had been concerned about the lives of the women; she made the first contributions to the summary statements: "The women missed many of the things they had left behind in their old homes in the colonies. They had to learn to use their environment in new ways and to do kinds of work they had never done before."

David added conclusions from his data about Indian attacks: "The worst year for Indian attacks was 1777, called the year of the Bloody Sevens. Many of the settlers had to leave their farms and move into the forts for protection. Almost every family had lost a member in the fight against the Indians."

Tim had investigated the building methods in various frontier communities. He summarized his findings, beginning in this way. "The environment provided the building materials for all the houses on the frontier, but the method of building was not always the same. For example, people in Fort Harrod used horizontal logs, chinked with wood chips and mud; those in Vincennes used vertical logs, and wide spaces between were filled with clay and whitewashed." And so the list continued.

━━━━━━━━━━━━━━━━━━━━━━━━━━━━━

At a second and higher level, Ryan and Ellis suggest that pupils try to relate their present study to things they have learned previously or to investigations others have made, perhaps comparing and contrasting results.

Generalizing: Broader Statements

"When our list of data statements was finally completed a few days ago, we thought it was a very good summary of life on the Kentucky and Indiana frontier in the days of the American Revolution. I remember that some of you commented about how different the frontier was from life in the colonies east of the mountains. We didn't have time to examine that idea, but it seems to me that it was important; after all, when people settled that area, it was a frontier, too. Let's build a retrieval chart of the data we collected earlier about life in the colonies and add the data we have just summarized about the frontier west of the mountains. Do you think we might find some likenesses and differences?"

With teacher guidance the children are able to move from such comparisons and contrasts to a third and higher level of statement, those that are generalizations of broader application and that may go beyond the data actually processed by the pupils. The teacher elicits the generalizations through questioning and, if necessary, assists in verbalizing the ideas.

Generalizing: Highest Level Statements

"As we study our chart of data about the two pioneer groups we have investigated are you willing to make some general statements about pioneers that you think may be true of all pioneers?" the teacher inquires. With help the pupils begin to generalize. Later on they will test these statements in new situations, perhaps in a study of moon pioneering or under-ocean living. Their generalizations included these:

1. Throughout history pioneers have sought new frontiers.
2. Pioneers move to new places for a variety of reasons.
3. Ways of living on any frontier are likely to be different from the life left behind.
4. Pioneers have reached most of the frontiers on our earth and have settled those that provide for the needs of people adequately.

Pupils may need some help in seeing how the statements they make may move from statements based on specific facts, through statements of increasing abstractness, to generalizations about a whole group of conditions or situations. Note that each of the following statements becomes less specific than the preceding one; each refers to an increasingly broad movement of people, a less limited theater of operations, and a more general purpose for pioneering.

1. Early settlers came to Illinois and Kentucky because the land was good for farming and the water and timber supplies adequate.
2. Pioneers moved westward in our country to provide a better life for their families.
3. Settlers came to all parts of the New World seeking better lives in more congenial surroundings.
4. Pioneers have pushed back the frontier to make life better for more pioneers who followed.

Types of Generalizations

Generalizations differ not only in level of abstractness but also in type. Some are explanatory, stating a relationship among descriptive data. The examples which follow are paired with an appropriate social studies problem which might be the vehicle for development.

1. The work of society is carried out through organized groups; group membership involves opportunities, responsibilities, and the development of leadership.[5]
   Problem: Why does our community have so many special clubs and organizations at work?
2. All nations of the modern world are part of a global interdependent system of economic, social, cultural, and political life.
   Problem: Why are we interested in preserving peace in the Middle East?

Some generalizations are causal and disclose a consequential relationship. These generalizations are significant, but caution must be exercised in ascribing a cause-and-effect relationship among concepts

---

[5] All listed items in this section on generalization are from *Report of the State Central Committee on Social Studies to the California State Curriculum Commission* (Sacramento, California: California State Department of Education, 1961), pp. 40–42.

where the relationship may be difficult to validate. Possible examples and problems follow:

1. Weather and climate and regional differences in land forms, soils, drainage, and natural vegetation largely influence the relative density of population in the various regions of the world.
   Problem: Why do some parts of the world have fewer population problems than others?
2. The culture under which an individual is reared and the social groups to which he belongs exert great influence on his ways of perceiving, thinking, feeling, and acting.
   Problem: Why is it difficult for people of different countries to understand each other?

A third group of generalizations are of the judgmental type. They state practical principles which should guide the behavior of people and groups.

1. Organized group life of all types must act in accordance with established rules of social relationships and a system of social controls.
   Problem: Why do we have laws in our community?
2. Man must make choices based on economic knowledge, scientific comparisons, analytic judgment, and his value system concerning how he will use the resources of the world.
   Problem: What would happen if each person or group used the environment without regard for others?

An illustrative problem accompanies each of these generalizations to further emphasize that generalizations are ideas to be developed through problem solving rather than statements to be given directly to pupils. Once pupils have formulated generalizations in a given situation, they can set about testing them in unfamiliar settings. The more facts they find in support, the more strength accrues to the generalization.

No pupil can study all the problems that might lead to a particular generalization, nor is there any one problem that is best to use in the development of that generalization. But because selected generalizations are content objectives of social studies, problem areas are selected partly in terms of their significance in developing these objectives.

Questions Which Lead to Generalizing

As we have previously noted, discussion of a somewhat structured nature is the vehicle for sharing information uncovered in the search for data.

This discussion leads to testing of hypotheses; application of data to problems; formulating conclusions, understandings, and higher-level generalizations. In this stage of problem solving, discussion reaches its highest point of refinement, as the teacher asks the questions designed to lift the level of pupil thought beyond the reporting of information.

Levels of Questioning

Considerable interest in the teacher as questioner has been spurred by research that has shown that teachers generally use a high proportion of fact-seeking questions and ask relatively few questions that foster thinking.[6] Bloom's taxonomy of educational objectives, particularly in the cognitive domain, has served also to focus attention on the levels of thinking encouraged by the questions teachers ask.[7] There is a strong feeling that the relationship between teacher questioning and the processes that lead to higher-level cognitive objectives is significant. Can you sense the increasing complexity of thought required by these two sets of questions organized according to the taxonomy:

Knowledge Level: What kinds of litter are common in our community?

Comprehension Level: How can we show on our map where most of the litter accumulates?

Application Level: How can we use what we have learned about litter to prevent more serious problems in the future?

Analysis Level: What patterns of littering can be determined by studying the locations where litter collects?

Synthesis Level: How can various groups that are fighting litter work together to do the job better?

Evaluation Level: What is the most useful thing an individual can do to solve the litter problem? Give your reasons.

*   *   *   *   *

Knowledge Level: How many people in our country are poverty striken?

Comprehension Level: Why is poverty in the world increasing?

Application Level: In what ways are proposed solutions applicable to the needs of poor in rural areas?

Analysis Level: What does data about the inner city environment tell us about the opportunities families there have to live comfortably?

---

[6] Claudia Crump, "Teachers, Questions, and Cognition," *Educational Leadership* 27 (April 1970):657–60; Theodore W. Parson and Fannie R. Staftel, "Thinking and Inquiry: Some Critical Issues," in *Effective Thinking,* eds. Jean Fair and Fannie R. Staftel (Washington, D.C.: National Council for the Social Studies, 1967), pp. 125–32.

[7] Benjamin S. Bloom, *Taxonomy of Educational Objectives, Handbook I, Cognitive Domain* (New York: David McKay Company, 1956).

Synthesis Level: What would you propose as a workable plan to provide better housing for the poor of the community?

Evaluation Level: In terms of meeting the daily needs of the poor, what are the merits of local efforts to improve living conditions in the inner city?

A consideration of questions according to the Bloom taxonomy is not a call for deliberate categorization of all questions teachers may wish to ask. In fact, it may not matter whether or not they can classify exactly each question, particularly since there is considerable overlap in the categories and likely some lack of agreement on the best classification. On the other hand, teachers who are familiar with the taxonomy can make certain that they are asking questions that encourage several levels of thought and that in most discussions questions include not only knowledge and comprehension levels, but also questions that go beyond.

A simpler classification of questions is proposed by Gallagher and Aschner.[8] They define four categories: the cognitive-memory question which seeks recall of facts; the convergent which seeks relationships and encourages pupils to produce an expected response; the divergent question which leads to hypothesizing and anticipates a variety of creative responses; the evaluative question which asks for supported choices among alternatives. Applied to social studies content, the categories may be illustrated by questions like these:

Cognitive Memory: On what date did Columbus discover America?

Convergent: Why did Columbus undertake his voyage?

Divergent: Which was probably more dangerous, Columbus's voyage or the first journey to the moon?

Evaluative: Which sources of data about Columbus appear to be the most reliable?

In another problem area, these questions are illustrative:

Cognitive Memory: What branch of government does Congress represent?

Convergent: Why are citizens interested in the work Congress does?

Divergent: How would our lives be changed if Congress lost its power to make laws?

Evaluative: In your opinion, what are the most effective ways for citizens to influence the actions of Congress?

---

[8] James Gallagher and Mary Jane Aschner, "A Preliminary Report on Analysis of Classroom Interaction," *Merrill-Palmer Quarterly* 3 (1963):183–94.

Sequence in Questioning

While recognition of levels of questioning is important, guiding a discussion which leads to generalizing requires a sense of sequence and timing which becomes part of teaching strategy only with training and effort. Taba and a group of associates, in their study of children's thinking, provided a real breakthrough in discovering techniques for lifting pupils' thinking from facts to generalizing and application. Their work has been very influential in stimulating teachers to give more attention to sequence in questioning and discussion. From their point of view, discussion of data, collected and organized for retrieval and reporting, has as an initial objective the identification of specific information leading to concept development.

In the Taba curriculum, the questioning sequence for concept formation required pupils to (*a*) enumerate items, (*b*) find a basis for grouping items that are similar, (*c*) identify the common characteristics of items in a group, and so label the groups, and (*d*) regroup and relabel as they see ways in which this could be done.[9]

Questioning: Concept Development

The second grade has returned from a field trip designed to answer questions about family homes in the community: Why do families in our town live in different kinds of houses? As Taba and associates suggest, the teacher asks, "What did you see?"

The pupils respond by naming the houses they saw: a log cabin, high-rise apartments, mobile homes, a camp tent, one-family houses, a duplex, hotels, motels, a condominium, a four-family house, and a dormitory.

Then the teacher inquires, "Do you see some kinds of houses in your list that go together because they are alike in some way?" One child groups hotels, motels, dormitory, and tent because people don't live there for a long time; another puts together those where one family lives; another may use cost as the factor for grouping; another, building materials.

When the pupils find criteria on which they can agree, the teacher suggests that they sort out the items and then asks, "What would you

---

[9] Paraphrased from Hilda Taba, Mary C. Durkin, Jack R. Fraenkel, and Anthony H. McNaughton, *A Teacher's Handbook to Elementary Social Studies: An Inductive Approach*, 2nd ed. (Reading, Massachusetts: Addison-Wesley, 1971), p. 66. Used by permission.

call each of these groups?" In this instance, the concepts developed depended on the children's decisions: single-family dwellings and multiple-family housing; temporary housing and permanent housing, etc.

●━o━●━o━o━o━●━●━●━o━o━●━o━o━o━●━●━o━o━o━●━o━●━●

Discussion then proceeds to the explanation of specific events or items by exploring relationships among facts, including causal connections if cautiously made, and the making of inferences based on the particular body of facts under consideration. Later, pupils will be able to build on these low-level generalizations toward generalizations of increasingly higher order.

The Taba theory refers to the phase of discussion beyond concept formation as the stage of data interpretation. The teacher asks questions that require pupils to (*a*) identify key points in data, (*b*) differentiate the relevant from the irrelevant, (*c*) discern cause and effect relationships, and (*d*) generalize. [10]

●━o━●━o━●━o━o━o━●━o━o━o━o━●━●━o━o━o━●━o━●━●━●

Questioning: Interpretation of Data

The second grade pupils are continuing to pursue the problem: Why do families in our town live in different kinds of houses? The teacher asks, "What did you notice about the differences in the houses we saw? What did you learn about the families who were living in the homes we visited?"

Pupils comment that students were occupying the dormitories; families on welfare were living in the low-rent housing; those in the tent were on vacation; the family of a road-construction worker lived in the mobile home; older couples were in the high-rise apartments near the shopping center.

The teacher inquires, "Why do you think these people chose these homes?"

The children share their ideas. "They haven't money enough to choose anything better. They move from place to place with the father's job. People live in condominiums because they want to own their own home but don't want to take care of yard or garden. Student families have to choose apartments that don't cost too much. Other people like to be close to stores where they can buy what they need. Some families might like another kind of home which isn't available in our part of the county."

---

[10] Ibid., p. 74.

When the pupils have exhausted the possible reasons, the teacher nudges them into making inferences based on the data. "What do these points mean? What can you say about why people choose the homes they do? What would you conclude?"

The children have come back with a statement they inferred from their data: People choose their homes for a variety of reasons: what they can afford, what is available, what is convenient, or what they prefer.

———————————————————————————————————

Discussion then moves to higher levels; pupils are encouraged to make predictions based on processed data but to go beyond that which is given to the formulation of generalizations of broader applicability. The Taba research identifies this stage as the application of principles in which pupils (*a*) predict consequences and hypothesize, (*b*) explain and/or support predictions and hypotheses, and (*c*) verify predictions or hypotheses.[11]

———————————————————————————————————

Questioning: Application of Principles

Discussion of family housing takes our second grade into the application stage when the teacher asks, "You have concluded that people choose their homes for a variety of reasons. What would happen if it were decided that only high-rise apartments could be built in the future and that the construction of additional low-cost housing would be discontinued?"

The children predict consequences. "There would be riots and protests, because people have a right to make their own decisions about where they will live. Some people would have to go on welfare if they could not afford the high-rise. The high-rise would be difficult for older people or for families with many children. Some people would decide to move out of the community; others would decide not to move in. Some people would protest having to give up their present homes to go into apartments if someone put pressure on them to give up their land for building new high-rises."

The teacher pursues a bit, "But why do you think these things would happen?"

---

[11]   Ibid., p. 84.

Pupils argue for the right to choose, the needs of poor people, the variety and beauty that would be lost to the community, the importance of housing that can be just right for families of different interests and desires.

Then the discussion leader suggests, "Would it always be true that people choose in terms of things that are important to them? Could you make a general statement that would apply to other things besides homes?" The pupils could—with help. In a while the statement comes out: The choices people make about how they will live is affected by needs, personal preferences, income, and the kind of place in which their community is located.

⬥⬥⬥⬥⬥⬥⬥⬥⬥⬥⬥⬥⬥⬥⬥⬥⬥⬥⬥⬥⬥⬥⬥⬥⬥⬥⬥⬥⬥

The pupils have formulated a generalization which has broad application to many other aspects of living not dealt with in the original study of homes. It shows a relationship between concepts, in this case between the concept *ways of living* and the concepts of *environment, economic level, needs,* and *preference.* The generalization may be thought of also as a tentative hypothesis to be tested further by application to a variety of new situations; it can be illustrated again and again by different content in a wide variety of problems that may be selected for study in the future.

It is at this point of generalizing and at this level that pupils come full circle to the place where goals and outcomes relate most fully to each other. The content goals are arrived at inductively by pupils as they study their collected data, infer from them to test hypotheses, and propose solutions to problems. Cognitive, affective, and behavioral goals are realized in the processes children use, the values they manifest, and the actions they may take as a result of their convictions.

The Teacher as Discussion Leader

From the analysis of questions and discussion which leads to generalizing, it seems clear that the teacher's principal roles are those of questioner and sequencer. Upon the teacher rests the responsibility of focusing questions and remarks so as to establish the point of the task, the content to be developed, and the operation to be performed. Teachers determine when adequate thought has been given to a particular level of information before they guide pupils to a higher level of thinking. When the transition is to be made, they pose the questions that will effect the transition. Throughout the process, teachers are most interested in challenging children to do their own thinking and in creating an air of acceptance to make free exchange of ideas possible. They are the facilitators of creative interplay as children pool data and move to increasingly higher levels of thought.

The teacher prepares the way for effective discussion by making sure that pupils have acquired necessary skills through direct teaching and through practice. Each participant should be able to hold in mind the question or topic being considered, to select information related to it, and to stay on the subject during the discussion. If pupils have organized their preparation well, they are ready with materials they may want to use—maps, diagrams, pictures, or quotations. Each pupil will be skillful in helping classmates join in the discussion, recognizing their right to contribute and listening to them. Each will know how to disagree courteously and how to state an opinion forcefully (but tactfully) and will be ready to prove ideas with facts and to concede when others have proven theirs. The teacher is the key person in guiding the acquisition of these skills, prompting pupils to set up discussion standards that reflect these skills and occasionally to evaluate their sharing to discover needed improvement.

From time to time the teacher analyzes a discussion session and its products, perhaps using a tape recording as the means of recall. In this period of reflection, the extent and breadth of pupil participation, the interest shown, and the general atmosphere are all considered. But because the discussion has problem solving and generalizing as objectives, concern for management is secondary. The teacher is especially attuned to discovering whether or not pupils have organized data for ready access and are able to dig beneath the surface to accept or reject their original hypotheses, to state understandings or inferences related to their specific problem, and to formulate generalizations, or higher-level inferences, which are applicable to new and perhaps as yet unidentified situations and problems.

Dissemination of Ideas and Action Proposals

When pupils become seriously involved in investigating a problem, they will often come to some important conclusions based on their data and have some actions to recommend. They are likely to propose that their ideas, feelings, and plans be shared with others. This sharing makes sense, particularly if the problem pupils have been studying is of current interest and concern to people in the community.

While pupils may conclude their study with group discussion as suggested previously, knowing that the outcomes will be or ought to be shared with others injects a new dimension of purposefulness into the closing phases of a study. There are other reasons, too, why appropriate sharing should be encouraged.

1. It provides incentive for identifying clearly the generalizations to be shared and for supporting them with data and illustrations.
2. It encourages pupils to evaluate the worth of what they have to share and to determine the values they wish to demonstrate to others.
3. It offers pupils the opportunity to take the role of citizen advocates for an idea or action.
4. It opens up possibilities for using creative talents to present ideas in attention-getting ways and for using skills acquired in other areas of the curriculum.
5. It gives children a chance to view and evaluate the results of their study as others respond to their efforts.
6. It demonstrates the pupils' skill in cooperative problem solving and illustrates to persons beyond the classroom the nature of the social studies instruction which engages the pupils.

Pupils may choose to make their findings known to others by sharing some of the products developed during their investigation, or they may devise new ways to present their ideas. In any case, they should now consider the dissemination of their work and their plans in as effective a manner as possible.

The vehicle pupils choose for demonstrating, reporting, publishing, or circulating their ideas is more likely to be successful if it meets these criteria.

1. It should be a natural follow-up to pupil investigation.
2. It should pointedly summarize the important findings of the study.
3. It should be appropriate to the kind of information to be shared and the actions recommended.
4. It should take into consideration the interests and attitudes of the "audience" for whom it is intended.

The methods pupils choose to put across their ideas and influence others are limited only by the practicality of the techniques. They may use some of the media they have seen adults employ in similar situations, or they may find unique ways of sharing their thinking.

While all types of mass media have possibilities for dissemination, the newspaper is the one most readily available to pupils. Drawing upon their writing and reporting skills, pupils can summarize their findings, describe their action proposals, and make their pleas for cooperation from those who read what they have written. They may write letters to the editor to support a position or propose a plan. If the local newspaper publishes a youth page on a regular basis, this outlet will be open to the children. If the study itself is newsworthy, it is possible to secure a photographic report for the daily news with children filling in the reporter on their findings and plans for implementation. The school newspaper is perhaps an even more available vehicle, since the pupils themselves can prepare the articles.

If the action proposals pupils plan to make are ones that have campaign characteristics, then posters and signs will help them spread the word. Pupils should be encouraged to make their posters informative as well as exhortative, combining both what should be done and why. Pupils consider strategic locations for their posters and make the necessary contacts in the school and community.

Some of the problems pupils study will result in plans for dissemination of helpful suggestions for accomplishing certain objectives. Here are some of the kinds of information elementary school pupils have prepared and distributed in decorative leaflets to their neighborhoods.

Disseminating Information: Leaflets

Conserving fuel. Ideas for maintaining family comfort and convenience while using energy wisely.

Spring clean-up. Plans for activities designed to encourage cooperative action to improve the appearance of the neighborhood.

Voting campaign. List of reasons why all citizens should vote and information about polling places.

Fire safety. Suggestions for getting rid of fire hazards in the home, together with cautions in using appliances and instructions to follow in case of an outbreak of fire.

Gardening guide. Suggestions for spring planting to insure a continuous supply of vegetables, together with recommendations to reduce the use of insecticides.

Pollution control. Suggestions for reducing water and air pollution in the home and for waste disposal.

Food preservation. Suggestions for canning, drying, and storing food supplies.

Holiday celebration. Ways to observe a particular holiday which will involve families and highlight tradition.

From organized and shared data, concepts are developed, conclusions drawn, and generalizations formulated. These children have arranged a fair about ways of living around the world and later will make summarizing statements based on their data.

Television guide. Recommendations for children's programs which pupils have evaluated according to criteria they have developed.

Safety tips. Ways to prevent accidents in the home and first aid suggestions in case of accidents.

Emergency tips. Sources of help—where to go and whom to call in various types of home crises.

———————————————————

Pupils may decide that demonstration or exhibition will be needed to encourage other people to follow through on some of the conclusions and plans they have formulated. These instructional assemblies are to be co-operatively planned and appropriate audiences invited. Enterprising pupils, with the help of sympathetic adults, can plan and implement presentations and workshops to put into action many of their ideas. Following are some examples, together with the problems that were previously investigated.

———————————————————

Dissemination: Workshops and Assemblies

Problem: How can we spend our money more wisely?

Presentation: Pupils plan instruction on how to read labels on products, compare weights, contents, and prices.

Problem: How can we reduce littering?

Presentation: Pupils conduct a workshop on recycling common throw-away items into useful products.

Problem: How can we make our community a more attractive place?

Presentation: Pupils display and explain their plans for neighborhood parks and recreation areas.

Problem: Why do we need a city art museum?

Presentation: Pupils arrange an exhibition of their own art and the work of community artists to emphasize the point that there is no official place where such exhibits can be given.

Problem: Why do people choose the work they do?

Presentation: Pupils set up a Career Day program in which they present a cross-section of careers found in the community, displaying materials and objects representative of each career and describing the training and skills needed.

Problem: How does our community help people with special needs?

Presentation: Pupils arrange a series of stations, each of which describes kinds of volunteer help needed by various service organizations in the community.

━━━━━━━━━━━━━━━━━━━━━━━━━━━━━━━

In the most optimum situations, pupils may take their findings directly to persons who can help them implement their plans. If children have worked out suggestions for improving some aspect of school environment or management, they are encouraged to take both plans and justification to the appropriate administrator. If their efforts have been concentrated on a community problem, adults should assist them in reaching the agency or official who can respond to their ideas. These experiences are good practice in citizenship, even when the results do not equal children's expectations.

Encouraging pupils to put their ideas into observable form and to influence others to participate is also a practical way of achieving the behavioral goals of social studies. While it is often impossible to gather evidence of pupil behaviors beyond the confines of the school or to know how well children may use their learning as they grow to adulthood, dissemination activities offer a challenging opportunity to reinforce the action component of social studies.

Other Points of View

Banks, James A. *Teaching Strategies for the Social Studies,* 2nd ed. Reading, Massachusetts: Addison-Wesley, 1977.
Chapter 3: Products of Social Inquiry: Facts, Concepts, Generalizations, and Theories; Chapter 4: Social Inquiry: Questioning Strategies.

Beyer, Barry K. *Inquiry in the Social Studies Classroom: A Strategy for Teaching.* Columbus, Ohio: Charles E. Merrill, 1971.
Chapter 6: Concepts and Inquiry Teaching.

Ellis, Arthur K. *Teaching and Learning Elementary Social Studies.* Boston: Allyn and Bacon, 1977.
Chapter 13: Questioning Strategies for Higher Level Thinking.

Giffin, Ronald D. "Questions That Teach: How to Frame Them; How to Ask Them." *Grade Teacher* 87 (January 1970):58–61.

Oliner, Pearl M. *Teaching Elementary Social Studies: A Rational and Humanistic Approach.* New York: Harcourt, Brace, Jovanovich, 1976.
Chapter 2: Concepts and Generalizations.

Ryan, Frank L. *Exemplars for the New Social Studies.* Englewood Cliffs, New Jersey: Prentice-Hall, 1971.
Chapter 5: Strategies—Questioning.

Ryan, Frank L., and Ellis, Arthur K. *Instructional Implications of Inquiry.* Englewood Cliffs, New Jersey: Prentice-Hall, 1974.
Chapter 7: Making Inferences.

Sanders, Norris M. *Classroom Questions: What Kinds?* New York: Harper and Row, 1966.

Taba, Hilda; Durkin, Mary C.; Fraenkel, Jack R.; and McNaughton, Anthony M. *A Teacher's Handbook to Elementary Social Studies: An Inductive Approach,* 2nd ed. Reading, Massachusetts: Addison-Wesley, 1971.
Basic reference for developing thought processes.

Using Maps and Globes in Social Studies

Maps and globes are useful tools whenever pupils search for data to verify hypotheses or answer questions that relate to space, location, the earth, its surface, and people's relationship to their world. Moreover, pupils are more likely than ever before to go to maps and globes for data. Improved communication and transportation have extended our contacts with the world, and the mass media, especially television and newspapers, are making ever-increasing use of maps in their reports of current events. Children are intrigued by maps, and both classroom experience and research studies assure teachers that pupils can learn to use maps and globes efficiently.

Functions of Maps and Globes

Maps and globes serve purposes no other sources of data can serve as well. They are the only in-hand representations of the earth and its surface available to pupils when they need a view of areas of the world which are beyond the range of their experience. They facilitate the search for specific kinds of data:

1. Those related to space and location.
   Where are the largest cities located? How far is it from the most inland city to the nearest coast? How does Ohio compare in size with its neighbors?
2. Data about the natural environment.
   Where are the highest mountains? Are lowlands or highlands characteristic of a given region? Judging from these maps, would you expect the climate to be hot or cold? Where are the deepest harbors?
3. Data from which inferences may be made about how people use the earth.
Why is the location of Chicago a strategic one? Why would you probably not expect to find wheat growing in Florida? Where could pioneers find a natural location for a trail to the west? If you were a farmer, in what part of the country would you choose to live?

Maps and globes are not equally useful or interchangeable, however, for the kinds of data each has to offer are unique to its characteristics. Globes make it possible for the pupil to see a model of the earth at a glance; to perceive the relationship of land and water areas and their relative sizes; to begin to understand how one may travel around the world and return to the starting place; how the turning of the earth causes day and night, and how locations on the earth's surface are related to home base. These relationships are not easily discovered from maps.

Maps, too, have their own special services. While it is impossible to view the world in true perspective through the use of maps, when pupils need to see the details of a given area on the earth's surface, maps rather than globes are selected. The amount of detail, of course, depends upon the size of the map, the size of the area it shows, and its level of sophistication.

Data from maps differ also with the type of map being used. Physical maps provide data for environmental features, mountains, lowlands, rivers, lakes, bays, peninsulas, and the like; physical-political maps provide additional locations of cities and other artificial features and land uses. Other maps emphasize particular aspects of the environment—rainfall, growing season, population density—data from which pupils can make inferences about the use of the environment. A variety of special maps is available: historical maps which provide data about land expansion and sequence of historical developments, vegetation maps which can be used to verify hypotheses about how land is used in a given area, economic maps which show the sources of natural resources and manufactured products, and many more.

This great variety of maps and the types of data they make available are resources that function in many aspects of problem solving. Social studies, more than any other curriculum area, offers a natural setting for learning to understand and use them.

Developmental Guidelines

Pupils' experiences with maps and globes will be most effective if the teacher bases them on knowledge of several developmental principles. Awareness of these guidelines sharpens the teacher's perception of the child's level of maturity and avoids the pitfalls of ill-considered and inappropriate experiences.

Children's concept of a map and its uses grows gradually from spontaneous reproduction of spatial arrangements to accurate representations of topographic conditions. Maps seem to be part of the early experiences of most children, though it is difficult to say when pupils first become aware of them. Television, newspapers, and magazines all bring maps into the consciousness of children.

Most first grade pupils do not hesitate when they are asked to draw a map of something. To some this request may mean drawing a picture; to others drawing a map indicates something not quite a picture. Note in Figures 8-1, 8-2, and 8-3 how diverse are the maps of their homes. First grade pupils drew these when they were gathering data on the problem, Why don't we all live in the same kind of house?

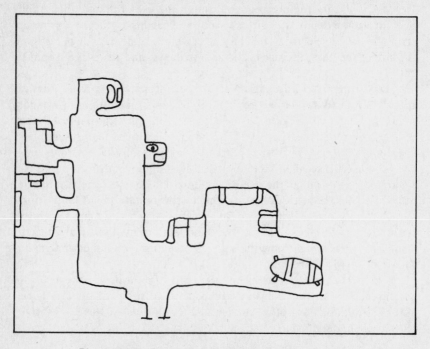

Figure 8-1. First grade child's map of his house.

In these early years, the maps children learn to read are very like the ones they draw—simple, uncluttered—a map of the school and playground, a map of the neighborhood or of the zoo they plan to visit, or a simple wall map of their country.

Several years later these pupils will disdain the maps of their early years. Maps of houses now become blueprints, and the maps they draw have the things maps should have—scale, symbols, and all. Note in Figure 8-4 the map of their school drawn by fifth grade pupils who were studying the problem: How are maps made?

The maps these older children read, while still appropriate for their maturity level, are more complex in the data they contain. A wide range of symbols represents a variety of physical and cultural features; scales become important for accuracy; location skills become essential tools in data gathering. Throughout the elementary years, children's awareness of the usefulness of maps and their ability to interpret them grow steadily.

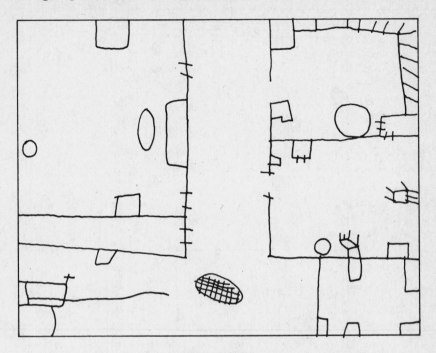

Figure 8–2. *First grade child's map of his house.*

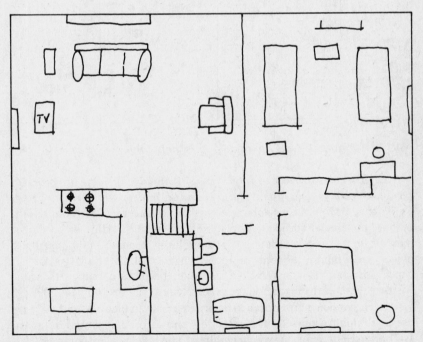

Figure 8–3. *First grade child's map of his house.*

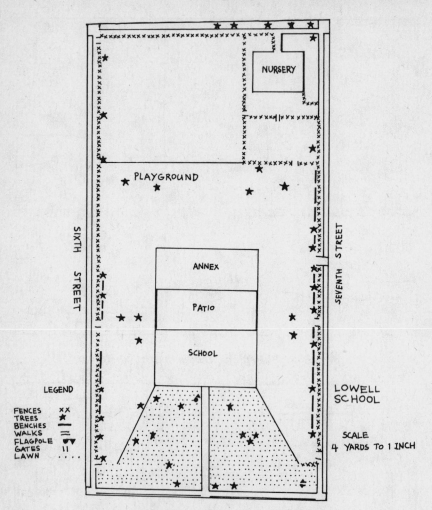

Figure 8–4. Fifth grade pupils' map of their school.

Children must learn to interpret the language of maps in order to recognize various geographic features and to understand their meaning. Pupils may begin to use symbols as they lay out on the classroom floor a map of their neighborhood. The streets are strings, strips of paper, or painted lines. Trees and houses appear. Pupils come to know that these objects are symbols; they only represent what is real. Later a large sheet of paper, also laid out on the floor or table, becomes a map with semiabstract symbols the teacher helps them devise, like those on page 209.

Such symbols may appear to be little more than pictures, but they are useful stepping stones to understanding more formalized and standard symbols used on maps for young children. The following are common.

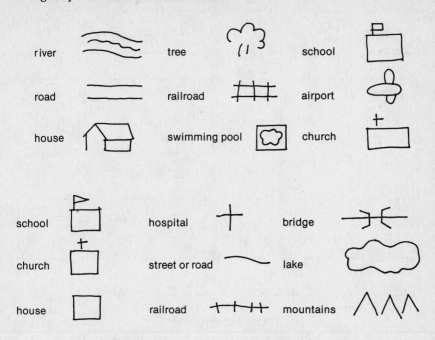

From these symbols, pupils move to more abstract ones. They interpret and use dots, circles, and stars which represent cities of various sizes;
lines of different colors which represent roads, rivers, railroads, and
airways. Color is interpreted in terms of elevation of land and depth of
water. The progress from simple to complex and abstract is gradual but
sure. At the intermediate level, the maps pupils use combine symbols of
many kinds. Ability to interpret these symbols is essential to data collection.

*Pupils need to develop an understanding of the advantages and dis-
advantages of various projections as a basis for accurate interpretation of
maps.* When pupils are working with simple maps of the local area, there
need be no special concern for projection and its attendant distortion.
Even maps of the United States show no significant distortion for the
purposes for which pupils use them. As they begin to use world maps,
however, possible distortion becomes of some significance. Pupils may
have tried previously to make a flat map from a spherical shape; for
example, to flatten half an orange peel or hollow rubber ball. From such
an experience it is easy for them to see why some older world maps like
Mercator projections were badly distorted at the poles as the map maker
tried to fill in ocean and land areas to make the map surface complete.
Fortunately, the Mercator projection is not now much used.

Pupils discover that the elliptical map gives a more realistic view of
the world, but when they compare the land and ocean areas with those on

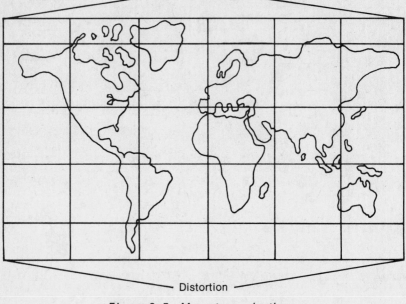

Figure 8–5. Mercator projection.

a globe, they become aware that distortion still exists, now at the east and west extremes more than anywhere else.

The equal-area map is most like the flattened orange peel the pupils may have experimented with. Because map makers preferred to leave the land areas intact, they placed the broken areas in the oceans. Now as

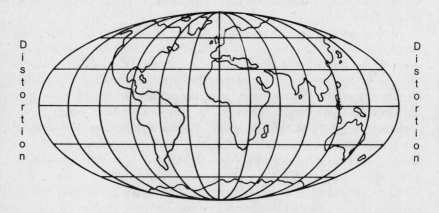

Figure 8–6. Elliptical projection.

pupils look at the map of the world, the land areas are less distorted than in the other projections, even though it is more difficult to determine the ocean areas exactly. It is a good time for the teacher to reinforce the idea once more that the most accurate model of the earth is the globe itself.

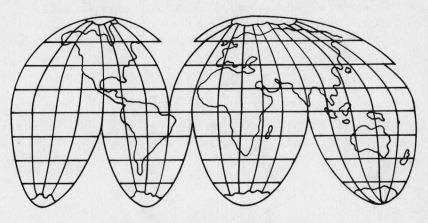

Figure 8–7. Equal-area projection.

Developing skill in map interpretation enables pupils to see relationships among maps showing the various environmental features of a region. Pupils become involved in many social studies problems in which they are trying to explain why people live as they do. Whenever these problems create a need for understanding how ways of living are affected by environment, maps are helpful. For example, pupils may be probing reasons why wheat is an important crop in the Middle West. Their search has revealed the conditions which are required for the growth of both winter and spring wheat. They study a rainfall map to find areas where rainfall is adequate for the growing of wheat. Similarly they find on a map of growing seasons the areas where the number of days is suitable for both varieties of wheat. Putting the data from the two maps side by side enables pupils to make some rather good guesses about the best locations for wheat culture. For confirmation they may check their ideas with a map showing wheat growing regions or use other references for such confirmation. Teachers can suggest other illustrations which show relationships between physical environment and routes for travel, between locations of cities and presence of natural resources, between cultural and physical features of the land, and so on.

Children's skill in interpreting ideas of latitude and longitude to find location on the earth's surface can be developed gradually and easily as the need begins to emerge. Children in primary grades have little use for location skills requiring a knowledge of latitude and longitude, but they often have an introduction to the use of grids on road maps used in family travel. The teacher may build on this knowledge, or half-knowledge, as the case may be, by challenging children with the problem of trying to describe a particular location without benefit of reference points or lines. For example, the teacher projected the following map of an imaginary island, asking the pupils to tell the exact location of Seaville and Hightown.

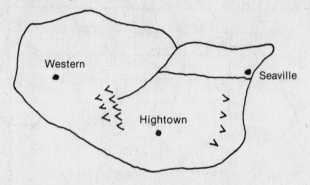

Figure 8–8. An imaginary island.

After the pupils had made some fruitless attempts to be exact in their locations, the teacher superimposed on the map a transparent grid, reminding the children that this grid would look like the ones they had seen

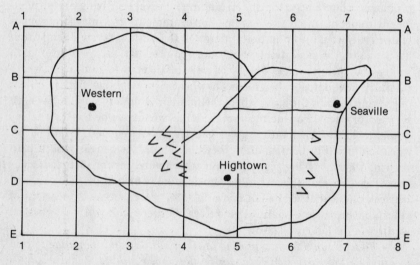

Figure 8–9. Map with grid.

on road maps. They were instantly successful in describing the location of each city. Since road maps are located by *spaces* rather than by lines, the teacher replaced the first transparency with lettered and numbered lines.

After using the grid to locate cities in their own state and neighboring states, the children were encouraged to look for grids on a variety of maps and globes. Later these would be labeled and the use of parallels and meridians developed.

These principles of instruction imply that there are specific understandings and skills which pupils must acquire if they are to use maps and globes effectively as data sources.

Understandings about Maps and Globes

What are the important ideas about maps and globes which pupils should come to understand through their experiences in learning to use them? Detailed lists of these ideas appear in various professional sources, but understandings about the globe generally include these:

1. The globe is an accurate model of the spherical shape of the earth.

2. The globe shows the physical features of the earth in their relationship to each other.

3. A grid system provides a scheme for locating points on the earth's surface.

4. North and south are definite points on the globe; east and west are not.

5. Great circles divide the earth into hemispheres; global distances are measured along these circles.

6. The earth turns on its axis; rotation of the earth produces day and night.

7. Revolution of the earth around the sun and the tilt of the earth produce the seasons.

8. Transfer of any portion of the globe to a flat surface results in some distortion; the larger the transferred portion, the greater the distortion.

Because maps differ from globes in significant ways, pupils also need to develop specific understandings about them. The following are among the most important of these ideas that pupils should acquire in the elementary years.

1. Flat maps show portions of the globe in greater detail than can be shown on the globe.

2. Flat maps of the very large areas are likely to be somewhat distorted.

3. Flat maps show surface features of the area in relation to each other.

4. Interpretation of maps depends upon an understanding of the symbols and scale used.

5. Map data must be translated into "landscape imagery" in order for them to be useful.

6. A grid system provides a scheme for locating points on a map as it does on the globe.

7. Map projections of various types differ in the nature and amount of distortion which result.

   Pupils grow toward these understandings as they use maps and globes in their data-gathering experiences and as they acquire the necessary skills.

Map and Globe Skills

Since problem solving provides motivation for perfecting skills and the opportunity to put to functional use those already acquired, the hierarchy of map skills thus becomes the focus of attention. These skills are usually ordered in terms of complexity. The outline which follows is brief, easy to interpret and use. The skills for each age group are identified, expressed behaviorally, and cumulative from level to level.

Age Six

1. The child points out land and water divisions on globes and maps.

2. The child uses east-west, north-south directions correctly.

3. The child makes simple maps on a flat surface with concrete objects.

4. The child reads simple large outline maps prepared by the teacher.

5. The child interprets pictures and simple symbols that represent places on such maps.

6. The child explains the differences between maps and globes.

Age Seven

1. The child uses in-between directions correctly.

2. The child constructs simple large-scale maps of school or neighborhood.

3. The child devises appropriate legends and keys for such maps.

4. The child interprets abstract symbols on simple commercial maps and globes.

Age Eight

1. The child points out hemispheric divisions on the globe.
2. The child reads directions on maps used on a flat surface, such as a table or the floor.
3. The child cooperates in making simple sketch maps needed in studying a problem.
4. The child develops legends and scales of miles needed for such maps.

Age Nine

1. The child identifies directions accurately when using wall maps.
2. The child uses legends correctly on various kinds of simple maps.
3. The child identifies symbols used for water and land features.
4. The child interprets the scale of miles on simple commercial maps.
5. The child compares two maps of an area in order to see relationships.

Age Ten

1. The child uses directions on the globe correctly.
2. The child interprets the use of color, dots, lines, and other such representations in addition to the usual symbols.
3. The child compares maps of different sizes of the same area.
4. The child chooses the appropriate map for a particular purpose.
5. The child uses latitude and longitude in determining location.

Age Eleven

1. The child uses the scale of miles to explain maps of the same size which show areas of different sizes.
2. The child interprets correctly the scale of miles on all maps used.
3. The child infers information about ways of living from studying related maps of an area.
4. The child relates latitude and longitude to other physical features to secure data about an area.

Development of Map and Globe Skills

The purposeful use of maps and globes in problem solving is strong motivation for acquiring skills. To develop map and globe skills needed in data gathering, teachers may from time to time engage children in exploratory or reinforcement activities apart from the learning experiences

Maps and globes are valuable sources of data which help pupils understand the real world. These children are engaged in a variety of learning experiences to gather geographical information about their country.

associated with problem solving. Children's interest in maps makes involvement easy to achieve. As they engage in exercises selected by the teacher, they acquire skills which can be used purposefully in the area of study.

The literature suggests many possibilities for such activities. Some of these activities may become the sources of data when adapted to particular problems; others may be related to aspects of the curriculum that are not part of social studies; still others are deliberately somewhat isolated (though planned) efforts to provide experience with skills. Following are a few such activities.

Direction

Primary Grades:

1. Pupils locate directions outside at noon as they stand with backs to the sun.
2. Pupils give directions such as "I go south to the library."
3. Pupils place direction cards correctly in the classroom.
4. Pupils locate direction finders on various kinds of maps.
5. Pupils use *up* and *down* correctly in relation to the center of the earth.
6. Pupils orient all maps they use to proper directions.

Intermediate Grades

1. Pupils practice giving oral directions to a given place.
2. Pupils practice telling what direction one place is from another on the globe.
3. Pupils identify directions taken from one place to another on field trip maps.
4. Pupils trace travel routes on globes and tell directions taken.
5. Pupils distinguish between *up* and *down* and *north* and *south* on maps.
6. Pupils practice using the compass to determine directions inside and outside the school building.
7. Pupils trace north-south and east-west lines on maps and globes and name them correctly.
8. Pupils refer to *parallels* when measuring north-south directions and *meridians* for east-west directions on maps and globes.

Location

Primary Grades

1. Before taking a field trip, pupils study a simple map on which their route is traced. They discuss points of interest along the way.

2. On a neighborhood or community map, pupils locate where they live and how they go from home to school.

3. On a simple map of the classroom, the location of a hidden object is marked. Pupils search for the object. The first person to find it hides the object and marks its location on the map for others.

4. Pupils take a walking trip in the neighborhood, using a map to locate where they are to make stops—where pets are located, for example.

Intermediate Grades

1. On a simple map of the world, pupils affix flags to countries where news events are taking place.

2. Pupils describe a place on the earth's surface—city, country, river—for others to guess and locate on a map. These places are then pointed out on the globe.

3. Pupils try to explain the location of an *X* marked on a blank globe; they try again when a grid is added.

4. Pupils match pictures of various distinctive environments with possible locations on the earth's surface.

5. Pupils compare an aerial photograph of the community with a community map; they locate specific places on both.

6. Pupils name places to be identified by giving the latitude and longitude; other pupils find the places and take their turns.

7. Pupils try to locate a given place on a papier-mâché globe that has no parallels or meridians; they add these lines with string or narrow gummed tape and number them.

Map Symbols

Primary Grades

1. Pupils make a large map on the classroom floor of some area near school which they have explored (an intersection, for example). They use gummed tape for streets and roads, blocks and boxes for buildings, and other concrete objects as needed for symbols.

2. Pupils study a simple picture map (of the zoo, perhaps) to discover the symbols used for various locations.

3. Pupils view from above an arrangement of doll furniture or toy cars on streets and draw what they see, using their own symbols rather than pictures.

4. On an outline map of the neighborhood, pupils add pictures to represent existing features. Later they replace the pictures with symbols.

5. Pupils use small globes to locate land and water divisions.

Intermediate Grades

1. Pupils match standard symbols with pictures of land features displayed on the bulletin board.

2. Pupils locate on a project globe (outlines of continents only) a particular island, country, ocean, etc., which another pupil names. The one who finds it first takes a turn.

3. Pupils devise maps of mystery spots, devising unique symbols and appropriate keys.

4. Pupils collect map legends, discussing likenesses and differences.

5. Pupils compare symbols used on road maps with symbols used on school maps, speculating on reasons for differences.

Scale of Miles

Primary Grades

1. Pupils travel to the top of a building several stories high. They note what happens to sizes of objects below as they ascend.

2. As pupils construct a map of the neighborhood on the classroom floor, they decide the distance for which one linoleum block stands.

3. Pupils locate places they know are one mile away. They draw maps of a walk to each place. They measure the distance on their various maps to make the appropriate scale of miles for each: (?) = 1 mile.

4. Pupils study road maps to find out how short a section of road represents one mile.

Intermediate Grades

1. Pupils compare the map scales from maps of the same size but showing areas of different sizes. They discover the relationship of the scale to the size of the area being shown.

2. Pupils look at several maps of the United States which are different in size. They study the map scales to note the differences.

3. Pupils use the scale on a blueprint of the classroom to compare the proposed size with the actual size. They may do the same with the blueprint of a house under construction.

4. Pupils use a large map of the United States (perhaps thirty feet across) painted on the playground surface to compute the scale used.

Teaching About Globes

Primary Grades

1. Pupils pretend to be flying or sailing around the globe with toy airplane or boats to discover that they return to the starting place without retracing their route.

2. Pupils draw routes around the world on a project globe to demonstrate that one can return to a starting place without changing direction.

3. Pupils cut in half a large, hollow rubber ball and try to flatten half of it to see how difficult it is to make a flat surface map from a globe.

4. Pupils use a flashlight and rotating globe to demonstrate day and night.

5. Pupils locate where they live on the globe.

Intermediate Grades

1. Pupils compare the scale of miles on globes of various sizes.

2. Pupils use a source of light and a revolving globe to show change of seasons.

3. Pupils use the globe to locate places which are the same latitude as their homes.

4. Pupils compare latitudinal and great circle distances between places in the northern or southern hemisphere.

Maps and Globes in Problem Solving

Some teachers teach skills in the use of maps and globes directly, as they would teach other subjects. But you may find that such skills are easier to teach in connection with problem solving. Pupils will sense the real purpose and will understand better how to use such skills outside the classroom. In the classroom we see children using maps, making maps, and studying about them as they try to interpret the real world through these representations.

Maps as Data Sources and Records

In their problem-solving experiences, children make frequent use of maps and globes as they attempt to gather data about the questions and problems they are investigating. They not only use maps to find information they need, but they also make maps on which they record facts and show relationships. The following examples have been selected from the problem-solving experiences of elementary school pupils.

Maps: Problem-Solving Experiences

The first grade pupils are trying to find out why families in their community live in different kinds of homes. At the moment they are gathering data on how their own houses are alike or different. After drawing rough floor plans of their houses, they are comparing them according to size, number of rooms, etc.

Next door in the second grade, pupils are working on the problem of how to reach school safely each day. One of their fact-finding questions asks about the best route for each of them to use in coming to school. They are studying a neighborhood map prepared by the teacher to determine the most direct route from their homes to school and to locate stop signs, signals, and crossing guards.

Pupils in a third grade are interested in why people live in communities. Presently they are trying to answer the question: How does our community provide electricity, telephone, and water for us? After identifying the kinds of community services citizens are unable to provide for themselves, pupils are using a community map to guide them on a tour of these facilities.

The importance of transportation in our world today is engaging fourth graders in considerable inquiry. They are researching how transportation helps countries exchange goods. Pupils are examining a large pictorial map of the world which shows important exports of each country. They plan to trace on a globe possible transportation routes for the exchange of products.

In the fifth grade, children have raised questions about how natural resources in the environment can be conserved. What is happening to our forest lands, they want to know. They are comparing maps showing the distribution of virgin forests in 1920 and the present with maps showing lands under cultivation in both periods.

Sixth grade pupils are studying tools around the world, and they are trying to find out how people use tools to meet their daily needs. On a product map of the world, pupils are constructing and superimposing a transparent picture map showing the important tools used in farm production in various areas.

Map and Globe Construction

As pupils use maps and globes as sources of data, they may find a need for constructing their own areal representations. When commercial maps do not serve pupils' purposes, they produce their own maps to illustrate relationships among data they have extracted from other sources. Such maps can be serviceable visual records from which inferences may be drawn.

Young children begin their map making with very tangible layouts—blocks on the classroom floor or objects set up in a sand table to show some aspects of an environment. Later outline maps of an area may be spread out on the floor, big enough for children to walk on, ensuring proper orientation to directions and a feeling for various locations to be added. They add semipictorial symbols to represent what was formerly shown concretely. After a time an accurate base map of a region can form the background for symbols that become more abstract.

When pupils need outline maps not readily available in the sizes or materials they require, smaller maps from various sources can be projected and traced in the desired scale. These maps can be developed into land-use and distribution maps helpful in illustrating various relationships that emerge as pupils study and record data. They can be made into a variety of special maps that help to make historical information more visual.

Such outline maps also form the base for relief maps of papier-mâché (wheat paste and strips of newspaper), sawdust and paste (five of sawdust to one of paste), or salt and flour (equal parts). Relief maps with elevations in color are converted to three-dimensional ones which more effectively clarify the earth's surface features.

Globe construction can contribute importantly to data gathering in problem solving. One group of fifth grade pupils constructed a globe six feet in diameter with a papier-mâché surface; on it they recorded a continuing stream of data gathered in their study of world problems and happenings. Small globes can be built around beach balls or large rubber balls, fishermen's glass floats, tree ornaments, balloons, and other spherical objects. When covered with papier-mâché of sufficient thickness to keep the globe from collapsing and finished with paint or plastic for a smooth surface, they are ready for data which pupils wish to record.

In map construction teachers and pupils have to decide whether or not the time required to learn the necessary techniques and to perform the actual construction is reasonable. The answer to the question resides in (*a*) whether or not the map construction produces data in the ideas and relationships that can be discerned through its use; (*b*) whether or not it provides an essential record; (*c*) whether or not an already available map or globe could meet the need; and (*d*) whether or not pupils see that the product of their efforts is more important than the process of construction.

Resource Unit: Why Do We Need Maps?

Not only do pupils use maps in their data search, but they may also make maps the object of their problem-solving adventures. Children are curious about maps; they pore over them without prodding; they collect them avidly. They can be encouraged to inquire about maps: their origins, uses, and construction by map makers. Following is an outline of such a search carried on by pupils in the intermediate grades. With some adjustment in content, it can be used with younger pupils.

Problem: Why do we need maps?

Objectives: Understandings

1. From very earliest times people have made and used maps to show locations and distances.
2. Maps have changed as people improved their map-making skills and as they found new uses for maps.
3. Maps can be useful only if one knows the meanings of the symbols used.
4. Maps are not all alike because each kind serves a particular purpose.
5. Cartographers are especially trained in the skills that are used in map making.

Objectives: Attitudes and Values

1. Interest in the history of maps and map making.
2. Desire to learn to use maps efficiently.
3. Awareness of the need for maps in everyday living.
4. Appreciation of the skills required in map making and map use.

Objectives: Behaviors

1. The child selects the appropriate map for a particular purpose.
2. The child sketches simple maps needed in daily activities.
3. The child reads and interprets correctly maps needed in everyday life.

Readiness Experiences

1. Children form small groups to play out situations similar to these: pioneers moving west by covered wagon without a map; travelers by car lost on a strange road without a map; scouts on a mountain trail for which there is no map; a pilot trying to land in an unfamiliar area. What will they do?
2. Children assume the role of travelers to an imaginary country; they must find out everything they can about this strange country from a map. What can they learn?

3. Each child makes a sketch map of some location near the school; other pupils try to read the map to discover the intended area. Why do they have difficulties?

Possible Problems Pupils May Raise for Study

1. Where did maps come from?
2. Why do we need maps?
3. Why are there so many different kinds of maps?
4. How are maps made today?
5. How can we learn to read maps correctly?
6. Why do maps change?
7. What if suddenly there were no more maps?
8. What new maps may be needed in the future?

Learning Experiences

1. Pupils collect and study the oldest maps they can find and compare the areas shown with modern maps.
   Purpose: To discover how maps have changed and to hypothesize why.
2. Pupils collect as many different kinds of maps as possible and identify their uses.
   Purpose: To compare maps made for different purposes.
3. Pupils interview a variety of persons to survey the ways in which maps are used in daily life.
   Purpose: To find out why people need maps.
4. Pupils visit a cartographer to observe the process of map making.
   Purpose: To identify the skills needed in map making.
5. Pupils map an area related to a current or forthcoming social studies or science problem.
   Purpose: To discover how environmental data is translated into map form.
6. Pupils read and enjoy a selection of trade books from school and public libraries.
   Purpose: To gather specific data to answer data-seeking questions.
7. Pupils read "The Story of Maps" written by the teacher.
   Purpose: To gather data about the history of maps and map making.
8. Pupils view two films, *Maps: An Introduction,* and *Globes: An Introduction* (Indiana University Audio-Visual Center).
   Purpose: To review basic skills in the use of maps and globes.

Related Skills

1. Pupils learn to interpret map symbols, scale, and legend.

2. Pupils learn new vocabulary: *location, direction, parallels, meridians, base map, atlas, relief map, scale, legend, grid, compass, cartographer, aerial photograph, sea level, altitude, projection.*

3. Pupils learn how to enlarge maps with a projector or pantograph.

4. Pupils use math skills in devising scales for their maps and in interpreting scales on other maps.

5. Pupils use letter-writing skills in their communication with resource persons.

6. Pupils use interview skills in gathering data about uses of maps.

Creative Experiences

1. Pupils make decorative maps of their neighborhoods.

2. Pupils draw imaginative maps of a make-believe country.

3. Pupils plan a treasure hunt and construct the maps to be used by participants.

Evaluation Techniques

1. Pupils match types of maps with statements of their purposes.

2. Pupils match common map symbols with their meanings.

3. Pupils arrange in order statements describing the steps in making a map.

4. Pupils interpret a community map to respond to questions about locations.

5. Pupils list the common uses of maps.

6. Pupils describe a situation in which the absence or loss of a map would be crucial.

7. Pupils respond to questions which require the interpretation of standard map symbols used on a map of a make-believe country.

8. Pupils map a country of the future—on the moon, for example.

For this study the teacher wrote "The Story of Maps," not just for children who could not read well, but for all pupils who were searching for hard-to-find data on the history of maps. In this case, very little information was available and that which was accessible was widely scattered in a variety of adult sources. Pulling essential data together from these sources, the teacher wrote the article for the children. Following is a portion of the story from which pupils were able to gather data related to the problem: Where did maps come from?

* * *

Teacher-Written Account: The Story of Maps

The story of maps began long before people learned to write. Early in the history of the world, people found that they needed maps to guide them as they moved about. They needed maps to show both location and direction.

The first maps were those which people made from their own experiences, the trail through the woods or the path to the nearest water hole. Hunters and warriors, who moved about a great deal, found that good maps were often a matter of life and death to them.

As people began to trade and to learn more about places farther from home, they were able to make maps of larger areas. The maps often were not very true ones, because map makers usually made their own cities or countries the center of the map and made them seem more important than any other part.

The oldest map we know about is now in a museum at Harvard University. It is made of baked clay and is so small it can be held in the palm of the hand. This small map shows part of a country where a river flows between mountains to a lake or sea.

Because clay maps were hard to make and harder still to carry about, people began to make their maps on skins or on papyrus, a paper made from the stalks of a reed-like plant. On the skins or papyrus landowners drew maps of their land, and kings drew maps of their kingdoms.

Some early maps tell us what people believed about our earth and its shape. Almost everyone at first agreed that the earth was flat. Some thought that it was flat and round like a dollar and that it floated in the ocean with the sky above.

Others thought that the earth was the shape of a rectangle. This earth, they said, was held up in space by compressed air.

Even before Christ was born, however, scientists had decided that the earth was round like a ball. Through their study of the rays of the sun they were able to measure the size of the earth. And they were very near its true size!

When map makers tried to make maps of this round world, they did not know what lands lay beyond the part of the world they knew about. They were sure that the lands they knew about would not fill up all the space as it had been measured. One map maker solved this problem by drawing on the globe some pieces of land he knew nothing about.

As the years went by, people continued to make maps of the places they had seen or had heard about. As they learned more about the world, it became more difficult to show on maps all these new things in their true relationships.

———————————————————————————————————

Such an in-depth study of maps enhances the acquisition of map skills and the use of maps in data gathering, emphasizing them as unique sources of data. There is merit in viewing these useful tools as the product of a long history of development and in speculating about new maps of the future.

The expanding horizons of children and adults in the present-day real world give new importance to the development of facility with maps and globes. Current news reports make continual reference to places unknown to former generations; startling views of Earth and Mars as seen by astronauts have enriched children's awareness of the shape and surface features of the globe; families are on the move, maps in hand as plans are made and destinations determined. Skill in handling maps that confront them in the everyday world and skill in using maps and globes as data sources in problem solving function significantly in the daily experiences of pupils.

Other Points of View

Carpenter, Helen McCracken, ed. *Skill Development in Social Studies.* Washington, D.C.: National Council for the Social Studies, 1963.
Chapter 9: Developing a Sense of Time and Space.

Ellis, Arthur K. *Teaching and Learning Elementary Social Studies.* Boston: Allyn and Bacon, 1977.
Chapter 12: Strategies for Making and Interpreting Maps.

Jarolimek, John. *Social Studies in Elementary Education,* 5th ed. New York: Macmillan, 1977.
Chapter 10: Teaching Children How to Use Maps, Globes, and Graphics.

Michaelis, John U. *Social Studies for Children in a Democracy,* 6th ed. Englewood Cliffs, New Jersey: Prentice-Hall, 1976.
Chapter 14: Using Maps, Globes, and Map-Making Activities.

Preston, Ralph C., and Herman, Wayne L., Jr. *Teaching Social Studies in the Elementary School,* 4th ed. New York: Holt, Rinehart & Winston, 1974.
Chapter 17: Teaching About Maps and Globes.

Wentworth, Daniel; Couchman, J. Kenneth; MacBean, John C.; and Stecher, Adam. *Mapping Small Places.* Minneapolis: Winston, 1972.
Activities for pupils.

Nine

Data Gathering and Problem Solving in the Open Classroom

The current interest in open classrooms and individualized study has raised many questions about social studies as a cooperative enterprise undertaken to solve problems raised by a group of children. How does a predetermined social studies curriculum function in the open classroom? How is the development of significant social studies generalizations achieved? Is it possible to encourage in-depth studies without violating the principles of individuality? Are there opportunities for pupils to pursue their own interests as fully as they wish? Is the teacher free to pursue the leads of pupils as they set individual goals and identify their own concerns?

Social Studies in the Open Classroom

It is noteworthy that there has been very little written which describes social studies in the open classroom.[1] Other areas of the curriculum—language arts, mathematics, the arts, and science to some degree—apparently have found a place in the developing ideas of openness. Social studies has received less attention. This is not to say that there is no interest in social studies among children in the open classroom; as yet this interest manifests itself in a rather casual way. Such a fluid situation is naturally of concern to teachers who believe that learning to identify and to attack social problems is essential to effective citizenship and to satisfying group living.

It is possible for the open classroom to be a dynamic setting for social studies without atomizing it into a collection of discrete tasks which may fail to zero-in on concepts, generalizations, and processes which characterize social studies as currently conceived.

Inquiring, hypothesizing, valuing, and data gathering imply both cooperative and individual effort and commitment. Cooperative efforts are centered on problem identification, on planning, and on certain types of group experiences in data gathering—role-playing, surveys, field trips, and the like—and in summarizing, generalizing, and evaluating. Individual effort manifests itself in varied avenues in data gathering, skill development, and creative expression, as pupils follow special interests and needs, just as they would likely do in the open classroom. Emphasis upon a wide range of data sources in the area of study, the flexibility of small and large

---

[1] One exception is Evelyn Berger and Bonnie A. Winters, *Social Studies in the Open Classroom* (New York: Teachers College Press, 1973).

group activity, the encouragement of individual investigation of interests in particular aspects of the problem being explored are not antithetical to the basic premises of openness.

The roles of the teacher as a stage-setter, as facilitator and guide, and as an evaluator in the problem-solving process are essentially the roles of the teacher in the open classroom. Observation of pupils to determine their growth toward concepts and generalizations, their development of skills, and their social actions are common elements in the open classroom and in the modern social studies program.

The open classroom and the social studies curriculum both depend much upon a challenging environment. The learning center in the open classroom surely facilitates inquiry and investigation. It intrigues pupils with its variety of materials in close proximity, objects to handle, new ideas to experiment with, bright colors everywhere, and a coziness that can be delightfully stimulating. Books, maps, pictures, realia, artifacts, and attractive "task cards" invite participation and stimulate children to become independent inquirers.

Openness has other advantages for social studies. The development of study and research skills is necessarily given high priority as essential to working on one's own. The presence of varied art media encourages creative expression of ideas encountered in problem solving. Valuing is continually exercised as children make choices of what activities to undertake and ideas to pursue; adventuring is stimulated as children are inspired to move out into uncharted and unspecified areas of exploration. Record keeping, the bane of many a teacher's existence, also plays a purposeful role in the open classroom because of the need to account for pupils' use of time and to chart their accomplishments. While attention to record keeping ought not to overshadow concern for children's learning, there is much to be gained by effort in this direction.

On the other hand, the open classroom as presently implemented and described in the literature appears to have some limitations for social studies as an organized component of the curriculum. While these limitations may not apply to all open classrooms, they seem to be rather common. Generally, learning centers in the open classroom are not especially designed to facilitate problem raising or to involve a class group in the exploration of a particular problem area; in other words, pupils seldom plan to mount a cooperative attack on problems as a result of their learning center activity.

Furthermore, usually plans are made by an individual with the teacher or a small group interested in the same idea or activity. Large group planning may be infrequent simply because there are no cooperatively defined problems that intrigue or concern the whole class group. While both the new social studies and the open classroom focus on learning processes, the social studies curriculum, which is sequentially developed and geared to definite outcomes, is concerned also with products—understandings and generalizations, attitudes and values, behaviors, and cognitive skills— deemed important for every child. The open classroom does not have usually such predetermined products for all in mind. While social studies promotes open-ended investigation through inquiry and hypothesizing, and in that respect shares with the open classroom lack of concern for closure, social studies does demand a certain degree of closure upon the products mentioned previously. The open classroom is much less concerned with where pupils are going than with how they are going; social studies considers both important.

As a result of such differences (or limitations as some social studies educators may view them), openness tends to focus upon self-evaluation or individual and small group evaluations rather than upon cooperative evaluation undertaken by the larger class group. To have little opportunity for the class group to examine its operation in social studies may seem to be a shortcoming not easily overlooked. Similarly other serious limitations reside in the lack of continual opportunity for group thinking and reflection upon data related to a significant social problem and in the lack of emphasis upon formulating generalizations which may be useful now and in the future. Whether or not these seeming limitations are valid depends upon the interpretation of those making the comparison. At least there is food for thought in the matter.

Problem Solving and the Open Concept

With the ascendency of both the highly planned program in social studies and the open concept in the classroom, it seems advantageous to explore ways in which the two ideas, already seen to have many points in common, may be interwoven to enhance both. The ideas which follow suggest a way in which the interlocking may be accomplished. It is not a compromise in which each idea loses something, but an opportunity which could strengthen both.

In such a union, the social studies learning center, as described later, serves as the locale for much of the action. It does, however, from time to time, change its focus as it stimulates pupils to become involved with particular problems or content. In other words, the teacher creates the learning center as an arranged environment which draws attention to a need, a problem, a dilemma of the past, present, or future. As pupils gather in the center, at the teacher's suggestion perhaps, they explore the challenges on display and talk about them. If other readiness activities are to be undertaken, these may unfold also in the learning center. Here pupils as a group

The social studies learning center combines group problem-solving enterprises and individualized activities. These children are using a learning center to collect data about the pioneer period in their own community.

begin to hypothesize about ways to gather data and about possible solutions. Proposals for individual investigations to complement the group effort are enthusiastically commended.

Following the cooperative problem identification and planning, the center takes on its new character; in other words, it is planned around the suggestions which came to light in the general planning. The center has teacher-constructed task cards that lead to appropriate data gathering. These cards present open-ended challenges which will encourage pupils to devise their own data-collecting schemes and exercises to develop specific skills. Sparking originality and creativity so that pupils will range far and wide over the content area will surely be a function of the learning center; branching out into previously unidentified aspects of the problem area will be welcomed and incorporated into the plan for the whole.

Obviously the learning center's simuli will change with the changes in problem area. Away with the antiques, the pioneer records, and the corn husk dolls, as well as the matching task cards, when the problem shifts to a study of the inventions that changed pioneer life into modern living. Basic resources will remain, so that as a pupil finds an interest in a tangential facet or problem, it can be pursued without undue delay.

Occasional group meetings will serve to focus attention on the original problem—How did all this begin? What were we trying to do? How are we getting on with it? Such meetings draw upon the pupils' original investigations as well. Who has discovered a new angle we didn't think of? Who has tried a different way of getting some useful data we didn't mention in our planning?

Some data gathering, of course, does not take place in the learning center. The field trip needed to understand various types of housing in the community, the visit of resource persons from the welfare agencies of the city, the film which provides background information for one of the facets of the problem—these are experiences which pupils share in planning, executing, summarizing, and evaluating.

As pupils and teacher move in and out of the learning center, they meet in small groups to discuss their experiences, to summarize what they have learned, and to talk about how it fits into the larger problem. But a larger fitting together is called for if the problem solving is to result in proposals for action inside and outside the school. Consequently, when the investigations appear to be coming to a close, the teacher propels children into the analysis of data and the testing of hypotheses.

The Social Studies Learning Center

The social studies learning center may well be the most interesting spot in the elementary classroom. It is composed of modules that may be arranged and rearranged to suit the problem being studied and to give it a new face from time to time. It requires storage units: book shelves with solid backs to serve as dividers, newspaper racks, low tables with chairs or cushions, picture files, bulletin boards, display space, task card file or peg board and hooks, burlap hangings for separation and display. Additions may be devised for special purposes: stacked large milk cartons make a good message center; egg cartons are laced together for attractive walls; cylindrical gallon containers hold materials needed for particular tasks; all sorts of boxes, jars, and bottles come into use. Pupils too are invited to be inventive in providing items the center needs. If the area is large enough for pupils to gather in as a large group, so much the better. And of course this space need not be used exclusively for social studies.

The learning center draws upon at least three types of learning resources: basics which are a permanent part of such a facility, large equipment which may be used there but stored elsewhere, and items which appear in the working area from time to time as the ongoing study requires them and which are then removed when no longer relevant.

The basic materials are those that need to be on call for research reading and study regardless of the problem in focus. They will naturally be chosen with the maturity of the children in mind. They may include print items such as single copies of many textbooks, children's encyclopedias, current fact books, children's magazines, cookbooks, daily newspapers from the local community and from a nearby larger city as well as classroom newspapers, and other specialized references. Sources of pictures are also indispensable: files of unmounted pictures in tear-sheet form, mounted pictures in standard categories, postcard collections, poster sets, magazines to be cut up for pictures. A learning center contains maps: a cradle globe; a project globe; a set of maps, wall hung or folded depending upon storage; outline maps of state, nation, and world; a community map showing appropriate detail; road maps of neighboring states and of the United States; an atlas; transparencies of maps; and a miscellaneous collection of other maps as they become available in current materials.

Some supplies and equipment may be used in the center but stored elsewhere, because they are not needed exclusively in problem solving. As construction activities develop, pupils need tools—hammer, saw, pliers, hand drill—and nails, brads, screws; scrap materials in great variety; discarded jars, boxes, spools, cartons, and the like; art materials—paper of many kinds, crayons, paints, brushes, and scissors. Audiovisual equipment will be in continual demand in the center and can be used there as needed even though stored elsewhere or borrowed. Filmstrip and slide viewers and projectors are easily used by individuals; the overhead projector is adaptable for a number of techniques; record players and tape recorders can be manipulated by most pupils. Supplies for making transparencies and strip films are also intriguing to experiment with. These items are used wherever group logistics allow, in the learning center or in another part of the classroom.

It is obvious that many things appear in the center only when particular problems are being examined. They are borrowed from libraries, audiovisual storehouses, parents and other community members. Pupils contribute items which they know will be helpful; other teachers in the school help, too.

Data Gathering

The social studies learning center becomes the focus of activity as pupils move into the data-gathering phases of problem solving centered on the problems they have raised. They choose their experiences according to their interests and their daily plans. Pupils work in the learning center at times they select, as individuals or in small groups. They find there many ideas for specific ways to collect information about the problem under study, suggestions which may have grown out of their cooperative planning, plus ideas the teacher and individual pupils may generate. In addition, the center will include some tasks designed to lead children to new explorations farther afield. Such adventuring is necessary in order to meet the free-choice principles which characterize openness. In general, however, pupils will be guided to plan their activities in order to meet both group objectives and their own desires and interests.

What kinds of tasks can be carried on independently in the learning center? How will these tasks contribute to the problem solving undertaken by the class group? Assume that the children in the primary group have become interested in some new toys and games which the teacher has brought into the center. The children speculate about whether children in other countries would like them. The experience leads them to make plans to find out why all children seem to like toys and games. The teacher converts their questions and their plans for finding out into a set of task cards, adding some others as well.

Task Card 1

Question: What games do children play around the world?

In your packet are cards that tell about ball games played by children in four countries. Study the cards and fill in the spaces in the chart.

Country	Name of Game	Kind of Ball	Directions

Think about these questions:
   How are these ball games alike?
   How are they different?
   What are some reasons why they are different?
   Which one is most like a game you play?

Task Card 2

Question: What kinds of games do children play around the world?

On each of these cards are the directions for playing a game used by children in another part of the world. Ask some friends to play one of the games with you.

Answer these questions:
   Did you enjoy the game?
   Does it remind you of one you have played?
If you enjoyed the game, perhaps you would like to try another one.

Task Card 3

Question: What are toys?

In each of these boxes are materials for making a toy. Using the things in one of the boxes, invent a toy which you think children would enjoy. Give your toy a name. Decide on directions for using it. Share it with others. Find out what they think of it.

Answer these questions:
   What makes a toy?
   Why are toys not all alike?

Task Card 4

Question: What are toys?

Here is a box which has in it many small toys which children enjoy. Divide the toys into two groups; put all the toys in one group that share something alike—color, shape, moving parts, or whatever you decide. Put into another group all the toys that are left. Then divide each of these groups into two more groups according to some way in which they are alike.

Answer these questions:

Tell why you put the toys into certain groups.

Do all toys have some of these likenesses?

Make a list of words which can be used to describe many toys you know about.

Would you like the toys as well if they had not been colored? If they were all the same shape? If they had no moving parts?

Task Card 5

Question: Why do toys change?

In this box are three very old toys from an antique shop. Most children no longer play with these toys. Look through the toy catalogs to find a toy of today which reminds you of each of the toys in the box.

Answer these questions:

Did the catalog have toys like the ones in the box?

Why do you think you didn't find them?

What toys did you find that were similar?

Why do you think the toys changed?

Task Card 6

Question: Why do toys change?

In this big envelope are pictures of toys and word cards to be matched with the pictures. Put into one group toys you think your grandparents played with and into another group put the toys you are quite sure they didn't play with.

Answer these questions:

How are the two sets of pictures different?

Why didn't your grandparents have all the toys?
How do toys change? Why?

<hr>

Intermediate pupils in a suburban school have become interested in local newspaper accounts about community problems of poverty and efforts being made to promote urban renewal. They have decided to investigate the problem: Why is it difficult to be poor? Because few pupils in the group have any notion of what it means to be in real need, the teacher has encouraged this exploration. Based on the subproblems the group has identified, task cards have been developed for the social studies learning center. Children will plan their own use of the center, and their activities will be interspersed with group progress meetings and data-gathering experiences in which all will participate. Here are some of the task cards.

<hr>

Task Card 7

Question: How does it feel to be poor?

Attached is a grocery list from a local supermarket and a diagram showing basic foods for a good diet. Plan a set of three meals for one day for a family of four, using the amount of money given by welfare agencies.

Think about these questions:
    Did your meals contain a balanced diet?
    How do the meals compare with those you have at home?
    What items did you want but couldn't afford?
    Ask your mother's opinion about the menus.

<hr>

For the following task card the teacher prepared two boxes, one containing paper, paints, brushes, crayons, scissors, and another containing a piece of plain white paper and a short pencil.

<hr>

Task Card 8

Question: How does it feel to be poor?

Ask a friend to work with you. Choose a box without opening it. Now open your box. Make the prettiest picture you can with the materials you find in your box. You cannot borrow from your friend. When you finish, talk about your feelings.

Use these questions:
Which one of you had the easiest time?
How did you feel just after you opened your box?
How do you think people feel who never can have what they see other people having?

Task Card 9

Question: How does it feel to be poor?

Use the catalog to select clothes for a person your age: shoes, stockings or socks, underwear, sweater, and jeans. Buy one set but spend as little as possible; buy another and spend as much as you wish. List the items, cost, and page number from the catalog.

Think about these questions:
How do the two sets of clothing differ?
Why did one set cost more than the other?
If you had all the money you needed, which set would you buy?
How do people feel when they must always buy the cheapest?

Task Card 10

Question: How does it feel to be poor?

You are a child who has been able to earn 80¢ for school materials you need at the beginning of the school year. In the envelope is play money to represent this amount; also a current price list of the cheapest school items available at the shopping center. Decide how you will spend your money. In the second envelope are $5.00 and a list of school supplies the teacher has requested. Plan how you will spend the $5.00, using the price list given to you.

Answer these questions:
How did you decide to spend the 80¢?
What helped you to make the choices?
Did you have enough money to buy what you needed?
How will you get the other things you will need?

How did your supplies compare with those you bought with the $5.00?

How did you feel when you were poor?

Research Skills

As pupils have need for specific research skills, the learning center can provide necessary practice for individuals and small groups. If all children need the instruction, it may be efficient for the teacher to give initial help to everyone at the same time, provided there are opportunities in the learning center for reinforcement. Sometimes the teacher simply reminds pupils of the practice resources available; on other occasions pupils are guided to the appropriate task cards when it is evident they can use them independently.

The learning center may contain a permanent file of task cards designed to strengthen basic skills; theses are the types of activities readily available in commercial form and need not be prepared by the teacher. Exercises in alphabetizing are good preparation for use of dictionaries and encyclopedias; crossword puzzles encourage use of reference materials; map location games give needed practice in certain map skills. The file may contain worksheets torn from old workbooks: exercises in finding main ideas in paragraphs, in summarizing content, in using location skills, in selecting meanings for words, in outlining, and the like. Worksheets and answer sheets mounted together facilitate selection and checking. Obviously many independent activities in conjunction with the developmental reading program or the exercises and task cards in the reading learning center contribute greatly to efficient research reading in social studies.

The learning center may include also teacher-constructed task cards which relate specifically to problems being studied. Here are several related to the study of toys or to the study of how it feels to be poor, which emphasize *skills* rather than *content.*

Task Card 11

Research Skills: Dictionary
On this card are some of the words we will be using in our study of toys. Find each in the picture dictionary. Draw your own picture of the word.

model   scooter
sailboat   tricycle
teddy bear   puzzle
electric train   dollhouse

Task Card 12

Research Skills: Library
On the card is a list of books in our library. Some of them may help us in our study of games. Find the book; look at it. Write YES or NO on the sheet after you decide whether or not the book will help us.

Task Card 13

Research Skills: Dictionary
Find each of the words on this card in your dictionary. Then find the meaning that you think fits our study of poverty. Write the meaning on the paper after the word.

urban renewal   tenement
unemployment   ghetto
welfare   slums

Task Card 14

Research Skills: Encyclopedia
On this card is a list of words related to our study of why it is difficult to be poor. Write the volume number of the encyclopedia which may contain each of the topics.

delinquency   inner city
vandalism   poverty
social work   prejudice

Task Card 15

Research Skills: Outlining
In this envelope are parts of an outline. Put them together correctly to show

1. what urban renewal does
2. how parts of the city are chosen for renewal
3. what kinds of problems are faced by people who live in the area to be redeveloped
4. what locations are on the list for renewal in our community

Assemble the outline, so that the information is well organized.

Task Card 16

Research Skills: Mapping
The areas to be redeveloped in our community are located

1. between Fleet Street and Ship Street; between Tenth and Twelfth Streets.
2. an area three blocks each way from the old Rice stadium.
3. both sides of Henderson Avenue from River Bridge north to Johnson Road.

Mark these areas on the attached community map, using a color code of your choosing. Put the color key and explanation on your map.

Creative Activities

Children will use the social studies learning center not only for data gathering and skill reinforcement but for creative expression as well. Creativity cards can encourage many avenues of adventure with art materials, poetry, music, and story telling, but pupils will no doubt invent their own ways of expressing what they are thinking and feeling about the problems or content they are studying. Ideas like the following can be used to spur the creative activities that may spin off from problem solving. The possibilities are many.

●━◦━●━◦━●━◦━●━◦━●━◦━●━◦━●━◦━●━◦━●━◦━●━◦━●━◦━●━◦━●━◦━●━◦━●━◦━●━◦━●

Task Card 17

Dramatics

> WHAT
> DO YOU THINK WOULD HAPPEN IF
> the toys in a toy store suddenly came alive and
> began to TALK?
> What would they say?
> What would they do?
> Who might hear them? discover them?
> CAN YOU

Write a story or play about what would happen? There are some books here that tell how to make paper bag puppets or stick puppets. Ask some friends to help you. Let us know when the show begins.

●━◦━●━◦━●━◦━●━◦━●━◦━●━◦━●━◦━●━◦━●━◦━●━◦━●━◦━●━◦━●━◦━●━◦━●━◦━●

Task Card 18

Arts and Crafts

> CAN YOU
> help the dolls in our
> center? They need some new
> clothes badly. Some of them come
> from other countries. The books show how
> they might be dressed. There are patterns, pins,
> cloth, needles, scissors, and other useful things in
> the sewing box. Any ideas about how to help these dolls?
> HELP! HELP!

●━◦━●━◦━●━◦━●━◦━●━◦━●━◦━●━◦━●━◦━●━◦━●━◦━●━◦━●━◦━●━◦━●━◦━●━◦━●

Task Card 19
Rhythms

WHAT DID YOU HEAR?
As we rode around the renewal
areas in our city, did you hear the roar of
traffic, honking of horns, boats under the old
bridge, voices of children playing in the streets?
Use the rhythm instruments to make the sounds you
heard. Put them together in an interesting pattern.
Use the tape recorder in the learning center to
record your composition. Name it and tell us
when we can hear it.

TOOT! TOOT
HONK! HONK! HONK!

Task Card 20

Poetry

Here are some poems written by people who lived in the slums of a very
big city. What do the poems tell you about their feelings and their problems?

Could you put your feelings into a poem?
Perhaps you would like to create a design or an illustration for
your poem.

Interest Centers in Preplanned Programs

Much that has been suggested about social studies learning centers in
problem solving is applicable to interest centers used as complements to
teacher-directed learning or guided inquiry strategies. In both these latter
approaches to social studies instruction, teachers may be seeking ways to
meet individual differences and to encourage special interests and explorations related to content presented by text or inquiry materials. Such
interest centers promote independent learning, the development of study
skills, and facility in following directions and using materials. They may
be required of individuals or small groups or they may be freely chosen as
pupils desire.

If these centers are neither a part of a problem solving strategy as described earlier in this chapter nor assigned as part of the ongoing social studies program guided by the teacher, they must in themselves attract pupil exploration and activity. Successful ones exhibit these characteristics:

1. They are organized and set up to catch pupils' attention and invite their participation. Bright signs, gay materials, and enthusiastic introduction by the teacher are helpful.
2. They indicate clearly the activities possible and how to begin. Task cards start the ball rolling and encourage pupils to create and invent other things to do.
3. They include experiences that will appeal to children whose interests and ability levels differ. Children are free to select and discard activities as they choose.
4. They change and present new materials and activities when interested pupils have participated in the current setup.

Interest Center 1

Objective: As a result of participating in the interest center, pupils will be able to state reasons why we have rules.

Materials: commercial game for four persons, local newspapers, set of puppets, materials for poster making, a quantity of small record booklets with each page numbered to correspond to the following activities.

Activities:

1. Ask three persons to play the game with you. The rules for the game are missing but play it any way you want to. In your record book write what happened.
2. Make a list of five rules which you think everyone in your class should follow. Ask five other pupils to mark the rules on your list which they agree are good ones. What did you find out? Record the results.
3. Interview your school principal about rules in your school. Find out which ones are most often broken.
4. Make a poster about a school rule which you think everyone should observe.

5. Use the puppets to play scenes that show what happens when people break a rule that was made for the safety of everyone. Ask for time to give the play for your class.

6. Think about the traffic rules you obey on your way home from school. Make a list of them. When you return home today, check the rules you see other children breaking. Report your findings in the record book.

7. Find five items in the local paper which tell about rules that are being made for your community. Choose one of the rules. In your record book tell why it would be a good rule or not.

8. Are all rules good rules? Invent the best rule you can think of to make school a happier place in which to work. Be sure to tell why you would like to have this rule. Put your ideas in your record book.

9. When you have completed all the activities you intended to do, please let the teacher know. Be ready to talk over why we have rules.

Interest Center 2

Objective: Following participation in the activities of the center, the pupils will be able to respond to factual questions about the states and their capitals, farm products, and physical characteristics of the country.

Materials: map puzzle of the United States, outline maps of desk-top size, modeling clay, physical maps of the United States, information sheet of states and farm products, outline map transparency, old magazines, drawing materials, large sheets of paper, packs of small white cards.

Activities:

1. Put together the jigsaw puzzle of the United States. Study the locations of the capitals. Make a list of those that are located on oceans, bays, or gulfs; on rivers; on lakes. Which ones are not on any body of water?

2. Use the clay to model a relief map on one of the outline maps you will find in the center. Use the physical map on the wall as your reference. Show hills, mountains, lowlands, lakes, and rivers.

3. Make a list of the states you have visited. Read about your favorite in the reference books on the shelves of the center. List the ways in which this state and the state in which you live are alike and different. Think about the climate, kind of land, products manufactured, things grown, the size, and the population.

4. Use the projector and a transparency to trace a map on one of the large sheets of paper. Using the information from the fact sheet of farm products for each state, make a product map for the United States. Use real materials, magazine pictures, or your own drawings to be attached to the map.

5. You all know how to play the game of *Old Maid.* Use the idea of this game and one of the packs of small white cards to make a new game. You might make one in which players match states and capitals, states and products, cities and locations, or any other ideas you have. Decide on what the Old Maid card is to be, too. Try out your game with other pupils.

6. Let the teacher know when you have done everything you intended to do in this center. Be ready to share what you learned about states, capitals, farm products, and physical characteristics of the United States, depending on the activities you chose.

Record Keeping in the Open Classroom

In the open classroom it is especially important for the teacher to develop records which (*a*) will enable children to report and evaluate their experiences, and (*b*) will be of assistance in keeping abreast of pupil activities and accomplishments. Because the children spend less time in a daily social studies hour in which all are engaged in pursuing the solutions to problems, considerably more record keeping seems necessary. In order for the teacher to account for the pupils' use of time and to make good use of opportunities to confer with pupils, children and teacher both keep records of the data-gathering activities undertaken by individuals and groups. The more freedom pupils have to choose and devise learning activities on their own, the more helpful their records become when guidance is needed. These records are also useful when teachers discuss pupil accomplishments with parents.

Indeed, the kinds of records being developed for use in the open classroom would be equally useful in the more group-oriented social studies program, too, where individuals and small groups are frequently examining aspects of problems which they have decided are not of sufficient importance to demand the attention of everyone.

Teachers' observations of pupils, so necessary to discovering their needs and guiding their experiences, undergird the whole of the open concept in social studies. As teachers move among the children at work, they note what their charges are doing in the learning center, what materials they are using, what skills they seem to have under control, what questions they ask about the problem they are attacking, and what research difficulties they may be having. These data recorded on file cards or in a notebook are indispensable for future planning.

The teacher may design a checklist for a particular group of skills, developing it as a class record kept close by for easy reference. If one of the pupils needs special attention, a running account of that child's daily activities in the center for a period of time may provide information for later reflection and diagnosis; or for these children a time-spot check (What was each doing at designated intervals during the period?) may be an effective data-producing idea.

The teacher's record will probably include also a scheme for noting what task card or individually devised project the pupil is currently engaged with. Although pupils have their own records of plans and accomplishments, as will be seen shortly, a briefer layout on class report sheets assists the teacher in seeing at a glance what is going on in the data gathering, skill development, or creative phases of the study.

Pupil-kept records are equally essential in maintaining the smooth flow of activity and learning, though care must be taken that they do not require an undue amount of pupils' time. There are many ways in which practical records may be kept; pupils themselves will have good ideas about devising them. These records should call for pertinent data in an easy-to-use form. Individual and small group conferences produce details that are not included in the report forms.

In the open classroom, children are stimulated to make choices about how they wish to use their time. They are usually free to use any of the learning centers which appeal to them, with the understanding, of course, that not everyone can use a particular center at the same time. On the other hand, some provision is usually made to make sure that pupils will give attention to all or most of the curriculum areas represented in the learning centers over a period of time. In the problem-solving approach it is necessary that all pupils contribute to the data gathering if generalizing is to follow. Consequently, the teacher may set some guidelines for planning the weekly schedules, asking that pupils give a specified portion of their time to the social studies learning center and calling to mind special group opportunities, such as film viewings, field trips, and similar experiences. The plan sheet like the one in Figure 9–1 may be used by children as they plan their daily activities over a wide range of language arts, science, mathematics, art, music, and social studies. When pupils receive their copies at the beginning of the week or at the end of the preceding one, they note the special events scheduled by the teacher according to plans children have made in their previous group meetings. Then each child completes a plan, either day by day, or a tentative one for several days. This schedule is shared with the teacher, and suggestions for revision are discussed and acted upon.

Individual Weekly Plan Name _____ Week of _____				
	Monday	Tuesday	Wednesday	Thursday	Friday
9:00					
10:00				Toy shop owner	
11:00					
1:00					Group meeting

Directions: You may plan for each day as it comes (or for the whole week). Use at least four periods in the week for social studies. You may use one period a day or put several periods together. Remember the visitor on Thursday and the group meeting on Friday to share data on our problem, Why do all children seem to like toys and games?

Figure 9–1. Individual weekly plan.

Children also keep personal records of their experiences in the learning center. One type of record is suitable for recording plans and accomplishments chosen from the task cards which the teacher has made available in the center and previewed for pupils in a group meeting. Others are better suited to plans which the child devises because of a special interest in a particular phase of the problem which may or may not have been identified in the problem-raising preliminaries. The records in Figures 9–2, 9–3, and 9–4 represent the kinds which pupils have in hand as they confer with the teacher about what they have done and what should be next steps. In the course of these talks, skill needs may surface and creative activities can be shared.

Task Card Record	Name		
Task Card Number	Date Begun	Date Completed	Teacher-Pupil Evaluation

Figure 9–2. Individual task card record.

The Teacher in the Open Setting

The teacher who views openness as a contribution to effective problem solving in social studies instruction assumes responsibility for much behind-the-scenes planning and much overt activity in guiding, conferring, and evaluating in order to facilitate children's choosing, planning, and executing. Beyond the record keeping required, what are the teacher's tasks and concerns?

Data Gathering Report   Name _____
Date Begun _____   Date Completed _____

The question I have chosen to investigate:

My plan for gathering data:

What I learned from the data I gathered:

Figure 9–3. Individual data-gathering report.

Diary and Self-Evaluation   Name _____
                                   Week of _____

This is a record of what I did in social studies this week.

Monday

Tuesday

Wednesday

Thursday

Friday

I think my work this week was:
all right   *better than I expected*   *not so good as I expected*
because:

I did my best work on

The part I liked especially well was

I plan to improve my work next week by

Figure 9–4. Pupil diary and self-evaluation.

It goes without saying, of course, that, as in any successful social studies program, the teacher in the open classroom makes basic decisions about the thrust of instruction for the group and foresees the possible outcomes of pupil planning and learning. Except for the emphasis upon openness, the predetermined learnings may be very similar to those in other programs. In any case, unless the teacher is clear about goals, it is unlikely that the social studies experiences of pupils will have the social focus that social studies implies.

Stage setting by the teacher is as crucial in the open classroom as it is in group-oriented classrooms, because upon it rests the generation of problems and the impetus for problem solving. The enthusiasm it creates and the feelings of purpose it develops make social studies come alive in the learning center. The teacher serves as the construction agent in the building of the learning center, gathering together its various components and energizing it with exciting things to do and to think about. While the teacher may be quite original in devising many of the experiences which the learning center promotes, much of the creation of these stimuli takes place *after* pupils have indicated their interests in certain phases of the problem. In a problem-solving strategy, the cooperative planning period which follows the raising of problems also provides suggestions for the preparation of task cards from which pupils make selections. The creative teacher plays an indispensable role in fashioning the learning center.

While children are at work in the learning center, the teacher observes, diagnoses, studies pupil records, guides, suggests, and encourages. Because not all pupils will be in the center at any one time for independent study, the teacher needs to be especially alert to the many things going on and will be shifting gears continually from social studies to other things that may be going on in the room simultaneously. Then at other times the teacher's role is one of refraining from interfering or suggesting or guiding, lest the thrust of the children's activity be turned from their own original purposes in becoming involved in the learning center.

Though most of the data-gathering task cards are structured in order to move children toward the making of inferences and ultimately to generalizing, the teacher furthers this process in consultation with small groups about the significance of what they did, helping them see how their research contributes to class objectives. Commendation is given for individually conceived explorations in diverse directions, and their special values for the group study are noted.

The role of the teacher also includes being alert to the need for the class group to assemble to share their findings, to report new and unusual investigations, and to discuss what it all means in terms of their original problem. Brought into play are the teacher's skill in questioning as children are assisted in the weaving together of their experiences and in generalizing on the basis of their collective data. The openness and diversity of learning in the open classroom make these sessions among the most exciting of all social studies experiences.

Openness in the classroom provides a setting for freedom, decision making, and personal development. Social studies contributes opportunities for children to explore the people of the real world and their problems and to consider how human beings may live more fully. Moreover, openness seems a logical step in developing creative citizens who are not afraid to attack whatever obstacles exist in the achievement of self-fulfillment in a very social world. Freedom and planning go hand in hand in such an undertaking. A flexible but planned social studies curriculum which focuses upon significant ideas, attitudes and values, behaviors and skills, and processes of inquiry and problem solving is compatible with the concept of openness. In the open classroom, with its philosophy of individual responsibility for learning, it is possible to achieve both social studies goals and personal ones. The interplay between them offers an exciting challenge to both pupils and teachers.

Other Points of View

Berger, Evelyn, and Winters, Bonnie A. *Social Studies in the Open Classroom: A Practical Guide.* New York: Teachers College Press, Columbia University, 1973. General guidelines and specific suggestions.

Davidson, Tom; Fountain, Phyllis; Grogran, Rachel; Short, Verl; and Seely, Judy. *The Learning Center Book: An Integrated Approach.* Pacific Palisades, California: Goodyear, 1976.
Chapter 5: In Social Studies.

Larkin, James M., and White, Jane J. "The Learning Center in the Social Studies Classroom." *Social Education* 38 (November–December 1974):689–710.

Oliner, Pearl M. *Teaching Elementary Social Studies: A Rational and Humanistic Approach.* New York: Harcourt, Brace, Jovanovich, 1976.
Chapter 3: Individualing Instruction.

Perrone, Vito, and Thompson, Lowell. "Social Studies in the Open Classroom." *Social Education* 36 (April 1972):460–64.

Piechowiak, Ann B., and Cook, Myra B. *Complete Guide to the Elementary Learning Center.* West Nyack, New York: Parker, 1976.
Chapter 9: Social Studies.

Preston, Ralph C., and Herman, Wayne L., Jr. *Teaching Social Studies in the Elementary School,* 4th ed. New York: Holt, Rinehart & Winston, 1974.
Chapter 9: 195–201 (Learning Centers).

Seif, Elliott. *Teaching Significant Social Studies in the Elementary School.* Chicago: Rand McNally, 1977.
Chapter 11: Organizing the Learning Environment.

Turner, Thomas N. "Individualization Through Inquiry." *Social Education* 34 (January 1970):72–73.

Welton, David A., and Mallan, John T. *Children and Their World: Teaching Elementary Social Studies.* Chicago: Rand McNally, 1976.
Chapter 12: Individualizing Instruction: From Independent Inquiry to the Open Classroom.

Valuing and Value Clarification in Social Studies

Whenever children and adults are involved in making choices and decisions, they necessarily engage in valuing; the decisions they finally reach
are indications of what is important to them, what they value. Whether or
not the valuing process and emphasis upon certain social values are the
legitimate function of social studies education is a dilemma for many
schools. While educators seem quite certain that values education is in
part their responsibility, the range of their commitment is great and the
diversity of their specific opinions is considerable. The following statements pinpoint some of the positions being taken.

1. Schools were established for the purpose of transmitting the values of
   the society and are responsible for achieving that purpose.
2. Since there are basic values which cannot be ignored if Americans are
   to survive as a free, self-respecting people, schools are obligated to
   teach these values.
3. It is hypocritical and impractical for schools to teach values which are
   continually negated by many members of the society.
4. Because values change with the times and from generation to generation, values we teach now may not be appropriate for the future.
5. Observable behavior is a good indicator of the values held by persons
   or groups; what the school does represents its values.

Perhaps the heart of the dilemma lies in the conflicting values which
the society represents, claiming to adhere to a given value but exhibiting
behavior wholly inconsistent with it. Most adults teach their young the
importance of being honest; yet they are frequently engaged in dishon-
esties, both large and small. Adults proclaim a strong belief in family and
family life but continually let business interests and pleasure lead to
neglect of their families. While professing love of country and belief in
patriotic duty, it is easy for adults to find ways to avoid such civic responsibilities as jury duty and voting. Many who would not let a child starve to
death in their neighborhood appear blind to the plight of deprived people
elsewhere. The value conflicts are many and to them may be traced many
of our social ills.

Public controversy over such issues as environmental protection,
integration of schools, civil rights, law and order, foreign aid, and urban

258

renewal is representative of some of the value conflicts that erupt in emotional outburst and alter the nation's self-image.

In face of such problems, some educators question the teaching of values in social studies, sometimes confusing values education with the *imposition* of values upon children, especially the values of the teacher. Much has been said about how various segments of the population may differ in values; how difficult it may be for teachers with middle-class values to understand the behavior of pupils whose family backgrounds are built on different values.

One focus of values education which can be justified is the development of a personal value system by which children can guide their own decisions and choices. It is this development of personal value systems which is the ultimate goal of the valuing process. Each person has such a value system. It may be achieved through continual effort to identify values, consider alternatives, and make decisions upon probable results of these alternatives; or an individual's value system may develop as a result of family background, experience, or other external influences over which the child has little control. If teachers choose not to leave value choices to chance, they seize every opportunity to encourage application of the valuing process to life-like situations and ideas.

On the other hand, many social studies teachers would go further to say that there are some basic social values characteristic of the American ideal which ought to be an integral part of social studies instruction; that without these ideals, citizens of the United States cannot be distinguished from those of most other nations. These teachers can marshal convincing evidence that these social values are part of the survival kit for the nation. Among these values are personal identity and worth, democratic principles, freedom from bias and prejudice, environmental protection, and world friendship.[1] How to help pupils incorporate these values into their personal value systems is a challenging responsibility in social studies instruction.

Values as Guiding Concepts

Values are concepts which a person accepts as guides for personal conduct and for the conduct of society. They are much stronger than attitudes, which are predispositions to action but which may be altered by circumstances, opportunistic considerations, or acquired by imitation or through

---

[1] Maxine Dunfee and Claudia Crump, *Teaching for Social Values in Social Studies* (Washington, D.C.: Association for Childhood Education International, 1974).

the influence of stronger individuals. Values are more than opinions, often stated on the spur of the moment and without very much thought, and more than opinions arrived at through analysis of pertinent information; such opinions may be indicators of values but not values themselves. Similarly, desires and goals may be value indicators, but they are simply things sought at a particular time in one's life and may be achieved or not as circumstances unfold; and in fact they may be discarded without undue effort toward their realization.

On the other hand, values represent what a person thinks is good, should be supported, should be carried out; they persist over a period of time, becoming clearly associated with the individual as representative of a consistent belief or course of action.

Lasswell identifies a number of universal values for which he believes all people and groups continually strive.

1. affection, or feeling love and friendship for and from others
2. respect, or being looked up to and looking up to others
3. skill, or feeling able and being able to do things well
4. enlightenment, or understanding meaning and using knowledge to do what one wishes
5. influence, or the feeling of power over others
6. wealth, or meeting basic needs
7. well-being, or experiencing a healthy self-image, contentment, and happiness through good mental and physical health
8. responsibility or rectitude, a feeling of being trusted and knowing what is right and wrong in oneself and others[2]

Raths, Harmin, and Simon describe a value as something which emerges as a result of choosing, prizing, and acting upon.[3] Their ideas have been adapted to this flowchart form on page 261.

The Valuing Process

The valuing process begins with children's discovery of their personal values. Children move through daily life, exhibiting values through their

[2] Harold D. Lasswell, *Power and Personality* (New York: The Viking Press, 1969), p. 17, as listed and explained in Maxine Dunfee and Claudia Crump, *Teaching for Social Values in Social Studies* (Washington, D.C.: Association for Childhood Education International, 1974), p. 11.

[3] Louis E. Raths, Merrill Harmin, and Sidney B. Simon, *Values and Teaching: Working with Values in the Classroom* (Columbus, Ohio: Charles E. Merrill, 1966), pp. 28–30.

behavior, but they seldom are asked or taught to consider what those values may be. By skillful questioning in an atmosphere of freedom and lack of pressure, teachers may help pupils look at what they are doing and the choices they are making in value terms. The child comes from the playground to report a fight over possession of a piece of equipment. The teacher may take a scolding attitude, an indifferent position, or may begin to question: "Can you tell me exactly what happened? Why do you think it happened? What did you do? Why did you do what you did? Why do you think your friend responded that way? What was important to you? What was important to your friend? What could have been done to settle the dispute? What would have been the consequences of each of these suggestions?"

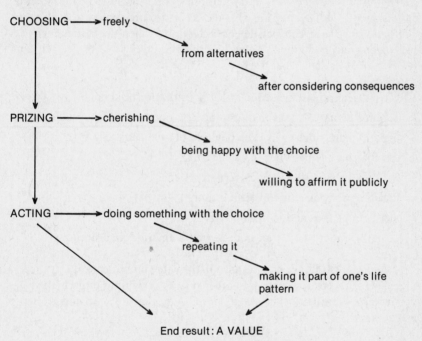

CHOOSING ⟶ freely

from alternatives

after considering consequences

PRIZING ⟶ cherishing

being happy with the choice

willing to affirm it publicly

ACTING ⟶ doing something with the choice

repeating it

making it part of one's life pattern

End result: A VALUE

Another child reports an exciting weekend visit to an historical restoration, recounting all the unusual sights and activities and the long automobile trip home. The teacher may comment, "How nice for you!" or "What was important to you about your trip to the village? Why do so many people like to go there? Would you like to visit there again? Did everyone in your family enjoy the trip as much as you did? Why do you think old villages like that are brought to life again?"

Many similar kinds of questions help children look at themselves in various situations, personal or group, and are good preparation for developing the valuing habit with social studies content and problems. If used frequently, value-directed questions begin to channel the child's thinking in directions which do not stop simply with facts and information. Not wishing, however, to rely only on chance opportunity to encourage valuing, the teacher may set the stage deliberately for the consideration of values as pupils pursue their solutions to problems. Fraenkel suggests a very practical approach to helping pupils value. He separates instruction into three phases: value identification, value conflict exploration, and the development of empathy.[4] The discussion and episodes which follow are based on his ideas.

Value Identification

Clarifying one's own values and identifying the values held by others are closely related skills; they are also necessary to any exploration of value conflicts, since such conflicts become clear only when the values involved have been sharply defined. Value identification directed both to self and to others follows somewhat the following flow of thought.

1. getting accurate information about the situation or action
2. defining what each person did in the situation
3. hypothesizing about why each behaved in a certain way
4. interpreting the behavior in value terms
5. relating the situation to one's own experiences
6. recalling what one did in the situation
7. interpreting that action in value terms
8. thinking about whether or not one would again act in a similar way

   Various techniques may be used in the value identification task, techniques which have application to other phases of valuing but which seem particularly useful at this stage. Several of these are included here; teachers will design others equally useful.

   The *survey* is employed to determine what people think about an issue or situation. Pupils may interview individuals with the question already formulated; they may construct a simple questionnaire to gather the data they need. They explain the purpose of their survey and exercise care in recording carefully and objectively. When data are collected and organized, pupils ask, "What are these people saying in response to our inquiries? How does what they say show what they value? Why do they not

---

[4] Jack R. Fraenkel, *Helping Students Think and Value: Strategies for Teaching the Social Studies,* © 1973, pp. 228–77. By permission of Prentice-Hall, Inc., Englewood Cliffs, New Jersey.

all agree? What does this information tell us about people and what they believe?" Some representative issues and inquiries follow:

1. Should our community build a new swimming pool with tax money?
2. Should bottled soft drinks, candy bars, and chewing gum be on sale in school buildings?
3. Should outside burning of leaves and trash be made illegal?
4. Should buildings of historical significance in the community be restored?
5. Should admission to all state parks be free?
6. Should our country trade with countries that are unfriendly?
7. Should we continue to explore outer space?

A *discussion* of an episode or incident drawn from social studies content and related to pupils' current investigation directs attention to the value components of such happenings. They begin to see the participants as real persons who did what they did for reasons and that these reasons reflect values.

Identifying Values 1

A pioneer family of the 1820s one day received a letter from a relative describing the need for a miller in a small village on the frontier. The new miller would find ready a log cabin, land for farming, and a mill needing only small repairs. After a family council, father, mother, and three children decided to leave their comfortable clapboard farmhouse, pack their choice belongings in a small two-wheeled covered wagon, and start out on a long trek over miserable roads to their new home. After a long and weary journey, they arrived at their destination. What would the future hold for them, far away from the surroundings they knew so well and the friends they were missing?

   Why do you think the family did what they did?
   What do these reasons tell you about what they thought was important?
   Do you think all family members agreed?
   Why might they have seen things differently?
   Would you have done what they did?
   How does your reply show what you value?
   What does this episode tell you about people and what they value?

Role playing an incident gives pupils an opportunity to get inside the personalities in the situation to better identify with them and to identify the values that influence their actions.

Identifying Values 2

Carlos and Roberto have come to Miami with their family from Cuba. Their father is hoping to find a job in one of the large hotels, but at present he is out of work; their mother has found work as a cook in the cafeteria where the boys go to school. Mrs. Ortez is an excellent cook but as yet has had no opportunity to learn English. Her supervisor knows both Spanish and English, so everything goes well in the school kitchen. Occasionally Mrs. Ortez helps out in the serving line, even though she has great difficulty in understanding the children who speak no Spanish. Carlos and Roberto have made friends rather easily, but today there has been a fight; the two boys jumped on Dick, who had begun taunting them with "Your mom is stupid, can't even speak a word that anyone can understand. She's real funny when she gives you a sandwich and you asked for beans. Boy, where'd you get her for a mom?" Soon many children were mixed up in the trouble, and all kinds of unpleasant things were happening. (Pupils assume the roles of persons in the incident. Discussion precedes role playing as pupils try to determine the motivations of the people involved.)

What made the persons do what they did?

How did their actions show what they valued?

What would you have done if you had been one of them?

How would your actions have shown what you value?

How could the fight have been avoided? Can you play it that way?

What could have been done after the fight?

How do these solutions show what you think is important?

Identifying Values 3

Henry and Mary Sunbear live with their son, Billy, on a reservation which provides areas for fishing and farming. The tribe earns a living from these areas. Recently, however, tourists have discovered the fishing grounds and have parked trailers and camping equipment on more and more of the farm land after paying a fee to some of the residents. Already attempting to manage on a limited income, the Sunbear family finds it harder each week to pay their bills at the trading post. Henry Sunbear has decided to leave the reservation and move his family to a distant large city where he hopes to find sufficient work. All of Billy's friends are suggesting that he refuse to go, make a big fuss over it, and even pretend to be very sick. Billy really is afraid to leave the reservation, because he has heard many things about the city he is sure he won't like. He is thinking about doing what his friends suggest.

Why has Henry Sunbear made the decision to move?
What do his reasons show about what he values?
Do you think other people on the reservation agree?
What will their ideas show about what is important to them?
What does Billy think about the decision?
What is important to Billy? To his friends?
Have you ever been in such a situation? What did you do?
Do you now think what you did was a good idea?

Value Conflict Exploration

When children have gained experience in value identification, they can more skillfully examine value conflicts and consider how they may be resolved. This exploration moves somewhat in this direction:

1. as in value identification, getting complete data about the situation
2. hypothesizing about why persons did what they did
3. interpreting the behavior in value terms
4. identifying the value conflict
5. considering what might be done
6. evaluating the consequences of each alternative
7. making a decision about what should be done
8. relating the situation to one's own experience
9. recalling what was done in that situation
10. drawing some conclusions about whether or not that action was good

Any of the techniques previously discussed would be effective at one time or another in dealing with value conflicts, with emphasis at this point on consideration of various alternatives to bringing about a resolution of the conflict. Several other strategies are well suited to this phase of valuing.

A *debate* approach is challenging if pupils have explored the conflict situation as thoroughly as possible at their maturity level and are armed with sufficient data to take the debate out of the opinion category. On the other hand, debate may be used to spur research of a conflict situation; and in that case it would be staged without the requirement of prior data. Teachers will be able to identify any number of debatable ideas involving possible value conflicts, but here are a few.

1. Resolved that all elementary schools in the community remain open, even though their enrollments fall far below normal.
2. Resolved that every citizen old enough to vote be fined for failure to do so.
3. Resolved that it was a mistake for the southern states to secede at the time of the Civil War.
4. Resolved that citizens of unfriendly nations should not be admitted to the United States.
5. Resolved that school libraries should be open for the use of pupils on Saturday mornings.
6. Resolved that the use of insecticides be made illegal.
7. Resolved that the animal shelter should not put to death any animal it has in its care.

In each of these debate situations a value conflict exists. Participants and observers deal with questions that probe: What values are in conflict? What are possible ways of resolving the conflict? What would be the result of each suggestion? What do you think should be done? Why?

The idea of *universal consequences* often throws into sharp focus the appropriateness of one or more of the alternatives suggested by children. The questions to be faced are these: What would be the consequences if this alternative were followed to its natural conclusion? If everyone did as you suggest that this person or group should do? Or if no action were taken to alter the situation and resolve the conflict? Application of the universal consequences technique is of course preceded by questions which identify the conflict and explore the alternatives. Try the idea on the following account.

Studying Value Conflicts 1

David goes to a school which has no Black students. There are rumors that Black pupils are to be transferred to the school. David insists that he does not like Black people and has formed a gang to impose punishment on the newcomers when they arrive. Some of the parents of the area do not wish to welcome the new pupils to the school, but law and school officials insist that this is a good arrangement for everyone.

If David persists in his ideas, what are the consequences?
What if these consequences became universal?
What values are in conflict?
What are the alternatives and the results of each?
What if each of these became a universal consequence?
Would you change your mind about its long-range effectiveness?

Studying Value Conflicts 2

Kathy's dad figures he gains a net profit of $50 for every hour he can cut off the time he must drive on the trip. In order to cut time on his trips, he does what many other people have done—uses a Citizens Band radio to ask the truck drivers coming toward him where the state police are. He tells the drivers coming toward him where he sees police cars. In that way the drivers know when they can speed without getting caught. Kathy's dad paid $300 for the CB radio. He said it paid for itself in two weeks.

What value conflicts did Kathy's dad face?
What alternatives did he have?
What would be the consequences if his choice becomes universal?
Were there other alternatives?
Would they have worked if applied universally?

A *simulation* experience attempts to create a situation which is life-like, but it assigns roles to participants in a planned way, and the roles themselves have definite predetermined characteristics. In this experi-ence, the situation is described, the role card characterizations are dis-pensed, and the action indicated. Pupils are to play the roles as described and to carry out the action indicated. For example, in a simulation called "The Poverty Game" pupils are given various roles in an inner city slum area: shopkeeper, police, welfare agent, some very poor people, a few middle-class persons, and a very few wealthy individuals.[5] Each person who does not have a specified community task is given an amount of money, ranging from none to sixteen cents, with which to buy from the

---

[5] Available from the author, James Egbert, 4418 Bridgetown Road, Cincinnati, Ohio, 45211.

stores materials to make a designated product—in this case, a simple collage on a paper background. The selling and the construction proceed, with the service people meeting a variety of frustrations generated by the fact that the poor are completely powerless to make the product because of lack of funds. In the debriefing that follows, feelings and experiences are shared and the consequences explored.

Some interesting simulations appearing in commercial game form may be used with more mature pupils to explore feelings and to generate problems and questions. Representative of these are *Dirty Water* (Cambridge, Massachusetts: Urban Systems, Inc.), *Tell It Like It Is: The Ungame* (Garden Grove, California: Aud-Vid, Incorporated), and *Woman and Man: The Classic Confrontation* (Del Mar, California: Psychology Today Games).

Teachers may convert current issues into simulations by specifying the action and the characteristics of each role. Possible actions may be designed and certain consequences the result of each.[6] Keeping an eye on the daily news for conflicts that arise on the local and national scene is a good starting point for the teacher interested in developing situations. Here are several fertile examples.

1. In northern California, 4,000 nurses from more than forty hospitals went on strike. A variety of issues was at stake. Hospitals were forced to send home all patients except those who were most critically ill. The nurses insisted that the principal issues involved the welfare of the patients rather than more pay. The hospitals had met a $60 monthly pay increase, but they were resisting an additional 6 percent increase for the near future. Meanwhile, hospital care came to a standstill.

*   *   *   *   *

2. Whales are in danger of becoming extinct. Japan and Russia are the only major countries that do not have any restrictions on the killing of whales, and they use hundreds of thousands of whales every year for food and other materials for human beings. Whale meat makes up a large portion of the meat needed by the Japanese.

*   *   *   *   *

3. In the pleasant Indiana city a great furor is out in the open because of the probable destruction of a well-known landmark in the community —a once-handsome Georgian mansion built by a Civil War officer. At one time the center of many gala balls and festive gatherings, the house

---

[6] For assistance in designing simulation games see Samuel Livingston and Clarice Stasz Stoll, *Simulation Games* (New York: Free Press, 1973).

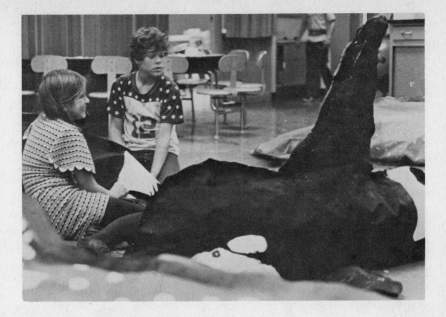

Social studies offers many opportunities for pupils to identify values and study value conflicts. The controversy over the killing of whales led these children to participate in the effort to save them.

is in very poor condition, its stately pillars are sagging badly, and its white paint has been weathering away. It has become a burden to its inheritors, who have announced its sale to business interests with an eye on its fine location on a busy thoroughfare. The local historical society has organized to fight, but the sale has been completed and the house apparently is doomed.

Situations like these may be lifted from current events, converted to simulations, or simply posed as problems for discussion or for role playing by various groups in the class. The implications for social studies investigation are quite clear, for the avenues for research which they open up have tremendous challenge and interest. Children must recognize, however, that even with adequate data the value conflict sometimes remains unresolved and that the values people hold are not easily altered by fact or logic.

A *role exchange* technique is useful in giving pupils a clearer view of both sides of a value question. Children play their assigned role and then change places to the opposite side of the question. They try to play each role as fully as possible in order to get a feeling for the situation. They discuss the action afterwards. How did values change when you changed roles? Were different things of importance to you? Was it difficult to take a role with which you didn't agree? Which of the alternative solutions did you prefer? How does your choice show what you value? Have you ever been in such a situation?

The role exchange works well too when the issue posed is one which is close to pupils' everyday experience or represents an actual conflict in progress. The teacher asks two pupils who feel strongly to argue a point between them and then for the class. A bit later they exchange roles and continue the argument. Such a verbal bout can be envisioned, for example, over the question of whether or not the girls may take part in the boys' team games or whether or not all pupils must buy their lunches in the school cafeteria.

Sometimes of course the value conflict is within the individual; a person may hold values that are in direct conflict with each other. These conflicts may be explored, the dilemmas recognized, and sympathy developed for the person faced with difficult alternatives.

Development of Empathy

Pupils have knowledge of many real-life situations in which they may be powerless to act or in which it would be inappropriate to do so. Some of these situations involve value conflicts which an individual or close friends must face, or simply events in which someone becomes embroiled because of the values held. Pupils need to learn to feel for others and to understand the values behind their actions. This more personal confrontation goes beyond identification of values and exploration of conflicts to a deeper awareness of what the other person or group may be experiencing.

Many of the techniques already mentioned—role playing, simulation, role exchange, and discussion—are appropriate in these situations. Good settings for the exploration of feelings and the building of awareness are these recent news items.

Exploring Feelings 1

It was discovered last week that, in the southwest part of the United States, land deeded years ago to a particular American Indian group has been lived on, cultivated, and hunted on by a neighboring tribe. Thinking the land was theirs, these people have built homes, corrals, and other permanent structures over thousands of acres. Now they are told that they must leave the area. An official has just given all the facts to tribal leaders and informed them that there is no alternative.

How did this situation come about?
How do the persons feel? The tribal leaders? The official?
Why do they feel as they do?
How would you feel in a similar situation?

Exploring Feelings 2

Not long ago welfare families in the state received word that those with dependent children would receive a 25 percent reduction in payments. Said one person, "What am I supposed to do? Go to my landlord and say he has to cut my rent by 25 percent because the welfare board has established a 25 percent reduction? The welfare department says we can get by with 25 percent less even though the federal government says it costs 25 percent more to live because of inflation."

What has happened in this situation?
How does this person feel?
Why does this person feel this way?
How would you feel in this situation?

Exploring Feelings 3

It is very difficult for people in Russia to go to America to live. One woman, now in Lithuania, has been trying for thirty years to get back to her native Brooklyn, New York. One man has recently been given permission to return home to Ohio, after waiting for twenty-seven years. The mother and father of one young man left in December, 1972, to join his sister in Pittsburgh. The son was told he could join them in six months. He has been turned down twice since then and lost his job after applying the first time. Another couple, born in Latvia, became citizens of the United States in 1960. The next year they returned to visit an ailing mother and have been trying to get out ever since.

How do you think these people feel?

Why do you feel this way?

How would you feel if you were one of them?

When the opportunity to develop awareness and empathy is the purpose of the experience, discussion moves along these lines:

1. recalling just what happened
2. identifying how the various persons felt
3. hypothesizing about why they felt as they did
4. taking the places of the persons and feeling as they did
5. recalling when one was involved in similar situations
6. remembering how one felt then

The separation of the valuing process into three phases—identifying and clarifying values, exploring value conflicts, and developing empathy—is well developed by Fraenkel, whose treatment includes some excellent charts specifying exactly what happens in each.[7] He includes a variety of interesting situations and episodes. Giving attention to these aspects of valuing discretely here does not imply that they are necessarily treated in that way when pupils are considering value questions. Quite to the contrary, they are interwoven and often appear as an integrative thought process, depending upon the situation that provokes them.

---

[7] Fraenkel, op. cit.

Valuing in Social Studies

Since social studies is a study of human relationships as people cope with problems of daily living past, present, and future, and since culture has much to do with the way in which people do things, how they perceive their world, and what they believe in, human values are inevitably the content of social studies. To learn what people do to survive in their world without asking why they do these things in their way is little better than reading an atlas about a country. Human beings are rational and have reasons for behaving in particular ways; and these reasons are rooted in the values they hold of what ought to be, should be, or has to be.

It is impossible to interpret accurately the events of the past without asking what values were held, what was important to the people of the times, how they made choices among the alternatives open to them, and why they made the decisions they did. Otherwise, history is merely a time line which illustrates only what was. This value-less approach to history makes it useless as a source of understanding or guidance for solving the problems of today. Without analysis of why it happened and what the consequences were, history becomes an exercise with little social significance. An interesting view of the heritage it may be, but little else.

As adults ponder their own value systems, they may wonder if their values were achieved through choosing, prizing, and acting as Raths indicates or whether they may not have been bred into them by family tradition and precept or imposed on them by the social groups—home, school, community—to which they have belonged. Social studies offers an unusual opportunity for pupils to identify their own values and the values of other people, explore value conflicts, consider the consequences of various alternatives, and to develop empathy for others. Although other agencies play their roles, values education has a very natural and logical setting in social studies.

From a broader point of view social studies implies a study of certain social values which no sociologist would fail to attend to in an analysis of any cultural group. In the particular case of American society, with its general acceptance of the principles of democracy, almost all social studies goals are geared to the development of democratic citizenship with a direct concern for values.

Finally, values education helps pupils combat many social forces which might otherwise make it impossible for them to arrive at wise decisions and defensible conclusions. Being able to implement the valuing process gives pupils skill in recognizing propaganda, analyzing evidence, detecting slanted writing and biased opinion, resisting pressure to choose an alternative which they already have rejected. Social studies provides the setting for investigation and research needed for just these purposes.

Valuing in Problem Solving

In terms of curriculum content, there is no problem worth studying which does not lend itself admirably to the valuing process. Some of the problems identified by pupils exist because of value conflicts (Why is it difficult for our community to provide adequate recreation for children? Why are pollution problems increasing? Why do people break laws? Why are dishonest people serving in government positions? Why are people not agreed on giving help to other countries?) In addition, every problem chosen for study has implications for values education if teachers are alert to the importance of values.

Problem solving encourages pupils to undertake in-depth studies of representative community and world problems; usually the more fully pupils explore a problem, the more they become involved with value questions. Their study of other peoples can be undertaken only with the realization that what people believe is important influences their behavior in the world family. (Why is our country involved in Middle East problems? Why do Canadians and citizens of our country value their friendship? Why is it difficult for Latin American countries to be democratic? Why is life in the South Pacific changing year by year?) Pupils' study of the past is more purposeful if it has a values orientation. (Why was there an American Revolution? Why do some people say that the Civil War is still being fought? How would we be different if our first settlers had come from the west instead of the east? Why were pioneers willing to risk an uncertain future?) Similarly, studies of community call for consideration of value conflicts which may exist and how these may be resolved. Even small children ask questions which have implications for the study of values. Why does everyone have to go to school? Why aren't all families alike? Why do we need police? Why isn't there enough money for better parks in our town?

The resources pupils use in their problem solving are also highly value oriented. Teachers are very much aware that print materials represent values both consciously and unconsciously, and that they should be screened for bias, inaccurate information, and opinion given as fact. Older pupils can participate in this analysis of print materials as good experience for a skill much needed in adult life. Resource persons who visit the children or whom they meet on school journeys will no doubt represent values important to them. Children need not accept these values arbitrarily; they are encouraged to ask, "Why did our 'experts' say what they did? How does what they said show what is important to them? What would be the consequences if everyone thought as they did? Is there another side to the picture?" Communication media also bombard children with value-laden stories, skits, song, dances, and news reports; when these are commented on in connection with the problem being investigated, valuing becomes a practical tool to put things in perspective.

Pupils bring their own values to any problem-solving task. If they are in the habit of identifying the values they think are behind their opinions and actions, the decisions they make will be more thoughtfully arrived at. Having considered the consequences of their choices, they are more willing to implement their decisions. Rather than simply agreeing that something ought to be or ought not to be done because of the teacher's influence or group pressure, children base decisions on their own thought processes and their own valuing.

As pupils delve into any social studies problem in which they are interested, the valuing leads in several directions. A beautiful example of the integration of valuing and social studies content is given by Hoffman and Ryan. They use the traditional content about Pilgrims to develop the concept of government, but in the development there is much emphasis upon feeling and valuing. For example, in one part of the plan of instruction they present to pupils a value sheet which describes how the governor and council of the colony issued laws which, when broken, were punishable in the uncomfortable stocks in full view of jeering villagers. Pupils are encouraged to consider the following questions. (Phrases in brackets have been added by the writer.)

a. If you had done something wrong, would you rather pay a fine or be put in the stocks for several hours? [value identification]

b. Tell why you make the choice you did. [value identification]

c. How might you feel if you were in the stocks and one of your friends came by and started laughing at you and calling you names? [exploration of feelings]

d. What would you do if this person were later in the stocks and you walked by? Remember some of the things he had said to you. [value conflict]

e. Have you ever teased someone or laughed at someone? How did you feel about this later on? [exploration of feelings]

f. What if paying the fine meant going hungry for a few days? How might this influence your decision? [value conflict]

g. Do you go along with the crowd when they are teasing someone even if you know they are wrong, or do you try to get others to see your way? [value conflict] [8]

---

[8] Alan J. Hoffman and Thomas F. Ryan, *Social Studies and the Child's Expanding Self* (New York: Intext Educational Publishers, copyright 1973), p. 177.

If valuing is to become an integral part of pupils' approach to thinking about a social studies problem, it cannot be something apart from the problem-solving process. If social studies objectives go beyond acquisition of knowledge and if instruction is geared to changing behavior toward making a better life and a better society, then valuing is prerequisite. Dunfee and Crump have given in-depth attention to valuing in pursuit of goals related to major social concerns. They propose a spectrum of strategies to stimulate pupils to look at these immediate and urgent problems from the valuing point of view. They draw upon classroom incidents, current news, and lively issues to provide incentive for valuing. They suggest moving into studies which take full advantage of problem-solving processes and are natural outgrowths of attempts to identify values and solve value conflicts. They also suggest many ways in which pupils may take action appropriate to the conclusions they draw from their valuing efforts. [9]

Conditions Which Foster Valuing

In a highly-structured social studies program which is carefully monitored by the teacher, the emphasis upon valuing may depend upon the materials being used and the concern for values held by the teacher. Fortunately there are several new textbook series which give attention to values, and teachers may inject into them creative approaches of their own. Sometimes, however, there is too little encouragement for valuing in an already overcrowded curriculum. A flexible schedule which permits exploration and discussion of ideas is a condition which favors valuing. Time to consider alternatives and to weigh their consequences is a positive encouragement as well.

Valuing in social studies also requires freedom to explore controversial issues freely. Even though teachers may be reluctant sometimes to become involved in such problems, they can hardly avoid those which are being explored in the communication media. Because children view television and hear adults discuss issues of the day, they naturally bring their questions to school. Teachers may respond simply by saying, "Yes, that seems to have been an interesting program" or, taking advantage of the opportunity to consider values, they may open up the problem by asking, "What did you think of those ideas? Do you think everyone agrees with them?"

Valuing flourishes best in an atmosphere where inquiry and problem solving are processes through which pupils gain facility in handling cur-

---

[9] Maxine Dunfee and Claudia Crump, *Teaching for Social Values in Social Studies* (Washington, D.C.: Association for Childhood Education International, 1974).

rent issues and in discovering how the past gives meaning to the present. Freedom to hypothesize, to brainstorm, to suppose, in an environment of trust, empathy, and acceptance creates an exciting setting in which valuing becomes almost as natural as breathing and speaking.

Assessing Pupils' Use of the Valuing Process

Values and valuing are significant components of the affective goals to which social studies instruction is devoted. While accepting responsibility for values education, teachers still are aware that the valuing process is not one which lends itself readily to evaluation in the usual sense. Teachers are, of course, interested in whether or not children have developed the habit of valuing and whether or not it improves the quality of the decisions they make. What can be said about assessing children's growth toward affective goals is included in a later chapter, but presently taking a look at pupils' use of valuing strategies is appropriate.

Obviously the best opportunity the teacher has for determining how pupils use valuing is to listen to their responses to situations in which questions with value overtones have been raised. Over a period of time the teacher observes what happens when children are faced with situations that require application of valuing processes, whether or not they accept the responsibility or avoid it, and how skillful they are in handling the valuing task once they undertake it.

1. Are pupils able to hold in mind the details of a situation?
2. Can they accurately describe what the individuals did?
3. Can they hypothesize about why they may have done what they did?
4. Are they able to identify possible values behind these actions?
5. Do they attempt to identify value conflicts?
6. Are they able to suggest alternatives for action?
7. Can they see the consequences of a given alternative?
8. Are they able to relate situations and conflicts to their own experience?

These cues guide the teacher's listening and observation when pupils are deliberately involved in valuing situations through the various strategies described here. But perhaps more important is whether or not the child engages in valuing when not prompted by an adult to do so. Does he apply his skill in situations that come about during the normal day? At

home? At school? On the playground? Is he exhibiting the habit of valuing as problems that arise in the environment are considered by family or
friends? Are decisions improving because of this habit?

Dunfee and Crump take the position that unless there is an observable
action of a positive nature supporting a value decision, social studies
instruction may be a rather hollow experience.[10] They propose that if, for
example, democracy is valued, pupils should make a contribution to its
realization at their developmental level; if valuing points out the unwhole-
some results of prejudice and discrimination, the real test of its success is
action on the part of children to overcome bias when and where they can.
What follows acquisition of skill in valuing is action; and evaluation of this
action constitutes the most telling evidence of whether or not valuing
makes a difference.

---

[10] Ibid.

Other Points of View

Banks, James A. *Teaching Strategies for the Social Studies,* 2nd ed. Reading, Massachusetts: Addison-Wesley, 1977.
Chapter 13: Valuing: Inquiry Modes and Strategies.
Beyer, Barry K. "Conducting Moral Discussions in the Classroom," *Social Education* 40 (April 1976):194–202.
Dunfee, Maxine, and Crump, Claudia. *Teaching for Social Values in Social Studies.* Washington, D.C.: Association for Childhood Education International, 1974.
Suggestions for developing values related to self-concept, democracy, world friendship, environmental protection, and the elimination of prejudice.
Ellis, Arthur K. *Teaching and Learning Elementary Social Studies.* Boston: Allyn and Bacon, 1977.
Chapter 8: Values and Human Relationships.
Martorella, Peter H. *Elementary Social Studies as a Learning System.* New York: Harper & Row, 1976.
Chapter 15: Analyzing and Developing Beliefs, Attitudes, Values, and Morality; Chapter 16: Special Tools for Affective Growth.
Michaelis, John U. *Social Studies for Children in a Democracy,* 6th ed. Englewood Cliffs, New Jersey: Prentice-Hall, 1976.
Chapter 7: Developing Values, Attitudes, and Valuing Processes.
Oliner, Pearl M. *Teaching Elementary Social Studies: A Rational and Humanistic Approach.* New York: Harcourt, Brace, Jovanovich, 1976.
Chapter 4: Values.
Raths, Louis E.; Harman, Merrill; and Simon, Sidney B. *Values and Teaching: Working with Values in the Classroom.* Columbus, Ohio: Charles E. Merrill, 1966.
Shaftel, Fannie, and Shaftel, George. *Role-Playing for Social Values: Decision Making in Social Studies.* Englewood Cliffs, New Jersey: Prentice-Hall, 1967.
Basic reference for techniques and problem stories.
Volkmor, Cara B.; Pasanella, Anne Langstaff; and Raths, Louis E. *Values in the Classroom.* Columbus, Ohio: Charles E. Merrill, 1977.
Teacher-education program including professional text and sound filmstrips.

Evaluating Learning in Social Studies

New programs in social studies usually generate questions about the evaluation of outcomes. Do they encourage lasting learning and the desire to know? Do they promote the pupils' progress toward content, affective, behavioral, and cognitive goals relevant to modern society? To answer these questions is the task of evaluation, a comprehensive and continuing process that functions through cooperative evaluation of day-to-day experiences in social studies, through teacher evaluation concerned with changes in pupil behavior, and through evaluation of the achievement of long-range objectives.

Cooperative Evaluation

Cooperative evaluation is the process by which teacher and pupils make some judgments about their social studies work together. It is a process that is geared to children's purposes: what they plan to do and what they hope to accomplish. It uses a variety of techniques and yet relies much upon discussion of successes and failures. Cooperative evaluation is continual, occurring at strategic points in the learning process and serving as a transition from past experiences to new ones.

When pupils need to see their progress, cooperative evaluation provides the opportunity; when it is important to identify strengths and weaknesses, talking it over makes this identification possible. When children ask in what way they may improve their efforts to solve problems, together they seek to answer the question as they constructively criticize their work. Pupils usually emerge from these evaluations with ideas of what directions they will take and how they can insure the success of follow-up undertakings.

Throughout the social studies experience there are many opportunities for cooperative evaluation; in fact, there are many points at which evaluation provides the bridge to more effective participation and more creative planning. Following are some of the natural occasions for teacher-pupil evaluation.

1. Following surveys of various kinds, pupils assemble and organize their data, discussing the effectiveness of the techniques they used, the validity of the information gathered, and the usefulness of the survey as a data source.

2. Following the visits of resource persons, pupils compare information learned with what they have read in books, identify still unanswered questions, and evaluate their skill in these social situations.

3. Pupils evaluate their time lines, graphs, and retrieval charts by checking carefully to make sure the information is correct and clear; they may suggest ways to improve such recording schemes.

4. Pupils identify questions to be used in viewing films and evaluate the films in terms of appropriateness to purposes and the adequacy of information.

5. Field trips into the community are followed by discussion of the values of the trip, quality of information obtained, methods of preserving information, and ways to improve the management of the experience.

6. Pupils evaluate their bulletin board displays with attention to arrangement and effectiveness in clarifying ideas.

7. They evaluate group projects and reports by recalling the purposes of each and discussing their success in achieving them.

Because cooperative evaluation and teacher evaluation are closely related, the two occur in part simultaneously. Although teachers must take a somewhat broader view of evaluation than do the children, they are alert to all aspects of pupil behavior and learning as cooperative evaluation sessions reveal them. These observations become an important source of data for the teacher who seeks to arrive at reliable judgments of pupils' needs and achievements.

Teacher Evaluation of Pupil Progress

The responsibility for finally evaluating children's development in social studies, however, rests with teachers. They are the persons best qualified to view learning as a whole, evaluating all aspects of pupil progress and relating the findings to the future experiences of pupils. One of the purposes of teacher evaluation is to assess children's growth toward selected objectives. Although cooperative evaluation gives the teacher some evidence about this progress, these impressions are likely to be general rather than specific. The techniques of teacher evaluation permit attention to the individual child's development in social studies.

Teacher evaluation also serves as a guide to the selection of further experiences. If the teacher finds that important concepts have not been well developed in the current study, future experiences to meet the need can be projected. If new interests surface in the group, the teacher can evaluate them in terms of needs and begin to formulate plans for things to come. If it appears that children need more contacts with their community in order to understand it more fully, these important school-community relationships can be strengthened in the days ahead. If careful analysis of available evidence clearly exposes children's inability to use certain basic skills required in successful problem solving, the teacher plans experiences with the development and functional use of these skills in mind. Because new adventures in learning grow out of and are built on previous ones, teacher evaluation gives direction to plans for future investigations.

Teacher evaluation also produces objective evidence that can be shared with parents in a variety of ways. In scheduled conferences teacher and parents together study test results, anecdotal records, checklists, and samples of a pupil's work to discover evidence of interests, needs, problems, initiative, creativity, and academic accomplishments. Shared is an analysis of the child's ability to use various skills—working with a group, doing simple research reading, using data sources efficiently, and actively participating in problem solving. Particular challenges that pupil and teacher have encountered are discussed as the teacher refers to notes made in preparation for the conference. When the teacher can base comments on concrete data, parents can be more objective in evaluating the child's performance and gain a keener insight into the objectives of social studies instruction.

Teacher evaluation, moreover, provides guidelines for developing the social studies curriculum as a whole. As evidence about pupils' behavior accumulates, the curriculum can be evaluated critically. Are children developing the understandings on which the curriculum is based? Do these understandings represent a balance among various content areas that are significant in the lives of children and relevant to the society in which they live? Are some aspects of social living being neglected? Are some included that now seem to be beyond the maturity level of pupils or far outside the range of their present or expected interests? Does the evidence indicate that children are developing values that lead to action outside the school? Are the skills learned in social studies being put to use in life in school and community? As the teacher takes a broad view of the results of the evaluation activities of the year, the scope of the program and the relevance of the studies undertaken by pupils come into focus.

Evaluation through Informal Techniques

Paper and pencil devices in the form of tests are commonly used instruments in the assessment of learning. While these techniques are often far from satisfactory, they do in a limited way make it possible to discover whether or not children have acquired certain knowledges and understandings about selected content, whether they recognize certain attitudes and values as desirable, and whether or not they can identify appropriate actions to be taken in problem situations. It is important to remember, however, that many of the most valuable outcomes of social studies instruction cannot be measured by testing.

Testing Knowledge and Understandings

Informal tests are most defensible when they are properly constructed to meet a clearly defined purpose. Keeping in mind specific points relative to the building of common types of informal test items may improve their quality.

The *alternate response* item requires the subject to recognize and select from two responses, one of which is acceptable. Responses are usually yes-no, right-wrong, true-false. The item which follows illustrates this type. Points to consider in its construction are suggested.

Test Set: True-False

Directions: If the item is true, write T in the blank to the left; if it is false, write F.

_____1. In our community the school board is appointed by the mayor.
_____2. Areas outside the city limits receive fire protection from the city fire department.

Points to Consider:
1. Are the directions clear?
2. For what objective is each item testing?
3. Are the items free of sly tricks and double meanings?
4. Are the blanks placed for easy marking?
5. How could pupils respond in order to reduce guessing?

In the *multiple-choice item* the pupils are required to select an acceptable response from among a set of responses. They may be asked to select one or more correct responses from the set, the best response, or sometimes the incorrect response when all others are correct. The following item is one in which pupils select the best response from a set of responses, each of which has some degree of merit. Points to consider in writing such items are identified.

Test Set: Multiple Response

Directions: In the blank in front of the item, place the letter of the *best* response.

_____1. You are concerned about some unattractive business buildings which are being planned for the residential neighborhood where you live. To whom should you take this problem to get the most direct action?
   a. the city building inspector
   b. the city planning commission
   c. the city surveyor
   d. the mayor of the city
   e. the city council

Points to Consider:
1. Are the directions clear?
2. For what objective is the item testing?
3. Is the item clear? Does it lead logically to the response?
4. Is each of the responses sensible to one who does not know the appropriate response?
5. Why are there five responses listed rather than just two?

In the *matching* set of items pupils are required to relate two sets of data, each of the sets being homogeneous in nature. Although a variety of things and ideas may be matched and the relationship shown in various ways, the following type is common.

Test Set: Matching

Directions: Match the community organization and its work by placing the letter from Column B in the correct blank in Column A.

Column A	Column B
	A. PTA

_____1. A group through which children can contribute to the life of the community.

_____2. A group which works to make the schools of the community better.

_____3. A group which helps people who cannot find work.

_____4. A group that makes life in the community safer.

_____5. A group that works to protect the community in case of war or disaster.

Column B

A. PTA
B. Peace Corps
C. Scouts
D. country club
E. police
F. employment agency
G. Civil Defense
H. hospital

Points to Consider

1. Are the directions clear?
2. For what objective is this set testing?
3. Are all items in each column homogeneous?
4. Will each of the choices be sensible to the one who does not know the correct match?
5. Why are there extra choices in Column B?

The *completion* item, unlike the alternate-response, multiple-choice, and matching items, requires pupils to recall rather than to recognize the response. Note the items below and the points to consider.

Test Set: Completion

Directions: Complete the sentence by writing the missing word in the blank provided.

1. According to the results of our study, the most serious current problem in our community is the inadequate supply of _____.
2. The responsibility for formulating policy concerning the problems of our community rests with the _____.

Points to Consider:

1. Are the directions clear?
2. Are the words to be supplied key words in the sentences?

3. Why are the blanks placed as they are?
4. Why are the blanks the same length?

━●━●━●━●━●━●━●━●━●━●━●━●━●━●━●━●━●━●━━●

   The types of items shown above are representative of objective items which appear in the tests many teachers give; even though the items are well constructed, they may fall far short of the criteria by which informal tests are judged. Do the tests reveal the pupils' progress toward objectives that go beyond information? Are the kinds of items used appropriate to the purposes of the tests? Do the tests stimulate pupils to think creatively?

   Casual examination of the previous illustrative items is enough to discover that their primary purpose is to test knowledge. While for the most part the items do test something other than trivial fact, they nevertheless do not emphasize higher-level cognitive and affective goals, nor are they likely to require critical thinking.

   Children's grasp of important ideas that have been developed through problem solving may be assessed in some ways that are practical. Admittedly, such assessment is more difficult to devise than tests of information, but the following suggestions may encourage teachers to try for more varied and creative evaluation techniques.

1. To match statements of cause and effect
2. To distinguish between facts and understandings in a given list of statements
3. To supply the generalization to be drawn from a given set of facts
4. To select the conclusion to be drawn from a chart, diagram, or graph
5. To support a given understanding with facts
6. To state the generalizations that can be drawn from a field trip or project
7. To match a generalization with its supporting data
8. To select the generalization that may explain why a given situation exists
9. To draw conclusions from an imaginary dialogue in which an issue is discussed; i.e., what person has inaccurate information, what person's comments reveal prejudice, etc.
10. To state the most important ideas learned from the . . . [study of a problem]
11. To state an opinion about why a particular . . . [topic] was chosen for study

12. To select responses to multiple-choice items which emphasize why something happened or why a condition exists

13. To match pictures with the generalizations they represent[1]

Determining Attitudes and Values

Attitudes are not easily assessed, but it is possible to determine children's ability to recognize socially desirable attitudes. At best, however, teachers can know only what the child reveals in the evaluation situation. These are kinds of tasks which may provide some evidence of the attitudes pupils hold.

1. To select from a teacher-prepared dialogue, comments that reveal [obviously] desirable or undesirable attitudes

2. To respond *yes* or *no* to questions which ask, "Do you think that . . . ?"

3. To respond to a list of statements of belief, feeling, or opinion by indicating degree—*always, sometimes, never*

4. To respond to statements that imply prejudice or lack of prejudice by indicating state of agreement—*I agree, I disagree, I am uncertain*

5. To match attitudes with likely resultant actions

6. To state what one liked about the . . . [area of study] being developed

7. To give opinions about described situations which reveal the attitudes of the characters

8. To give reasons to support action that should be taken in a described problem situation

9. To write the ending to a story which describes a problem situation

10. To complete an unfinished sentence such as, "Our [study of _____] has changed my ideas about. . . ."[2]

Values which pupils hold with regard to some facets of their study can sometimes be uncovered in a forced-choice situation. Pupils are asked to make the choice and give reasons for their decisions; reasons may be given in writing by older pupils; younger ones respond orally on tape. Following are some choices relative to possible problem investigations pupils may have completed.

---

[1] Maxine Dunfee, "Evaluating Understanding, Attitudes, Skills and Behaviors in Elementary School Social Studies," in *Evaluation in Social Studies,* ed. Harry D. Berg (Washington, D.C.: National Council for the Social Studies, 1965), p. 165.

[2] Ibid., p. 166.

You are the owner of a very valuable, forested piece of land which later the city would like to develop as a park. You are now offered a large amount of money by a famous maker of hamburgers; an elaborate drive-in restaurant is planned. Would you sell the land or keep it for a future park?

You are a member of a family that lives comfortably and does not need anything. Your family has just received an unexpected amount of money as a gift. If you put it into your business, you will double the amount of money you can make next year. Since you did nothing to earn the money, some relatives have suggested that it is just the right amount to start a new day care center in the slum area of your city. What would you do?

The value sheet may be used to discover the pupils' ability to think through a value situation and to identify the consequences of alternatives. This example is based on a news item which appeared during a gasoline shortage.

Directions: Read the following account and respond to the questions which follow.

Recently when gasoline sales were being limited, a woman stopped at a station and asked for $2.00 worth of gas. The attendant left and for some reason another one put the fuel in her car, saying, "That will be $3.00." When the woman said that she had asked for only $2.00 worth, the man replied, "Look, lady, what's another dollar? Besides with this gas shortage, you're lucky." The woman had only $2.00 with her but said that since she lived nearby she would come back right away with the other dollar. However, she really didn't have any more money at home for the gasoline, so she never went back.

What happened at the station?

Why was the attendant angry?

How did the angry remark show what was important to the attendant?

Why did the woman fail to return to the station?

How did this action show what was important to her?

What could have been done?

What would be the consequences of each of these alternatives?

What would you have done?

Have you ever been in a similar situation?

What did you do?

What do you think now about what you did?

Similarly, many of the techniques suggested in the chapter on values and valuing may be adapted for use in informal evaluation sessions, especially if individual responses can be arranged.

Assessing Behaviors

Assessing behaviors may be a part of informal written evaluations but obviously on the verbal level only. Items which present problems to which pupils are asked to react reveal only what pupils say they would do; if they give an expected appropriate response, the teacher may hypothesize that children may take acceptable action, but there is no way to guarantee the action in the real world. As in the case of values, the teacher does not have much opportunity to discover how pupils will respond outside the school. Nevertheless, responses made to items of the following types are more helpful than mere guesswork. Children may be asked to perform tasks like these.

1. To indicate what they would do about a [described] problem situation
2. To choose from a number of suggested solutions to a described problem
3. To write the ending for an unfinished story which describes a problem situation
4. To suggest and evaluate several possible solutions to a described situation
5. To complete an unfinished sentence, such as, "This . . . [study] has helped me to. . . ."
6. To select a course of action in a problem situation and justify the choice made[3]

Evaluating Skills

Evaluating skills in planning, research reading, and independent work is significant in determining success in problem solving. Classroom experiences in social studies offer many opportunities for pupils to learn and practice a variety of skills. In addition to informal assessment of understandings, attitudes and values, and behaviors, teachers can prepare exercises to test skills. The following are types of tasks pupils may be asked to perform.

---

[3] Ibid.

1. To interpret an imaginary map, locating physical and cultural features and answering questions calling for an interpretation of information provided

2. To answer questions which require the reading and interpretation of data on a graph or table

3. To match kinds of references with types of information to be found in them

4. To arrange in order the steps in cooperative planning or problem solving

5. To select the duties of a . . . [committee head] from a list of responsibilities of committee members

6. To supply a missing step in directions for doing something that involves a skill

7. To list the characteristics of a good discussion, a good report, etc.

8. To describe how to take notes, how to locate information in a library, etc.

9. To demonstrate how to conduct a meeting, how to give a report, etc.

10. To use a table of contents or index in locating specified information[4]

This discussion of informal assessment indicates that there are ways to discover pupils' growth toward the goals of social studies and to assess pupil achievement of a variety of skills. Whether or not critical thinking is encouraged by such test items depends entirely upon how well they require levels of cognitive behavior of increasing complexity.

Testing for Higher Cognitive Levels

In a discussion of questioning in a previous chapter, mention was made of current interest in studying the relationship between questions and the level of cognitive behavior they evoke. Similarly, this interest is relevant to any consideration of the types of items teachers use in informal evaluation.

Bloom's taxonomy of educational objectives has served as the point of departure for educators who have become interested in analyzing the cognitive behavior of pupils and in particular for those like Sanders who have special interest in teachers' questions.[5] Bloom and his colleagues classified cognitive behavior into six categories on a scale of increasingly complex

---

[4] Ibid., p. 167.

[5] Norris M. Sanders, *Classroom Questions* (New York: Harper & Row, 1966).

thought.[6] It is possible to study a given test item to determine the level of cognitive behavior toward which it is directed. It is also possible to consciously construct items that emphasize the ascending levels of reflection and thinking. Each of the categories identified by the taxonomy is defined and illustrated in the following section.

Knowledge, the first and lowest level in the taxonomy, is the most frequently emphasized level in teacher-made tests. Evaluation items focusing on knowledge are usually represented by the recognition and recall exercises previously described. In these situations pupils are required to respond to or reproduce information without changing it from its original form. An example follows.

Test Set: Knowledge

1. Match the dates with events in Afro-American history by writing the letter of the event in the blank before its date.

   _____1. 1619   A. march on Washington
   _____2. 1770   B. Emancipation Proclamation
   _____3. 1831   C. first slave in America
   _____4. 1863   D. death of Crispus Attucks
   _____5. 1964   E. Civil Rights Law
                        F. Nat Turner Rebellion
                        G. death of Martin Luther King

2. Complete the sentence by writing in an appropriate word.

   A. Carver, Drew, and Banneker are famous Afro-Americans in the field of _____.
   B. Democracy assumes that every citizen is entitled to equal _____.
   C. Discrimination is the result of ideas and feelings called _____.

Comprehension, the level of cognitive behavior above that of knowledge, requires the pupil to do more than simply recognize or recall information. At this level, understanding is revealed through *translation,* a

---

[6] Benjamin S. Bloom, *Taxonomy of Educational Objectives: Handbook I, Cognitive Domain* (New York: David McKay, 1956).

behavior in which the child must change the form though not the content of what is known. In other words, the learner translates knowledge from one form to another: words to maps, pictures to words, detailed accounts to summaries, and the like.

●━○━○━●━○━●━○━●━○━●━○━●━○━●━○━●━○━●━○━●━○━●━○━●━○━●━○━●━○━●━○━●

Test Set: Comprehension (Translation)

1. Using a graph showing leading oil producing countries of the world, list the countries in order of their production, from largest producer to smallest.

2. Demonstrate the meaning of each of these terms, which describe land features, by writing the term at the appropriate location on the map.

●━○━●━○━●━○━●━○━●━○━●━○━●━○━●━○━●━○━●━○━●━○━●━○━●━○━●━○━●━○━●

At a higher level of comprehension is *interpretation,* which requires the subject to take a new view of the material, seeing relationships, comparing, generalizing. The following are some of the varieties which emphasize interpretation.

●━○━●━○━●━○━●━○━●━○━●━○━●━○━●━○━●━○━●━○━●━○━●━○━●━○━●━○━●━○━●

Test Set: Comprehension (Interpretation)

1. From the list of sentences below, select those that are understandings about community life. Mark them with an X in the blank in front of the number. Do not mark sentences that are merely statements of fact.

    _____A. Communities differ partly because of their environment.

    _____B. There are 5,000 people living in our community.

    _____C. There is no train transportation to the community in which we live.

    _____D. Everyone in our community is responsible for the care of its natural resources.

    _____E. People in a pioneer community depended upon their surroundings for many things they needed.

    _____F. In the pioneer community the houses were made of logs.

    _____G. A community changes when the needs of the people change.

_____H. Many people in the community work together to supply its needs.

2. Here are pictures of three farms, one from prehistoric times, one from pioneer days, and one from today. Study them carefully. Then put an *X* before each of the sentences in the list which is a reasonable inference to be drawn from the pictures.

_____A. Methods of farming have changed very little since early times.

_____B. Hand labor is becoming more common on modern farms.

_____C. Machinery helps modern farmers do more work with fewer helpers.

_____D. Crops were better in early times because the soil was not worn out.

_____E. Animals were used for farm work in early times.

_____F. Farmers today make many of the farm implements they use.

_____G. Scientific farming was unknown in primitive times.

_____H. Many members of the primitive family helped with the farming.

3. Match the community problem and the appropriate program by writing the letter of the program in the blank in front of the problem.

_____erosion
_____floods
_____water shortage
_____worn-out soil
_____slums
_____air pollution

A. Program to encourage use of fertilizers
B. Program to extend urban renewal
C. Program to clear forests to make farm land
D. Program to encourage tree planting
E. Program to build levees
F. Program to provide reservoirs
G. Program to beautify roadsides
H. Program to reduce smog

Application, further along the scale of complex cognitive behaviors, asks pupils to apply to a new situation an inference or principle previously arrived at.

Test Set: Application

1. On this mythical map four cities are shown; one city is missing. Locate the missing city and list reasons for your location.

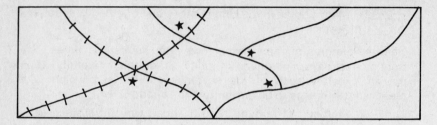

2. Write one statement in response to each of the following:
    A. How would living in your community be different if the rainfall decreased to less than 5 inches a year?
    B. How would living in your community be different if latitude were changed to zero degrees?
    C. How would living in your community be different if the hills became very high mountains?

Analysis requires a still higher level of cognitive behavior, a thought process in which an idea or a whole is broken into its parts. Producing evidence to support an understanding, discovering elements that do not belong to the whole, and relating cause and effect are examples of the analysis level of thinking.

Test Set: Analysis

1. Mark with an X each of the statements in the list which supports the understanding: Communities are different from each other partly because of their environment.

    _____A. More people prefer to live in the city than in the rural areas of the country.
    _____B. Because of weather and climate, living in Florida is different from living in our community.
    _____C. Seacoast cities offer some kinds of recreation that are not available in inland countries.
    _____D. Many communities make good use of their environment for public recreation.
    _____E. A community often carelessly destroys its natural environment.
    _____F. Many of the things we need we must buy from other communities.

_____G. Some communities are different from others because of their customs and beliefs.

_____H. Communities in mountain areas are more likely to be engaged in mining than communities in lowland regions.

2. Give evidence to support each of the following inferences.

    A. Discrimination against minority groups is contrary to the beliefs on which our country was founded.

    B. Many of the good things we enjoy have come from the people of minority groups.

3. In each of the sets below are four items, one of which does not belong with the others. In the blank provided write the letter of the item that does not belong.

    _____A. tea tax
    B. Sugar Act
    C. income tax
    D. Stamp Act

    _____A. postal service
    B. military protection
    C. money system
    D. educational system

    _____A. The Declaration of Independence
    B. The Monroe Doctrine
    C. The Constitution
    D. The Articles of Confederation

Synthesis is cognitive behavior that results in an original product. It is essentially formation of a whole by combining parts; for example, making a prediction based on a set of conditions, drawing a conclusion from a collection of data, or creating a design or plan.

Test Set: Synthesis

1. Study the following sentences; then write a statement which will summarize and emphasize the important idea the sentences suggest to you.

    A. The national government protects forests in national forests and parks.

    B. State and local governments pass laws to protect forest areas.

C. Each person who uses the forest area must handle fire very carefully.
D. Park officials and fire rangers are responsible for detecting and
   extinguishing harmful forest fires.

2. Every day when people are going or coming from their jobs in the
   city, there is a traffic jam. Pretend that you have been given the task
   of solving the problem. Basing your ideas on data you now have
   about the situation, devise a plan you think might work now or in the
   future.

Evaluation is at the highest level of cognitive behavior. At this level
the learner must judge or evaluate in terms of some criteria.

Test Set: Evaluation

1. Some businesses in your community have been asked to support a
   program of urban renewal. Which of these actions would you think
   most useful in solving the problems such a project might create?
   Mark your choice with an X. Be ready to support your choice in the
   follow-up discussion.

   _____A. One person suggests that it would be best to let the
            people in the ghetto work out their own solutions to the
            housing problem.
   _____B. Another proposes that the people of the ghetto should be
            participants in planning for the renewal.
   _____C. Another gathers information to prove that urban renewal is
            not needed.
   _____D. Another agrees to help only if tax money will not be used
            in the project.

2. Assume that you are seeking up-to-date information about ways of
   living among American Indians today. Evaluate at least five possible
   sources in terms of the recency and completeness of data.

3. Respond thoughtfully to each of the following.

   A. Why was it important to study about conservation?

B. What was the most useful contribution you made to the study? Why do you think so?

C. What was the most important idea you gained from the study?

D. What part of the study of conservation was most interesting to you? Why?

Any discussion of levels of cognitive behavior and their evaluation through informal techniques must be tempered by the realization that exercises at the higher levels of cognition are not easily constructed for elementary school children; it may be that eagerness to evaluate learning in terms of the taxonomy may lead to oversimplification. Nevertheless, whatever emphasis the teacher gives to techniques that go beyond the knowledge level represents a distinct gain.

Evaluation through Group Discussion and Interview

Whenever pupils are sharing data, expressing opinions, drawing conclusions, and planning the next steps during the development of a problem area, the teacher catches from pupils evidence of their knowledge, their growth toward significant ideas, their attitudes and interests. This evidence is useful in evaluation of children's progress, regardless of how fleeting the data may be.

However, discussion planned specifically to reveal the quality of the pupils' thoughts and attitudes toward the subject under study is even more useful in evaluation. This discussion may be group or individual; it may be directed or nondirective; but in any case, it is planned with an objective in mind: to produce evidence about pupils' learning.

The group discussion takes place in an informal, relaxed atmosphere where pupils exchange ideas freely. The teacher usually starts the ball rolling by throwing out a challenging question. Pupils examine the proposition openly, without the formalities that accompany the usual recitation. For example, pupils who have concluded their study of the problem, "How has education helped people meet the problems of daily living?" may discuss such questions as these:

1. If you could start a school of your own, what new things would you teach your pupils? Why?

Evaluation is a continuing process through which teacher and pupils assess their progress in meeting objectives. These children are providing evidence of their learning through positive action in a school beautification campaign.

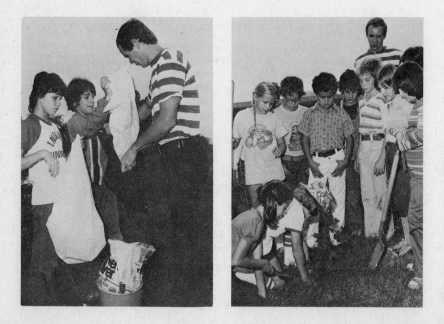

2. What would you do to make sure that every child in our country has a chance for a good education?

3. Why is the school you attend different in some ways from other schools?

After study of the problem, "How do methods of production, exchange, and distribution meet changing needs?" these questions may spur discussion:

1. If our community were located in mountains or near the ocean, how would our industries and their products be different?

2. If we had to produce at home everything we use, what would be our most difficult task? Why?

A study of transportation in the world today suggests these discussion questions:

1. How would our lives be different if we were unable to share beliefs, customs, and ideas with other countries?

2. How would our community be different if we used only simple methods of transportation?

How do people live in our own and other communities? This problem may lead to these discussion sessions:

1. Would you be willing to live in a community that was not democratic?

2. Should people of the community be able to use their natural resources as they please? Why? Why not?

3. What is your opinion of people who did not help in our recent community clean-up campaign? What reasons might they have had for not participating?

As the discussion continues, the teacher, whether leader or listener, gathers some evidence about the pupils' involvement with the content of the problem they have investigated. If the teacher can arrange to record the sessions without interfering with the flow of ideas, the discussion can be reviewed later for further evidence of the pupils' understanding of the content. This evidence may be supplemented with individual interviews that are planned to reveal facets of the child's understanding which were not brought out in other ways. The teacher chooses carefully the questions to be asked, sometimes varying them to suit the child. Responses are recorded on paper or on tape to make them available for later study. The following are possible interview questions.

1. What did you like about our study of the United Nations?
2. What was the most important or useful things you learned about the United Nations?
3. Why do you think we studied this problem?
4. What special contributions did you make to the study?
5. How are you going to use the ideas you gained from this study?

Although the interview questions will vary widely from one situation to another, the teacher can learn some kinds of information more easily in this way than in any other. Some ingenuity in finding odd moments when the interviews can take place and some skill in helping children talk freely are prerequisites to success.

Evaluation through Observation

Among the important goals of social studies instruction are the behaviors which pupils acquire as a result of the understandings and attitudes developed during the study. Many of these behaviors are not readily tested in any sense beyond the teacher's asking pupils what they would or should do in a given situation. Moreover, many of these behaviors appear outside the school, in the neighborhood, in the family, and in the community, and some of them only in adult life. Opportunities to observe these behaviors are, therefore, likely to be limited. Nevertheless, the teacher should not pass by the possibilities of such observation, even though it may be less than systematic or thorough. For example, surely there are behaviors the teacher expects pupils to exhibit as a result of their study of the problem, How does prejudice create problems in American life? If so, what are some of these behaviors? What kinds of observations can be realistically employed?

1. Do pupils identify problems of discrimination in their classroom?
2. Do they avoid making generalizations about people of minority groups?
3. Do they discuss current events dealing with racial problems?
4. Do they greet visitors and newcomers from other groups with kindness and sincerity?
5. Do they challenge adults and peers who are expressing prejudice?
6. Do they select for their own reading literature written by persons of minority groups?

7. Do they avoid making unkind remarks about persons of other groups?

8. Do they work enthusiastically on projects designed to help others?

9. Do they report on evidences of discrimination which they see in the community?

10. Do they speak out against practices which they consider unfair?

Equally worthy of attention in evaluation are behaviors related to the problem-solving process, behaviors which can be observed in the school setting.

1. Do pupils independently investigate various aspects of the problem?

2. Do they show skill in gathering data from various kinds of sources?

3. Are they able to relate data to the problem being investigated?

4. Do they use new vocabulary with understanding?

5. Are they able to formulate big ideas derived from their study?

6. Do they challenge inaccurate statements and generalizations?

7. Are they able to support their own ideas with appropriate data?

8. Do they apply the understandings developed in this study to related situations?

Teachers may devise simple records to aid in organizing information gathered through observation. A simple checklist, kept in a convenient place on the desk, is easily available for marking when the teacher has good evidence that a pupil has control of specified behaviors. The chart in Figure 11–1 is an example.

The teacher may prefer a separate check sheet for each pupil with space to record specific notes as supporting evidence. Such checklists, although time consuming, generally provide more objective information for teacher evaluation and for reporting to parents. For example, a study of data on the chart of participation skills reveals the answers to a variety of questions about pupils. Which children are making successful growth in these skills? Who has difficulty cooperating with others? Who has special skill in organizing a group for work? Who completes independent work quickly and well? Which pupils know how to use many kinds of materials and equipment?

Relating Evaluation to Objectives

In spite of efforts to improve evaluation procedures on the classroom front, much more needs to be done. Critical studies of curriculum guides

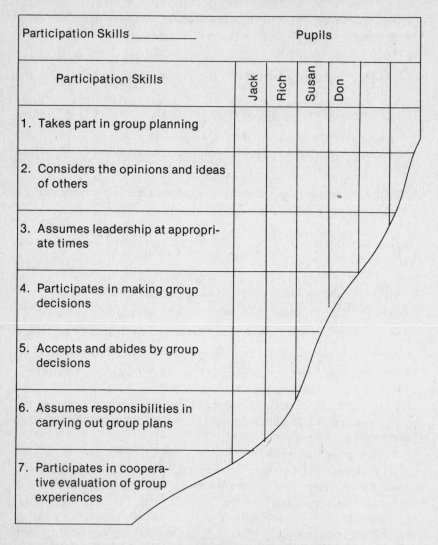

Participation Skills _____						Pupils	
Participation Skills	Jack	Rich	Susan	Don			
1. Takes part in group planning							
2. Considers the opinions and ideas of others							
3. Assumes leadership at appropriate times							
4. Participates in making group decisions							
5. Accepts and abides by group decisions							
6. Assumes responsibilities in carrying out group plans							
7. Participates in cooperative evaluation of group experiences							

Figure 11–1. Participation skills checklist.

produced for state and local use have shown clearly that plans for evaluating pupil progress toward stated goals have been widely neglected.[7]

Failure to clarify objectives obviously invalidates evaluation efforts. If the objectives clearly state what it is the pupil will be able to do as a result of experience, then it is possible to devise appropriate evaluation measures for these performance objectives. The question remains, however, as to

[7] Dorothy McClure Fraser, ed., "Review of Curriculum Materials," *Social Education* 33 (May 1968):576.

whether or not there are objectives which cannot be stated in performance terms; and, if so, how the attainment of these objectives can be determined. Certainly objectives in the affective domain are of this category unless the behavior which results from particular attitudes and values can be identified sharply.

Consistency between objectives and evaluation is essential and should be apparent to both teachers and pupils. If you look back on your own education thoughtfully you can attest to the fact that evaluation procedures very soon teach pupils what the teacher considers important. If evaluation is restricted to information recall, pupils know that the facts encountered along the study route are to be memorized and retained until the study and testing are completed. If, on the other hand, more significant objectives are emphasized, pupils come to know that creative thinking, valuing, and action are the expected outcomes; their ways of working are therefore directed to these goals and their learning has a different meaning and purpose.

Evaluation of the Social Studies Program

Evaluation of the social studies program from the point of view of the curriculum as a whole goes beyond the evidence gathered by teachers about the progress of their pupils. What has been learned through observation, from interviews, and from informal testing will either support their belief in the teaching strategy employed or will indicate in what ways pupils have failed to meet the immediate objectives of a study. Data gathered from all teachers in the school can be marshalled to point up successes and weaknesses in pupil achievement of the goals of social studies.

Evaluation on a broader base than suggested by the teachers' analysis and discussion of pupil achievement is particularly timely when social studies curriculum issues are quite fluid, when a variety of new programs and textbooks is being proposed, and when the ideas of national assessment and accountability are current. How will a school committed to its beliefs about a modern social studies program manage to view its progress objectively?

Typically schools have employed standardized instruments to examine their success in teaching the various elementary school subjects, although there are few tests which measure social studies objectives beyond the information level. Two tests, however, have proven helpful in assessing some aspects of modern social studies programs. One is the *Iowa Every-Pupil Tests of Basic Skills: Test B, Work-Study Skills* (Boston: Houghton Mifflin Company). This well-constructed test for pupils in grades 3–9 evaluates skill in a variety of study techniques needed in social studies research reading and problem solving: map reading, selection and evaluation of reference materials, use of dictionary, interpretation of data in graphic form, and the use of table of contents and index. The other is *Sequential Tests of Educational Progress: Social Studies* (Princeton: Educational Testing Service). This test for grades 4–14 is built on the premise that what pupils can do with knowledge is as important as what they know. Each item of the test requires application of a skill as well as understanding of an important idea; the skills and understandings on which the items are based are closely related to content and cognitive goals identified earlier in this book.

If the school has chosen a preplanned program using a teacher-directed learning strategy or a guided-inquiry approach, teachers will no doubt use whatever built-in evaluation techniques the program suggests. If these measures do not give a broad view of the outcomes of the program, or if the school is moving into a problem-solving approach to social studies, a more comprehensive evaluation effort may seem desirable.

To gather necessary data, the faculty of the school may undertake the task themselves or may decide in the interests of time and objectivity to seek the assistance of qualified observers who know the field of social studies well, who are committed to goals beyond the knowledge level, and who have a workable plan for looking at the teaching-learning process in social studies. It is important, of course, that teachers welcome an objective view of the program and that the data gathering is clearly nonthreatening.

Although observers may develop varied plans for their work, they may begin by making a preliminary survey of teachers to determine their response to social studies in their classrooms and in the school as a whole. The survey questions, adapted to interview form or questionnaire form, will attempt to tap the level of satisfaction teachers feel, the problems they may be experiencing with the current social studies program, innovations they are making, and their views about what they want students to learn.

Observers then may turn their attention to studying the entry behavior of learners, apply available data-gathering techniques to arrive at tentative answers to questions. What kinds of programs and processes in social studies have learners experienced previously? Interviewing teachers and supervisors, examining textbook and curriculum guides, and observing classrooms will yield appropriate data. What kinds of interests do pupils bring to the social studies classroom? Interviews and a variety of paper and pencil devices can be used to produce this information. Observers may ask children, "What questions about how people live in our world would you like to have answered? What puzzles you most about things that are happening today? If you could find out about any place on earth, what would you choose? How do you feel about what you and your teacher do in social studies? Are there other things you would like to do? What is your favorite school subject?"

A study of entry behavior also calls for information about the inquiry and problem-solving skills which pupils may have acquired previously. This evaluation, of course, is closely related to the objectives of the curriculum and the relative emphasis given to content, affective, behavioral, and cognitive goals. These goals influence the criteria used and the way in which pupil behavior is described.

Pupils bring their entry behavior to their first encounter with any new content or problem in social studies. Observers may note how pupils are introduced to an area of study and the extent to which a need is created and interest aroused. They analyze readiness experiences as they are staged in the classroom, recording evidence of enthusiasm pupils display and the range of participation. They give special attention to the problem areas selected for study at each level of the curriculum, encouraging teachers to consider how the content may be justified in terms of stated objectives. If problem solving is the strategy employed, observers note especially the vitality and challenge of the problems and questions identified by teacher and children.

Observers then study the pupils' involvement with the social studies program. From curriculum guides and textbooks they infer the extent to which children are likely to be participants in planning their experiences; they gather information about the types of data-gathering activities in which pupils are likely to engage. Resource materials are examined for variety and quality. Returning to the classroom, observers look on as pupils interact with textbooks or inquiry materials or set about their data collection in problem solving. If children are working in an open classroom, observers move in and out of the learning center, talking with pupils and studying the records pupils and teachers are keeping of the work in progress. Depth of involvement may indicate the degree to which activities are meaningful to pupils; and, while this assessment may be somewhat subjective, differences from group to group usually become clear.

Exit behavior is also of concern to the observers, because of its relationship to desired outcomes of instruction. As a result of their social studies experiences, what exit behaviors are children exhibiting? What skills in formulating tentative generalizations based on data? Are they eager to investigate more deeply? Have they developed habits of valuing? Do they try to devise new ways to discover facts and ideas? Do they want to carry into action their proposals for problem solution?

Interviewing pupils about how they plan to use what they have learned is possible; engaging pupils in discussion sparked by divergent questions which call for application of learnings to new situations is another approach. Creating ways to observe pupils' behavior beyond the classroom is more difficult but can be accomplished with the cooperation of parents, teachers, and other community members. The level of achievement of objectives which pupils exhibit at any evaluation point, of course, becomes the entry behavior for their further adventures with social studies.

As teachers begin to analyze and discuss the data their observers have gathered, they enter the most challenging phase of the evaluation process. They recall their feelings about social studies instruction in the school and their hypotheses about its strengths and weaknesses. As they look to the future, these criteria may help them synthesize their findings and make plans based on their conclusions.

1. Are program objectives clearly defined, emphasizing affective, behavioral, and cognitive as well as content goals?

2. Is the content of the program relevant to the lives of children, stimulating them to inquire about problems and topics significant to them?

3. Does the program generate the enthusiastic participation of pupils in learning experiences that are realistic in terms of their background and maturity?

4. Does the program help pupils develop understandings, values, and skills of continuing applicability in their world?

5. And finally, is the program likely to challenge pupils to translate their learning into actions characteristic of citizens in democracy?

Other Points of View

Banks, James A. *Teaching Strategies for the Social Studies,* 2nd ed. Reading, Massachusetts: Addison-Wesley, 1977.
Chapter 13: Evaluation Strategies.

Ellis, Arthur K. *Teaching and Learning Elementary Social Studies.* Boston: Allyn and Bacon, 1977.
Chapter 5: Evaluation Strategies.

Fraenkel, Jack R. *Helping Students Think and Value: Strategies for Teaching Social Studies.* Englewood Cliffs, New Jersey: Prentice-Hall, 1973.
Chapter 2: Diagnostic Evaluation; Chapter 7: Summative Evaluation.

Jarolimek, John. *Social Studies in Elementary Education.* 5th ed. New York: Macmillan, 1977.
Chapter 13: Assessing Pupil Achievement in Social Studies.

Michaelis, John U. *Social Studies for Children in a Democracy,* 6th ed. Englewood Cliffs, New Jersey: Prentice-Hall, 1976.
Chapter 15: Evaluating Children's Learning.

Oliner, Pearl M. *Teaching Elementary Social Studies: A Rational and Humanistic Approach.* New York: Harcourt, Brace, Jovanovich, 1976.
Chapter 9: Evaluation.

Ploghoft, Milton E., and Shuster, Albert H. *Social Science Education in the Elementary School.* Columbus, Ohio: Charles E. Merrill, 1976.
Chapter 14: Evaluating Progress in Social Science Education.

Preston, Ralph C., and Herman, Wayne L., Jr. *Teaching Social Studies in the Elementary School,* 4th ed. New York: Holt, Rinehart & Winston, 1974.
Chapter 22: Evaluating Pupil Performance.

Ragan, William Burk, and McAulay, John D. *Social Studies for Today's Children,* 2nd ed. New York: Appleton-Century-Crofts, 1973.
Chapter 14: Evaluating and Reporting Pupil Progress.

Thomas, R. Murray, and Brubaker, Dale L. *Decisions in Teaching Elementary Social Studies.* Belmont, California: Wadsworth, 1971.
Chapter 14: Test Construction and Use; Chapter 15: Observation Techniques.

Welton, David A., and Mallan, John T. *Children and Their World: Teaching Elementary Social Studies.* Chicago: Rand McNally, 1976.
Chapter 15: Evaluation Strategies: Beyond a Necessary Evil.

309

Epilogue

Citizens for
the Real World

The real world of the present and the future is the setting in which our children will play their roles as citizens. We know something of this world of the present; the world of the future we can only surmise from the predictions of the futurists.

We know that now the real world is a world of contrasts: majestic beauty sometimes shrouded in pollution; magnificent cities marred by slums; democratic ideals denied by individual and corporate actions; pleas for peace and cries of conflict.

The real world in which American citizens live is a changing world. Old values on which our country was founded are being questioned, leaving citizens without the guidance these values once provided. Institutions responsible for the early education of our citizens no longer seem to have the influence they enjoyed in the past. The American scene is more and more mobile; people feel less and less committed to a group or an idea. Mass media have an increasing impact upon citizens, swaying opinions, channelling thoughts, and sometimes implying that many problems are without solution.

The real world demands of its citizens something more than complacent acceptance of the society as it is. Coping is not enough. Of very high priority are the actions citizens will take because they believe that life in the world is worth improving, that it is possible to make the world a better place in which to live.

Can elementary school pupils take beginning steps along the road to a better America, a better world? Let's return for a few moments to the children of our prologue who were planning the redevelopment of the slums of Hunters Point. Their project is an excellent illustration of what can be accomplished by an inspired and determined group of youngsters and a creative teacher. When the children presented their report to a group of college students who had been following their progress, the discussion was recorded on tape—what they had planned for Hunters Point and how the plan would be accomplished, complete with a wall map showing the details. These excerpts from the presentation illustrate how these young people were practicing the skills of cooperative thinking, effort, and action.

In the first selection, some of the children were concerned about how the people of Hunters Point will be taught to live in the cooperative housing planned for the redevelopment. Others were thinking about human feelings and values as people find new ways of living in new settings.

Child: . . . in this cooperative there's going to be a lot of play areas and different things, and I think it will be a place where your kids, older than tots, can play; and before people can move into this cooperative they have to go through the training center.

Teacher: Could you tell us a little about this training center? I think this was your plan, Yvonne. Why are you having a training center for getting into this cooperative?

C: Well, we decided that most of the people in Hunters Point, they weren't ready to move into a cooperative right away from the beginning, so we decided to make a training center and in this training center there will be apartments and people will stay here, and they'll pay about $50 a month for rent; they'll stay here and they'll have inspection every week, and some inspectors will have, will see if the person can be cooperative, and when he's finally learned to keep up his house and everything, well then he can move into the big cooperatives.

T: Dan, I remember that you didn't like that idea much.

C: Yeah, because when we went on that trip to Hunters Point, we didn't see all of Hunters Point. We only saw part of it so how does Yvonne know that all the people of Hunters Point are the same?

T: Good argument, good point. I wonder if they are. . . .

C: Well, I thought that if some of the people are more cooperative than the others, we'd move them into the cooperative and if they do anything wrong they have to go through the training center like the other people.

*   *   *   *   *

T: Dan, still don't like it?

C: Well, if the people do do like she said back there, they don't like to be taught. Well, a lot of people will stop moving into cooperatives.

T: In other words, you think a training center would keep people away because they will resent—

C: Yeah.

T: —going into a training center?

T: Dan, you said the other day you had a plan how you would train people to be cooperative, and you said something, I don't know if this is right, correct me if I'm wrong. You said, "The best way to be cooperative is," do you remember? (Pause) Does anyone remember what he said? I think he said, "To do it." Is that what you said? (Pause) What did you mean?[1]

---

[1] Association for Supervision and Curriculum Development, *Hunters Point Redeveloped* (Washington, D.C.: Author, 1970), pp. 14–16.

This discussion about whether or not people should be "trained" to improve their living habits led the teacher to ask the pupils how *they* had learned to be cooperative. Did they go through a training center, or, did they, as Dan had suggested, just *do* it?

T: . . . Let me ask you this question. Did you have to cooperate all together to make up all these plans?

C: Yes.

T: How? Tell us some of the problems that you ran into.

C: Well, we had a lot of problems of the cost, and we all had to work together on figuring out the cost because there's some people that are good in mathematics and some aren't, some people are good at finding out the dimensions. And then we had to work together on the mathematics and all the dimensions.

T: Any other ways you had to work together?

C: Well, in making this plan we had to work together because, like, some people took—like, I took making the cooperatives and the park. Well, and some other people took—like, Rosa took making these buildings over here, and Ed took the making of the zoo, and then Dwight he took making the schools and Rosa did too. So we all worked together to get this finished.

T: Now, did you go to a training center or anything? Dwight?

C: Well, no we didn't go to anything. We just sort of like worked together. Just kept our heads, and that's what we came out with.

T: Well, how then, how do people learn to be cooperative?

C: Well, we learned to be cooperative as we went through it.

T: You mean as you went along day by day? You think that's a good idea or not?

C: Yes, I think it is a good idea because I remember when we first came into Mr. Edison's class we didn't know anything about independent reading or working together. And then, he showed us some of the things that other children had done and so we thought we'd like it and so we started then to do different and everyone had to work together and it wasn't very hard because we all knew that we'd like this job so we just all worked together.[2]

When we listen in on the creative thinking of children and see how deeply they can become involved in problems that are important to them, we are encouraged to believe that social studies can make a difference in

[2] Ibid., pp. 21–22.

their lives. Will it also prepare them for their future as citizens? What will these children do when they meet the inevitable problems that lie ahead for our country? Will they strive to make democracy work, to preserve the wonderful gifts of our heritage, to make friends with the world's people, and to use wisely our natural resources?

Equally significant will be the methods citizens use to achieve these goals. If they follow authoritarian principles, expecting their problems to be solved by impersonal agencies, they will lose the rights and privileges of democracy. If, on the other hand, they have learned how to solve significant problems, how to carry plans into action, and to give priority to human relationships, feelings, and values, we can be confident of their future as citizens of the real world.

Index

Affective goals. (*See* Goals, social studies)

Anthropology, generalizations, 9–10

Arranged environments
learning centers, 234–36, 245–48
for readiness, 72–76

Arnsdorf, Val E., 126

Aschner, Mary Jane
classification of questions, 190

Attitudes
definition, 28
development of, 28
evaluation of, 289–90
as goals, 28–29

Behavioral goals. (*See* Goals, social studies)

Behaviors
definition, 29
evaluation of, 98, 299
as goals, 29–30

Berger, Evelyn, 230

Bias
classroom episodes, 63, 64–65, 149–50
in nonprint sources, 274
in print sources, 47, 149, 274
resource unit on, 88–98

Bloom, Benjamin S., 189, 292

Bloom's Taxonomy of Educational Objectives
applied to questioning, 189–90
applied to test items, 292–99

Brainstorming, 80–81, 108–9

Career education, 122–26
behaviors, 123
classroom episodes, 64–65, 125–26
data-gathering experiences, 123–25
data sources, 123–25
stages in, 122
understandings, 122–23

Charts
classification, 162
as data records, 168–72
as data sources, 161–64
narrative, 161
organizational, 162–63, 168
process, 162–63
pupil-made, 168–69
tables, 161–62, 165
time lines, 169
retrieval, 170–72
skills needed, 164–65
understandings about, 163–64

Civic education. (*See* Political-civic education)

Citizenship education. (*See* Political-civic education)

Classroom episodes, processes
application of principles, 193–94
arranged environment, 73–76
brainstorming, 108–9
building readiness, 61–76
concept development, 182, 183–84, 191–92
concluding a study, 180–82
data gathering on current